Presented to the
Library of
Temple Beth El
in Honor of

Ellen Weiss
Bat Mitzvah

by

Joan, Robert &
Andrew Parmet

D1058911

No Words
to Say
Goodbye

No Words
to Say
Goodbye

A Young Jewish Woman's
Journey from the Soviet Union
into America

The Extraordinary Diaries of
Raimonda Kopelnitsky

By Raimonda Kopelnitsky
and Kelli Pryor

First two sections translated by

William Spiegelberger

HYPERION

New York

J B
K

Library of Congress Cataloging-in-Publication Data

Kopelnitsky, Raimonda
   No words to say goodbye : a young Jewish woman's journey from the Soviet Union into America—the extraordinary diaries of Raimonda Kopelnitsky / by Raimonda Kopelnitsky and Kelli Pryor. — 1st ed.
      p.   cm.
   ISBN 1-56282-867-3
   1. Kopelnitsky, Raimonda, 1977–   —Diaries. 2. Jews—Soviet Union—Diaries. 3. Jews, Soviet—United States—Diaries. 4. Immigrants—United States—Diaries. 5. Jewish girls—Soviet Union—Diaries. 6. Jewish girls—United States—Diaries. 7. Soviet Union—Ethnic relations. I. Pryor, Kelli. II. Title.
DS135.R95K6445   1994
973'.04924047'092—dc20   93-12423
                                                               CIP

Designed by Holly McNeely

First Edition

10 9 8 7 6 5 4 3 2 1

FOR DAD, MOM, AND SIMON

ACKNOWLEDGMENTS

Our gratitude goes to Robert Miller and Martha Kaplan for recognizing what could be and to Leslie Wells for making it happen. For buoying us always, we thank Daniel Strone. We are grateful to Carol Gold for her kindness, to Amy Virshup for getting us started, and to James Seymore for his support. Also, thanks go to Marina Belotserkovsky, William Spiegelberger, Andrew Hurwitz, Jeffrey Mendelsohn, and Craig Newman. We are indebted for countless reasons to Jerry Pryor, Meredith Berkman, Kate Meyers, Robin Saex, and Suelain Moy. Of course, this book could not have happened without Igor, Klavdia, and Simon Kopelnitsky, or without Andrew Rosenstein: Thank you.

—R.K. and K.P.

CONTENTS

INTRODUCTION

BY KELLI PRYOR

Raimonda Kopelnitsky wasn't acting her age on that day in April 1990, the day I saw her for the first time. She had been in the United States only three weeks, living with her family in a Manhattan welfare hotel. That afternoon, she had come to a place of truly foreign dimension—offices in a skyscraper. There, she was helping her father translate his Soviet career as an illustrator into an American one. Her poise seemed that of someone older, not someone twelve years old.

A tiny girl, she was remarkable for her huge eyes, framed by expressive eyebrows that were pulled to a V-point over her nose because this was such a serious occasion. She was solemn, sometimes perplexed, often concentrating on conjuring the right words in English. But when I mentioned the diary I knew she had been keeping, suddenly she became a child: she grinned in a tight-lipped way that held something back warily, but her dimples revealed a playful spirit and eagerness dawned in her eyes. That was the moment that persuaded me to find out more about Raimonda and the diaries she has kept as poignant testament of coming out of the Ukraine and into the uniquely complicated realm of enticement and disappointment that is America. Since that April day, I have spent hours at the family's kitchen table, sifting with them through their memories, their secrets, their silences.

A certain Old World stillness abides with the Kopelnitskys in their apartment on a wide avenue in Brooklyn. It is almost as if it was something that they had packed in their trunks, something that traveled with them when they came across the ocean from the Soviet Union. It might have nestled among folded linens and black and white pictures of people they might never see again. That stillness stays with them, even here where movement seems required of them, where in daily life each member of the family moves persistently, each trying to prove that by excelling at school or working overtime there is good reason to hope for a better life, for some peace at last: Peace from the anti-Semitism that stalked them daily, from the horrors of Chernobyl that almost killed Raimonda, from dreams too big for Soviet life.

As I came to know them, I discovered each member of the family to be rich in character and personal lore. The father, Igor, is a solid, compact man in thrall to his creativity. He is an illustrator who spends hours laboring over his ink drawings, deepening them line by line into an elaborate filigree. He frowns in his concentration, in his worries, his sadness. He cries when he is moved by a film or a book or a poem. But he can also burst open with mirth. He is a fine one for stories and jokes and toasts with good vodka.

His wife Klavdia is naturally cheerful, with a lovely smile. But, often, she feels the walls of her home. She has too often grown tired by looking at her husband's back bent over his work. She chafes, ready to bend to her own tasks. If she cannot work as an artifact restorer as she did in the Ukraine, she will sell real estate, anything. Anything not to have to look at his back.

Their son, Simon (affectionately known as Sima), is a hard worker, with a fine-boned face and hair pulled back in a severe ponytail. He is proud of his hair; his family often is not. Simon is a boy becoming a man in too small a space to hold him—the space of his family.

Together, they have moved across a vast distance. While everything around them has changed, these four hold between them the one certain world—these four people, bound by a family name and by blood, and by something more.

When they gather around the metal table in their kitchen and begin to eat the food from Brighton Beach, the fish brings a rush of memory because it tastes, to them, of the sea lapping Odessa. They settle. They rest from their persistent American pace. And they begin to talk together, to forget the difficulties of making a new home, to remember the comforts of that lost place. And to remember also what made them leave. It is then that the stillness seems a possession that they pass among themselves, something old and cherished that they have retrieved from a suitcase.

The stillness is their memory, a story they tell each other. Through my years with them, they have shared what they could of that memory with me, have described the terror of Chernobyl and revealed the insidious tenacity of anti-Semitism. They have told me in extended interviews about what happened in the years before Raimonda began keeping her diary. Here, listen.

No Words
to Say
Goodbye

A Life of Believing:
The Second World War
to Chernobyl

An Oral History of
the Kopelnitsky Family

Raimonda: My grandfather Adolf talked to me about our family. At first he would not—because I was just a little girl, and he did not want me to know. Then he told me of his childhood: He went to synagogue, and he studied in the Jewish school. He told me about the war and going to the front. He told about how his mother was burned to death in a fire.

Klavdia, Raimonda's mother: My parents—his name is Adolf, her name is Sofa—met in a little Ukrainian town, very little, in the countryside, next to Kelmentsy, Gorodok. Before the Second World War a lot of Jewish people lived in this town.

Igor, Raimonda's father: Before the war, Adolf's town had the biggest pogrom ever. Adolf watched. Adolf remembers. He was a young man. All his family hid with him under a building, in a basement.

Klavdia: He was in the basement for days. Afterward, there were a lot of wagons with horses taking bodies to bury. Three days it took to take the bodies. Almost all the people were killed—after they were robbed for candlesticks, dishes, pillows, and money, for food, drink, and dress. Everything.

When he was still a young man, he met my mother, Sofa. She was alone because her parents were very old when she was born. She was the last of twelve brothers and sisters, born when her mother was fifty-three years old. So, when she finished school, she studied alone in another town.

Her mother gave her bread, and sent her far away to this school to study. My mother didn't have anything except this bread.

RAIMONDA: When we slept together at night, Grandmother Sofa always told me stories about her life. She showed me some photos of when she was young. She was very beautiful. But all her stories were sad and of a very hard life.

KLAVDIA: My parents were already married when the second war came. And they had a daughter—my sister.

My father went to the front. My mother only wanted to hide. She knew about pogroms. So she left in the evacuation—from her home in the Ukraine to Uzbekistan. She wanted to hide.

IGOR: Do you know how long people traveled from Ukraine to Uzbekistan? Sometimes three months, sometimes five months. A lot of people died because they were without horses, without food.

KLAVDIA: Mother was walking, alone with her baby. It was a trip with a lot of changing trains, cars, horses, sometimes by foot. A very long way. And sometimes airplanes fired at this stream of a million people.

Her child was killed on the way—my mother's baby girl caught a cold and she died. And so little. She didn't live even for one year.

And, at the front, Father was shot in the breast. It was in the big battle of Kursk, in 1943.

IGOR: The front was one hundred kilometers long. One part of the Soviet army was attacked by German airplanes. A lot of people were shot, millions. It's not against one man, that kind of fighting. It's a lot of bombs, a lot of artillery from the sky.

KLAVDIA: When Father was wounded, he was evacuated to the hospital in Novosibirsk. They cut out his lung to save him.

My mother came to him there. And she told him that their baby had died. She stayed with him.

RAIMONDA: Afterward, Grandfather returned to look for his mother and his father and his sister; they were gone. He didn't know where—because he had been on the front.

KLAVDIA: Later, my parents found out. All my father's family was killed. His mother and sister were killed, were burned in the fire by the SS. The Nazis usually dug holes and then they shot the people. But my father's parents and his sister were burned alive, without shots.

So my young parents were left alone. They didn't know where to live. At a train station, some people near them said, "Do you know there is a very beautiful part in the best of Ukraine? Chernovtsy. It is a little Switzerland."

IGOR: Chernovtsy, a little Vienna. It is near Kiev and about two hundred kilometers southwest of the town called Chernobyl.

KLAVDIA: My parents came to Chernovtsy, and they chose to stay in that town.

IGOR: Many Jews had lived in Chernovtsy before the war. After, they had mostly disappeared. But there were apartments there that hadn't been destroyed. So a lot of both eastern and western European Jews who had no home to return to ended up in Chernovtsy. Among the Jews was a big difference between ones from East and ones from West. The ones from the West had more culture. They came from bourgeoisie.

But most of the Jews—from both east and west—didn't know the Jewish culture: they had a lost language, a lost religion, and lost habits.

KLAVDIA: In 1946, I was born in Chernovtsy. I was the child born after the war. My parents gave me the name that had been my sister's before she died. They named me Klavdia.

IGOR: I was also born in 1946. But my father and mother met only after the war—when my mother, Galya, was still a very young woman.

My father had lived in the Ukraine in a little Jewish town near Kiev, and when the war began, he was a young man. He became a soldier, and he fought the whole war. Three times he was wounded. Each time, he was treated for a half year, and then he would go back to the front. He was a tank man, a real soldier.

After the war, my father was never the same. He was not Jewish anymore; he was a Russian soldier. He told me his mother was killed in Germany. And his father, my grandfather, was probably killed at Babi-Yar, near Kiev, where 150,000 women, children, and old people were killed. So my father was without relatives. He was a Jew, but he was a Soviet Jew. He went to a big war, lost all his family, lived alone among Ukrainians. He lost all Jewish habits, all his religious moments.

Our parents' life was war. It changed all minds, changed all people. My father was alone. And then he left us alone. He began to drink vodka. He went away when I was three years old. I lived with my mother and grandmother in a communal apartment all my life—before I became a university student. A lot of people in the Soviet Union lived two or three families together. We had three people in my family: my grandmother, my mother, and me. Another family had seven. Sometimes someone would die or another person would move. But for ten years we lived together with those other families.

My mother worked all her life in the post office. It was a very empty life, very poor.

In my class at school, I was the poorest among the boys. And the poorest among the girls was my future wife.

KLAVDIA: Igor didn't have shoes. And I didn't have a dress for parties. I had a uniform for school, only this. In all my years at school, I never had any dress. I didn't want to have a dress; I wanted to have a job.

My father didn't work ever, because of his wounds from the war. He was ill all the time, and he couldn't work even though he is an intelligent man. He had finished school in Yiddish. He went to the Institute a long time ago, before Stalin.

When I was growing up, he had a very little pension, very little. He had the status of disability, but the money was very little because he was just a soldier. He wasn't an officer.

And all the time my mother was working as a teacher in school. Three jobs she had, all the time. And Father was in a hospital often because one lung was cut out and the other lung had holes in it. All the time he had to go to the hospital. I didn't see him sometimes for a year, half a year. He went from one hospital to another.

In the morning, my mother taught little children. In the evening, adults. I was alone all the time. And sometimes I didn't have food.

RAIMONDA: My little mother went to school, and when she came home, it was dark and she went to sleep on the couch, still hungry. It was cold and she slept and slept and slept. They had nothing to eat. Even to buy apples was expensive.

IGOR: Some things were very good, though. Someone in my apartment had a radio. It was very difficult to work, and I was very small. But I twisted the knobs until one day I heard different sounds: *Voice of America . . . Washington, D.C.* I ran to school and told everyone.

KLAVDIA: It was very dangerous for him to talk about it at school. The KGB . . . He should not be listening. But he was so smart, so curious.

IGOR: I was always sneaking around, listening, taking everything in. I had no father to take me to the bathhouses, so I went with my mother. I had very big eyes, looking at all those big bare women. Ahhh.

And I had a friend who lived in a communal apartment with a soldier who went to Hungary in 1956. I remember waiting to cross the street one morning, and a tank came by like thunder on the street stones. And when the soldiers came back, this man brought record albums from Hungary, silly songs about chocolate. We played the songs again and again. It was the first time I ever touched something really good. I could touch it and know that it was not Soviet. It was something better. I remember smelling those records; they were different in every way.

KLAVDIA: When Igor met my father, he felt the same about the foreign newspapers and magazines that my father had. He was so happy that my father let him take some of them. He has kept them all his life.

IGOR: Klavdia and I knew each other a lot of years, eleven years. But it was not until we were apart that we came together. First, we studied in universities in different cities. Klavdia was in Yaroslav, near Moscow, and I was in Novosibirsk.

Jewish students could not go to university in the Ukraine because of anti-Semitism. And nobody Jewish could go to a famous Moscow or Leningrad university. It was understood. They would say you had a bad grade on an exam, even if you were a genius. So a big company of young Jews went a thousand kilometers from our town. We took our famous trip—days by train—to Novosibirsk. There, for a few years, it was a good time for good Jewish students. We scored great exams. We lived in dormitories.

I had grown up in a nineteenth-century town; I had a nineteenth-century education; I had a nineteenth-century mind and way of thinking. The first time I broke this old view was at university. I studied in one of the best universities in the Soviet Union for science. That's why I have more freedom of mind. It broke all my old life, all my limits. That's why I'm different from my mother. Between my mother and me, there is a very big distance. Her generation of Jews lived in closed ghettos. But for us, in the Sixties, we wanted to break from the ghetto to go to a big world with culture and science, where we could sometimes forget about our parents. For that reason, there were broken families: Jewish sons started new lives with Russian families. Most of my friends married non-Jews, Russians.

For me, I broke with my small-town Jewish life and became

involved in a big life and never returned—at least my mind did not. My whole life, I've moved and moved. Nothing is stable. I've been a refugee all my life—from anti-Semitism, from my town, from my country.

What do I know about being Jewish? I don't know the language. I have only one habit as a Jew—being hated.

We never studied religion. We didn't have a yeshiva or any chance of Jewish education. Under law, we could not. We might have been able secretly to celebrate holidays. We could go to synagogue, but we were afraid. In the workplace we were told, If you go to synagogue, you will be sent away. Never go to synagogue.

I never knew about prayer, that I could go to God. People didn't know anything about religion. I know people who didn't know the difference between Judaism and Christianity.

Some families kept on being Jewish, more culturally than religiously. But I didn't have grandparents. My grandparents were killed in the second war. If you don't have grandparents, religion is broken.

Yet I could never forget that I am a Jew. When I was at the university, involved in Russian culture and language, I grew farther from a Jewish community. But I would only be truly happy when I returned on holiday to Chernovtsy and all my Jewish student friends would get together.

Every summer vacation, all the students went back to Chernovtsy and met with each other, had parties. Occasionally, we spent vacation time in Odessa.

KLAVDIA: I had a relative in Odessa, and I stayed in their apartment. Every day, Igor and I began walking together, swimming together in the Black Sea. When vacation time was over, we couldn't stand to be apart.

IGOR: One month, I flew altogether five thousand kilometers to be with her. I never did the trip the same way twice because I didn't have money. Some friends taught me how to get a flight for free—without a ticket. It was easy. Eleven, maybe twelve times, I flew in a big plane without money from Novosibirsk to Moscow.

Sometimes the plane was delayed or had to land in another town where the weather was better. The passengers all had to leave the plane, and then I would be stuck in another city, without money, without an address to go to, without anything. I stayed in the airport for one, two, or three days—until I could sneak on another plane.

Once, I changed clothes to look like a soldier, to travel with a lot of soldiers. One man gave me his long soldier coat and under it I was wearing civilian clothes. My shoes were sticking out.

Always, when I got to Klavdia, we would have only a little money—just enough for an electric train that went to Moscow, the most interesting place in the Soviet Union. All our time together, we spent in Moscow.

KLAVDIA: Sometimes we would sneak into theaters. Sometimes we bought tickets and went without eating meals. We only wanted to go to theater. We were interested in culture: theater, movies.

IGOR: It was a good time—Khrushchev Spring. There were interesting movies from the West. It changed our minds; we became more clever and understood that communism was not good.

Hemingway called his a lost generation. We had a *broken* generation. We didn't read in English. But we read Hemingway and Salinger, only three or four other writers. It seemed a lot. For us, it was enough to change our minds. We knew Stalin was bad, and communism. And we knew that there was another life.

KLAVDIA: We married in 1968.

IGOR: Klavdia wanted to change schools, to be with me at mine. But because of the bureaucracy, she couldn't. She was afraid to lose the chance for education. And if I changed schools, I would go into the Army, be drafted. Every young man must go to the Army unless they are studying.

So we still had to travel to see each other, sometimes only once every three months. It took three days on the train. Sometimes we saw each other only on vacations, sometimes between.

After the university, we began to live together. It was 1970.

That year, Simon was born. Klavdia lived with her mother before he was born. We both worked, two professionals. She was a chemical engineer. I was a radio engineer—until later, when I drove a taxi and did cartoons for foreign publications.

KLAVDIA: Raimonda was born in 1977.

IGOR: The first people were beginning to move to Israel. Only a few people emigrated because Israel was open only a short time. But people could think about it. The government personally looked through everything. But some people could go and live in the West.

It was a historic moment for Jews. But we waited twenty years after that moment. From that time on, all our life we talked about it: *"Do you know X moved? What did they write?"*

All life changed then.

KLAVDIA: For Raimonda, it is all she remembers. All she knows.

RAIMONDA: Papa's mother lived two buildings away from us. And Mama's parents were ten minutes on the bus, one hour walking.

The town was small. The central street, Lenin Street, where Grandmother Sofa lived, was old and very nice. It was an old road made with small stones, and all along it were bars and cinemas and ice cream and stores where you could buy toys. It was a very nice street because all the houses and the stores, all the buildings were old and very ancient and nice.

There was the theater, that was called Kobelianskaia. It had a gold ceiling, red velvet seats. I was a very little girl when I went there with my grandmother. And then once I went with my class and teachers to see theater in the Ukrainian language.

In my school, there were a lot of Ukrainians. I could hear Ukrainian everywhere. Even my friends—some of them—in kindergarten were Ukrainian. In my kindergarten, my best friend was a Ukrainian girl. Then I went to another school, and I didn't see her for years.

I liked my kindergarten. Everything that I remember was great. Except the soup from peas. When I was small, I did some bad things with it. I threw up on the table.

Once, there was a fire in our apartment. We were eating supper in the kitchen, and we were talking a lot—quiet and very good. And then I wanted to open the door to go out of the kitchen, but I couldn't because I was too small to reach the knob. And my brother came, and he helped me, and when we opened it there was smoke and we looked and we couldn't believe. And my brother screamed, *Fire!* My father came running from another room.

The radiators had not been giving heat. So we were heating with a plug-in heater and some paper from my table had fallen on the heater. As always, there was no water in the apartment, so my parents took my favorite blanket to put over the fire. My brother screamed at me and said, *"Go to Grandmother."* And I said, *"Where are my shoes?"* And he took them and gave them to me, and I put on one but the other I didn't get because he closed the door behind me. And it was winter, so I went to my grandmother with one slipper and only a bathrobe. And she lived five, ten minutes from me, my father's mother. She opened the door: *"Oh, child!"*

I stayed a lot with my grandmothers. My father kept me out of kindergarten until I was four—so I could stay with them.

I can see that Grandmother Sofa is really a good person, a real woman. She was working all her life—because Grandfather was sick and she had to do everything, to cook, to clean. It was all her job. My grandfather didn't clean, did not do anything.

IGOR: It is true, he cannot even use a hammer.

RAIMONDA: He was always reading the paper, talking with me, eating.

IGOR: It looked like an Italian movie. Grandmother would say to him, *"You reader. You don't do anything. All the time."* But he would only grin.

RAIMONDA: All the time, she would scream at him, "You are lazy. *You are so lazy!"*

And she'd slam the door on him, and he would wave her off. And when my grandmother started to clean, he would be on the sofa, and he would put on a hat, a very hot hat. Even in summer, he would put on this winter hat. And he would put his ears inside the flaps, and sit like this with his arms crossed, waiting for her to finish. It was funny.

And all the time he wanted everything to be hot. And my grandmother wanted always fresh air. So they argued. Whenever she was opening the windows, he was screaming, *"Close the window! I'm so cold, I'm gonna DIE!"* There was a big old oven covered with tiles, from old times, from Romania. Built in 1920. Grandfather would stand by it all the time. Heating with papers.

IGOR: When I lived as a young man, there was no hot water; I washed only with cold water. People went to the bathhouses. Our apartments didn't have hot water at all. When I was young, we didn't even have a bathroom.

RAIMONDA: In our apartment, we had warm water in the morning, then only cold water, then no water, then at ten o'clock in the evening, hot. We were at the top of building, so it was worse. My grandmother Galya lived on the second floor, and she almost always had hot water. So when I wanted a bath, I went to her.

IGOR: We lived in a cultural town, but we did not have water. We didn't have gas. We didn't have anything. But the buildings were beautiful from the Romanian time.

Klava's family lived in a separate apartment—single, not communal. Their building was very old, with a balcony around the inside court. And they lived on the fourth floor, the top. In the court, a lot of people walked around the balcony and talked together. And inside this building, almost all the people were Jewish; they spoke in Yiddish. It was unique, a court from nineteenth-century Eastern Europe.

It was a microclimate, the building. Sometimes you forgot about real life. I really liked it when I was inside. It had a specific mood, a feeling. It was a poor building. The steps were dirty, very dirty. But sometimes we would think: *"All the people around are the same as me."*

RAIMONDA: Grandmother Sofa made a home. All the time she talked about how hard she worked. How long ago she was alone with my little mother, and how Grandfather had always been away from home, and even if he was home it didn't make any difference. But she always cared for him.

When I think about her, I see that she's really a good woman. It's hard to be with a man who is sick all his life, and never makes money. Grandmother cooks quickly. The best thing is knishes with cheese or cherries or meat.

KLAVDIA: My mother made parties. Very good chicken, little mushrooms. We had natural food because we didn't have anything in the store. Everything was in the market.

Every day we had very bad food, but when we had some party— a birthday, New Year's—we bought everything. My mother always did a big table, and she spent a lot of money in the market. We could afford only once in a while to do this—a big table, a lot of food, the cakes.

RAIMONDA: There were two markets. The one near my grandmother had everything. There was a little store with meat, like rabbits. Another store had cheese and white cheese with salt. You could buy sour cream.

There were fruits, vegetables, meat, cheese, and nuts, different kinds, and sometimes clothes and domestic honey. Also, there were barrels and inside these were apples or tomatoes or cucumbers in salt water. There was salad from carrots and cabbage in salt water. Everything in the market was made or grown by these farm people.

But every day it got more and more expensive. Sometimes we couldn't buy anything; sometimes we carried home empty our plastic bags, our cloth bags.

We had no fruits and vegetables in winter—only in summer, so in spring when it just arrived it was expensive. Then in summer it was less.

Once, I got lost in this market. And my mother walked and looked for me, and she couldn't find me. I stayed on the steps of the store, a high place so I could see her. But I could not see her. And then I looked down, and I saw my father running and looking for me. And I screamed, *"Papa!"* He was running for the police because I was lost. I was maybe six. Next time, they held onto me.

I usually went with my grandmother. I called her "Babula." Often we call them "Babushka," but if you are close to her, "Babula." And I went there with her and she bought me the black nuts of the sunflower.

When we came home from Odessa in the car, outside Chernovtsy, there were big fields with sunflowers. We went to the field and picked them, cut them with a knife. And then we brought them home, a lot of them. Sometimes we took apples, too, because it was empty roads and there weren't other cars. Nothing around but big fields. We brought a lot of sunflowers home and put them in the oven and made them hot and watched TV and ate them.

IGOR: Every year the holidays became less and less. We had good parties in the sixties and seventies, but after that the food disappeared.

RAIMONDA: Once, with my grandmother, I waited four hours for butter and didn't get it. We went at 6:00 P.M. and came home at 10:00 P.M.

SIMON, RAIMONDA'S BROTHER: When I was little, in Moscow when we would visit, the stores were filled with mandarins, oranges, bananas. Mama and I had a sandwich with caviar for fifty kopeks. Ten years later when I came as a student it was a big problem to eat, to get even sausage.

RAIMONDA: Poor children, no caviar.

SIMON: Grandmother used to have bottles of black caviar . . . for the New Year. New Year's is the biggest family holiday. But when I became a teenager, I wanted to leave for the square with my friends.

RAIMONDA: On New Year's, all children believe that Father Frost comes with his daughter, Snow Girl. They have to come in the night and leave presents under the green tree. I am always too tired to wait up and watch.

One morning, Simon told me he saw Father Frost and Snow Girl. Father Frost was wearing Papa's trousers and Snow Girl was wearing Mama's bathrobe.

SIMON: I remember when I was six or seven years old, I got two cowboy pistols, silver. I played American cowboy and Indians, or Fascists and Russians.

RAIMONDA: When we were little, we would steal fruits and flowers. There were small private gardens with nuts and cherries. There was one old woman who caught us up her tree. She said, "If you're not going to come down, I'm going to bring the hatchet and cut down the tree." We hated her.

The yard was the most important place. In the winter, we would make a snow castle and a lot of children came. And Simon and I defended our castle in a snowball fight. And we could skate everywhere. We could go out from our building and start skating.

Sometimes, I could not even play—my head was so fat with schoolwork that I couldn't play. I went to school six days. I had to work on my homework for a very long time.

In fifth grade, I had English every day. I had it almost every day from first grade. Other schools taught it only from fourth grade. But I studied *"mother—father—1-2-3"* from first grade. I learned a lot those four years, and other children only started it.

With English, I had bad, bad grades and also in Russian language and Ukrainian language. Once in first grade, I had a score of 2 [the equivalent of a D]. And my father saw, and he came to me at night, angry, and he woke me up and he beat me. I was crying. He took my English book, and he said, *"Read it!"* And I read it for two hours. And Papa said: "If you do it again, if I see a score of 2 or 1 anymore, I'll beat you again." He never had beaten me. It was the first time: I was surprised.

And the next day I got a 4, like 90. And then only 5-5-5, which is like scoring 100. Then after that I loved English. I loved English more than Russian, and my dream was to be an English teacher or translator. And my English teacher was proud of me, and she always picked me in class and talked about me to the other teachers. But she was Jewish and she soon left for Israel, and another woman came. She was also Jewish.

I remember becoming a Pioneer. This was when children felt proud because they wanted to become older. And if they were becoming a Pioneer, they were becoming older.

When we became Pioneers, we were all soldiers of some kind. The teachers picked the uniforms for us. In the parade, my class was border guards. Simon had been a sailor.

We practiced. They taught us to march stiff-armed and to salute. We sang songs. We practiced three weeks in special movements. My class did the best, and we got the honor roll—a red flag to hang in the classroom.

There were thirty-six kids in my class. Some of them had KGB parents; some of them had parents in prison. Nobody talked about it. Everybody knew.

For the ceremony, we stood next to the statue of Lenin in the center of town. We swore to be true. All around us were the beautiful buildings with the mosaics from the Austro-Hungarian years. There were flowers around the statue of Lenin. During the ceremony, I was watching, there was a pigeon sitting on the outstretched hand of Lenin . . . and then on his hat.

I was nine years old. Before that, I was a Child of October (for the month of the Revolution). Then I wore a star with five points. It had a photograph of Lenin when he was a child. When I became a Pioneer, I wore a red tie and another button with a picture of Lenin as an old man.

SIMON: When I became a Young Pioneer, I thought, *"Wow, I'm growing up. I have the red tie."* But soon the teachers had to force me to wear it.

When kids turned fourteen, you were supposed to join the young Communist organization, Komsomol. Then you wore a button of a flag with Lenin on it.

I was lazy. I didn't want to memorize everything. Girls were fond of it. They even studied Mao's book and swore to be a good Communist.

I went to winter camp in Odessa when I was twelve years old. There I met my first girlfriend. We were supposed to study but we ran around.

While we were there, Brezhnev died. We were watching television and the ceremony and how they buried him. We had to watch TV and hold the salute—our left hand angled above our foreheads.

I was the last one in my class to enter Komsomol, when I was sixteen. If you're not a member, you can never enter college.

I understood that it was bullshit. I wasn't anti-Communist. I was just laughing at *everything*.

RAIMONDA: There was no God, only communism. Lenin was a God. And he was only a dead leader. We had to memorize it from first grade to sixth grade. And live with it the rest of our lives.

My parents were laughing at this. And I believed in my parents more than I believed in this philosophy.

I would have to study these things. And my father would say, "I don't care if you do study it. It doesn't matter." But I would go to my grandmother's and she would say, "You are going to live here. And you must study it."

Once I wrote a poem. The teacher asked us to memorize a poem about war. Everyone else memorized from the book, but I wrote a poem. All the poems from the book were alike: *They are heroes, we love them, dee-dee-duh-duh.*

But I wrote that, *Yes, they did. They were heroes. They fought for us, but now we don't remember them.* Because it is true that no one remembers. Always someone says: *Nothing is forgotten. No one forgets.* But it isn't true; everyone has forgotten about it. They don't care. So that's why I wrote this poem. And in some newspapers—like three newspapers—it was written about it, that no one cared. And my poem was like: *The heroes, they lost their lives and blood for us and now we don't care, and if they could wake up and look at us, they would say, "Why did we do it? For what? It's empty."*

And my teacher became so angry that I wrote this poem, and she said, "What does it mean? It's not true. How could you write it? Sit down." And I said: "But what happens now?"

After, not only my friends but even my enemies came to me and said: "That was so great. That was true, and we're proud of you because it is true."

My grandfather was wounded in the war, and he told me that everyone is forgotten, everything is forgotten. I know it is true. But my teacher looked at everyone and at me and all the boys and girls who were standing around me, and she felt so stupid. She was afraid. She felt the same as we did, but she was afraid.

Always, always, our teachers had to be right. They were going to teach us that everything was so great, no matter what. But the kids understood anyway. Even my enemies, Ukrainians, stood up and came to me and said that I was right. I didn't know that they would do it, but the teacher was looking so stupid and she was so afraid. And I knew that she was Jewish and she understood everything very well and that she would go to Israel. Her daughter had already gone to Israel. She knew everything.

IGOR: In Chernovtsy, there were maybe forty thousand Jews. And then in 1987 they began moving, emigrating. We don't know exactly how many. But it was a very important moment for our town.

Once, there were a lot of Jewish people, a whole Jewish culture from Germany. In Chernovtsy, before the war, maybe forty thousand Jews lived there. They had real freedom: synagogues and houses, beautiful buildings and Jewish centers and newspapers—a big culture. You know Kafka and other Jewish great names in Austro-Hungary and Prague. It was the same, a little, in Chernovtsy.

But it all changed when the Nazis killed all the Jewish people. Before the war, Jewish families lived together—three, four, ten families—in the countryside. Some Ukrainians and Moldavians helped Germany by pointing out these Jewish families. A lot of people were killed and robbed by Germans. But this is tradition. It is a very anti-Semitic region.

In our time, the tradition continued. Take Grandmother Sofa's house as a model. This is a Jewish building, surrounded. All around our town is countryside, a lot of little farms of people who live inside the radius of Chernovtsy. And all these people are not Jewish. Fifty percent Ukrainian; fifty percent Moldavian. And they all hate the Jewish people who live inside this building and this court. And all these Ukrainians and Moldavians know exactly who is a Jew.

KLAVDIA: My mother had a problem in her school with anti-Semitism all the time. It was the atmosphere.

IGOR: Everytime, everyplace.

KLAVDIA: Everywhere, all the time.

IGOR: It's normal life.

KLAVDIA: In the Soviet Union.

IGOR: All my life, even when I was very young, I understood that other people at a minimum didn't like me and at maximum hated me: Hate, hate, hate. I was a very sensitive young man. It was in the air when I breathed: *You are different. You are a Jew.* And you have to be afraid. I had that big fear all the time in the Soviet Union.

I never met with a Ukrainian who wasn't anti-Semitic. Sometimes they were good, and didn't hate us. They would say, "Oh, you're a good Jew." But, in their minds, there was always a bad Jew.

When I was a university student, I was surprised to meet very good Russian people. I became friends with good Russian people, without any anti-Semitism in mind. They never had it in their family. But also in Russia I met with dark anti-Semitism, darker than the Ukraine. They were the new Fascists.

Very soon you recognize who is who. You keep friends only with a good man or woman.

KLAVDIA: In our town every year, a school director distributed hours of work to teachers. The director of my mother's school was very anti-Semitic, and he did not want to give her more hours, more work. But she needed work because my father couldn't work.

Two times in her life the director fired her. He told her, "You finished Jewish school and Jewish university. You cannot teach Ukrainian students."

And so my mother was without a job. She wrote complaining to Moscow, and they came to check her work. She demonstrated. A lot of teachers analyzed all her lectures, and afterward they told her: "You are excellent." And she began working again.

My mother gave all her life to work. We didn't have food because she didn't have the time to prepare anything. If she didn't work, we didn't have bread at all, except if friends gave us food. But still my mother believed in justice.

IGOR: She believed that all the government said was true.

KLAVDIA: My mother was communist in her thinking. She grew up inside Soviet life, and for fifty years she had only good news about the Union. My mother cried when Stalin died. She is a sacrifice of Soviet propaganda.

She believed Stalin all her life. She believed Brezhnev. *Her life is believing.* It's nothing else.

IGOR: Before people began moving, Chernovtsy didn't have contact with the world. But after the people began leaving for Israel and America, they began to write letters. We began to have a lot of information—only inside our family and friends. There was almost no official word. But somebody would tell somebody about somebody visiting America.

Before that, some people never even thought about moving. But then a neighbor moved and wrote letters: *Good and very good and very happy, oh, oh, oh.*

I felt uncomfortable *all the time.* I felt that if I stayed it meant that I wasn't good, not clever, not powerful, not an active man, not brave.

KLAVDIA: We knew one man who didn't even know English. But he was brave: he left.

IGOR: Finally, it was not about being brave. It was about the child. It was about going away to live, or staying to die.

RAIMONDA: One night, I slept, and then I heard the voices of my parents. And they were looking out the window and gasping, *Ach, Ach.* And I opened my eyes and what I saw through the window was a blue light, a very nice light in the sky. I liked this, and I thought my parents were saying it was so nice. I didn't understand at first that they were so shocked. Then I thought maybe that soldiers were making that light.

It was a very, very nice picture—the blue sky, the bright light. It was raining, and the sky was different. There was a lot of lightning, a lot of different colors, even red.

I felt kind of warm and comfortable. Outside, it was raining and horrible. But I was in my room, soft and warm. I thought it must already be day, the sky was so bright. But I went back to sleep.

IGOR: Only a few people understood: my friends and I listened to Radio Liberty and the Voice of America and Polish radio. They began to speak about an atomic explosion and about a nuclear cloud. And we began to understand.

That nuclear cloud brought rain to us. On May Day, there was the first rain after Chernobyl, which happened on April 26.

The first thunderstorm was normal. Then in four or five days there was another thunderstorm. The lightning did not turn off—just stayed on like a fluorescent light in the night. We were afraid. We were shouting that this was unusual. It was flashing, flashing.

I noticed that when the rain fell down against electric lines and ran to the ground, it was flashing like the Northern Lights. It was luminescent, flashing white. All the little leaves in the tree were flashing like ghosts. The rooftops were glowing. The TV antennas were lighting up, anything iron.

SIMON: I never saw it rain so much. My friends and I were out together, seeing a movie. And we danced in the rain, got soaked, and made jokes about a nuclear storm. We danced in the night, in the rain.

KLAVDIA: There were a lot of people in that rain. We didn't have broadcasts to forecast the weather, and if we had, it would have been absolutely different from the truth anyway.

RAIMONDA: On May Day, we didn't go out to celebrate. It was the first time we didn't go out to the parade.

IGOR: We watched the parade on television. It was raining in Kiev. I watched the rain run down the faces of the little drummers. I cried for them. I kept my family inside.

RAIMONDA: My papa was talking about it a lot. He was using some kind of instrument to measure the radiation. He measured the radiation in a big jar of honey my grandmother bought. She was afraid of it.

IGOR: I had a friend in physics, and he had a Geiger counter. In the office where the Physics Institute and laboratory were, where people used Geiger counters, somebody official (we don't know if it was KGB) told the staff: "Please remove Geiger counters from the lab."

But some of these men hid Geiger counters at home. It was a big secret about the radiation—except for the scientists who had Geigers. They showed the highest rating, much higher than normal. With the Geiger counters, we could only count light iron. We could not count heavy iron.

All night, we measured in the ground and three feet above the ground, and the leaves, and the bread, and the water. And we knew that this week was the highest radiation. We were all sick in our throats, and we coughed. Our lymph nodes were swollen, and we wanted only to sleep. Our bodies felt bad all over. There was the taste of iron in our mouths. This is usual for radiation poisoning.

The Soviet government, radios and newspapers, kept silent. For days after the explosion, all was silent. After ten days, Gorbachev explained. But still the Ukrainian minister of health was saying: "It's normal. An explosion, yes. But dangerous, no. All things are normal."

It made fools of us.

Finally, after the rain, school was closed for four days—but only for the littlest children. The children in child care began to drink iodine to draw off the radiation. Plastic covered our food for four days. The only word from Sanitation was to cover food in the street. In this whole big town no one knew exactly what had happened, what to do. And we could find no advice from radio or TV, which only kept saying, "It's good, don't panic. Work, don't stay at home."

We had nothing but "underground instructions." Xeroxes exist only in offices. But someone managed to give special instructions by Xerox and pass them underground.

The Xerox said that no people should remain in Zone One. All animals should be killed from helicopters. All the wheat and vegetables should be buried. Everything must go under the ground; everything is dangerous. In Zone Two, wild animals could stay, but people must not. We lived in Zone Five. Our instructions were to wash the dust with water and to wear gas masks. In our apartment, we closed the door and closed the windows. We cleaned the floor. We cleaned the dust, especially on the window sill, all the time. We cleaned with water. We washed our hair three times a day with a lot of shampoo. We avoided eating any fruit with water inside, like grapes or cherries.

After twenty days, the official Soviet radio began finally to say: One, clean with water. Two, don't eat food from the ground. But in the early, dangerous time, they had kept silent. The government was pig shit. Only animals would keep silent. All people hated the government in this moment. All people understood that the Ukrainian government was guilty.

Finally the government called an emergency. The reserves were put to work. Young drivers from Chernovtsy went to Chernobyl under orders from the military. I have one friend who works in Sanitation. He drove a truck that looked like a fire truck—but it was really for public showering. After a chemical or atomic poisoning, you must wash. And so the military called in these trucks from across the country.

When my friend arrived in the most dangerous zone, there was panic. It looked like war. When he was sent there, he was told only to drive there and wash people. He arrived at his place, and there were fifteen trucks there like his. He waited two, three days. Nobody was washing. But he had no permission to leave, even though the crowds were elsewhere.

No vehicles were allowed to leave the zone. People could return home—if they had a reason. My friend created a reason, that his wife was dangerously sick. Some other people stayed. They thought that because the weather was good, everything was fine. But really there was dangerous radiation, and there was an army of workers there— one million workers in the zone. My friend spoke to a young soldier who didn't understand that it was dangerous. The soldier was just doing what the officer ordered him to do—wash and wash the street.

In Kiev, all the streets and buildings were washed. The situation in Kiev was more dangerous. We had only a cloud in the atmosphere and the rain to bring it down. But then it went away. So in Chernovtsy, only three buildings were washed: the Communist Party building with its Romanian architecture, the city government building, and the regional government building.

Our homes didn't get washed. In Chernovtsy, we always had difficulty with water. The water is deep in the ground, and the river runs only a little. Water is a big problem.

We lived on the fifth floor, and on the morning and evening when they washed the streets, we didn't have water at all. They washed their buildings; we didn't drink water.

That May, there was good weather. In the forest there was a

natural pool with no stream leaving it. It was dangerous because it accumulated a lot of radiation. But a lot of people—simple people—didn't believe it could be dangerous. They went swimming. "Chernobyl is too far," they said. They developed dangerous symptoms.

That summer, when June came, most people understood that it was dangerous to live in this place. So the children went with their mothers and fathers to Odessa to swim in the sea. A million people moved to the Black Sea, where a big panic started. The sea was radioactive, we heard. Everyone talked about it all the time. Everyone became more friendly, talking about the problem. We needed help from each other. There was never any official word.

That autumn, a lot of mushrooms grew to be a foot tall. But they rotted very quickly. The apples were big. The walnuts were the most dangerous because they accumulated radiation; so did the mushrooms and the strawberries.

RAIMONDA: The strawberries were big as apples. All the fruits and vegetables were spoiled; they were yellowed and grew spots. And the next year, the cucumbers grew twisted.

KLAVDIA: Under our apartment window, there was a quince tree. It grew double its size. And the quince were huge. But if you cut them one day, they were spoiled by the next.

I worked in a museum, and our director didn't understand the danger. It was an anthropology museum with a garden. We had to dig ground for the flowers. Forty women and men began to do it. After two days, everybody was ill with a sore throat and cough. Three young gardeners who worked outside all the time were ill with pneumonia.

We had a meeting, and everybody was coughing. And the director then began thinking. We understood it was because we worked in the soil.

In the villages around Chernovtsy, people liked to grow vegetables. It was their work. They were ill, absolutely ill. All harvest, they dug in the ground. And they ate the vegetables.

IGOR: Only a few people understood. When they saw the lightning, they understood. And then they forgot. When the fruit grew big and bigger, they said, *Ah, the air is fresh. The sun is good.*

But we could tell that in Kiev, *everyone* knew. You can only change apartments in the Soviet Union if you exchange identification numbers with someone else, like prison. Most years, a thousand families in Chernovtsy want to exchange with only ten families in Kiev.

Kiev is a capital, a center of culture. But sometimes someone from Kiev wants to live in quiet Chernovtsy. So they will exchange one room in Kiev for three rooms in Chernovtsy and a lot of underground money.

RAIMONDA: There was a big chance for us to exchange our apartment for one in Kiev. All the people from Kiev wanted to exchange apartments to get away from the radiation. It was a good deal for us, but we didn't because of the sickness.

IGOR: After Chernobyl, millions left Kiev to stay with relatives and friends. There were big crowds. There were a lot of people, a lot of children without their mothers. It was an evacuation. In our forest, there was a summer camp at a beautiful place. Then, only children, hundreds of them from little towns around Chernobyl, came to the camp, where they could eat good food with more vitamins. Raisins. I cried in the street because it looked like the war . . . little children without their parents . . . children with their backpacks and little caps.

SIMON: I saw kids from Chernobyl. The kids were so skinny and so sad. They almost never spoke. It was like the Twilight Zone— they were so slow, drifting around the city. They weren't normal. They almost seemed not to have emotions. They didn't run, didn't play.

IGOR: Thousands became ill. It continued long after the explosion. The most dangerous sickness began in Kiev. Radiation accumulated because every day there was a new portion of nuclear dust and rain.

A friend of ours was a physician in Odessa. She met many people from Kiev. In Odessa, the hospitals and clinics and science hospitals began to treat people. But the Soviet Union itself took no special action against this illness. If someone had pneumonia, they treated against pneumonia only. If someone had skin burns, they treated only the skin. If someone's stomach was bad, they treated only the stomach.

KLAVDIA: In Kiev, young women who were pregnant were put in clinics and forced to have abortions. Other times, they just lost the babies. Some women ran at the thought of abortions, screamed that they couldn't.

Inside the hospital it was a real hell. People cried on the floor because there were no beds. They lay on the floor, waiting to have abortions. The doctors would explain to pregnant women that the radiation was not good, and sometimes they would understand. It's a black place in history.

In the Odessa hospital, our friend said that if she pushed a woman's skin with her finger, it would bruise and stay pushed in. If someone was cut, it didn't heal, it began to spoil. The wounds from old operations opened again and spoiled.

Women suffered the most because of their insides. There was too much blood. They grew mustaches. Young women stopped bleeding forever. Other women never stopped.

IGOR: It was a little nuclear war. We thought it was finished for humans.

KLAVDIA: Women lost their hair.

IGOR: In classrooms close to Chernobyl, a little boy fainted because he drank milk—from a farm where the cow ate green grass that was radioactive. Even the babies didn't have milk.

RAIMONDA: It was a big problem with vegetables and fruit. That was the main problem, for all people. The market was part of our life. The food was always fresh from the ground. And suddenly we couldn't buy anything.

Grandmother once bought me nuts. They were so big. But they were black. The water turned black when we washed them. She just threw them out.

KLAVDIA: In Chernovtsy, we kept going to the markets because the stores were empty. Finally, after two months, there were officials with Geiger counters. But people were hiding food from the counters because they thought the officials just wanted to take the food for themselves.

IGOR: I saw a peasant woman hiding meat under her skirt to avoid examination, even though the other meat in the store was tainted.

Nobody knows exactly how much bad food was mixed in. Nobody was controlling it.

RAIMONDA: For me it seemed a big problem of another world, not mine. It wasn't my problem. Because I was just a child, I didn't understand anything.

IGOR: A cartoonist I knew in Kiev had three young children. They all got very terrible nuclear pneumonia after the accident.

The next year, the pneumonia came to Chernovtsy. At first people didn't believe they would get sick. The weather was good, and they vacationed near the river. Then the next day they woke up sick, and got sicker and sicker every day.

RAIMONDA: I know why I became sick. In May, I went to swim in the cold water from the mountain. That's why I think it happened. I only went inside the water and then went out again. I don't think it would have made me sick normally, but I was weak because of the radiation. If I had been strong and there had been no radiation, I wouldn't have been sick because I just went inside the water and out again. Very fast.

I was a child. No one else was swimming because the water was so cold coming down from the mountain. I felt like if I went in, I'd be the hero—the only child who went in the cold water. I jumped in and out. I couldn't really get that sick—not pneumonia—just by jumping in two times and that was it. Mama didn't really worry about it.

But the next day I woke up and felt very bad. Because it was Saturday, I had to clean the apartment. I said I felt sick. My parents didn't believe me. They thought I just didn't want to clean. I said I felt hot. Papa told me to wash the floor. When I was cleaning, I was sort of dancing because I couldn't stay properly on my legs. Then I got so tired I thought I was dying. They measured my temperature. It was 40 degrees Centigrade [104° F.]. They put me in bed, and Papa told me I should go to the hospital. I wanted to do anything but that. The hospital was the scariest thing for me.

At first I felt like I wasn't very sick. I had a boyfriend, and he came to me and said, "Close your eyes." And when I opened them I had a red ring on my finger, and he told me, "I'll wait until you get better." And I became red on my face because my grandfather was sitting next to us reading the newspaper. But he cannot hear. He did not hear a thing, just kept reading.

I wasn't so sick then. But, of course, my doctor was stupid. She came and said that I just have the sniffles, that I am not sick at all. And then when my temperature got higher, she came again and said, "Oh yeah, she has a cold." And then the next time she said I had flu. The next time she came and saw that I was really sick. Then she said I had pneumonia on my left side.

So for three weeks, I became more and more sick, and then I thought that I was going to die and my grandmother Sofa always called and screamed: *"You have to put her in the hospital. What you want—for her to die? You don't care."* It was terrible. Then my temperature was 41.

Every day, I felt worse and worse. My temperature would go

down and then up and then too low. It made me feel worse. At night, I felt like an object, not a person. My grandmother Sofa would call at two o'clock in the night and tell me I had to go to the hospital.

Papa had a friend from the hospital, a Jew, who came to me with three other doctors. They were examining me, four people in my room looking at me. They told me to go to the hospital immediately. But I started crying, and they finally said it was a problem, but that I could stay at home and take my medicine.

The next day, I felt so bad. I had such a high temperature, Papa drove me to the hospital. Someone else was with him, but I was so sick I don't even remember whose face I saw.

Two old women doctors examined me at the hospital. There were three floors at the children's hospital: the first floor, for babies born too early; the second floor, for children with heart problems; and the third floor, for pneumonia. One of the old doctors thought it was my heart because I was having pain there. So she was examining my heart and the other was examining my back. One started screaming for me to go to the second floor because it was my heart. The other screamed for the third. Finally, Papa's friend took me to the third.

Then they put me in a room with about twelve children and twelve mothers. And some of them were just babies, little kids, but they weren't as sick as I was. And of course mothers—they care about *their* children—they started screaming: *"She's got a 41 temperature. She could die. She can make everyone sick. Get her out of here!"* I remember it as though through smoke. I couldn't understand anything because I was so sick; I imagined things. When I woke up, I was in another room with two beds, one for Mama and one for me.

I hated it. I could not sleep, only sweat. And I would think that I was going to die, that I was full of water and nothing more. That I was not a human. I was so sick.

The doctor finally said that my sickness was so terrible that I was going to die. In the morning my father came and his teeth had fallen. He was so nervous that his teeth had dropped—the gum stayed up but the teeth slipped down. He was so worried.

Then my grandmothers met inside the hospital. I saw my father's mother every day. But Grandmother Sofa did not come often because she is old. So when she came, she met Grandmother Galya, and she started to talk about how my parents were bad. I was lying sick, and my grandmothers started to talk about my parents. Grandmother Galya was looking at me, but Grandmother Sofa just screamed and talked about my bad parents. And by the time she went away, I had a big temperature again.

Then they started to test. They saw inside of me with X-rays, and they saw something so strange: My pneumonia was so bad and so unusual for children that they couldn't even understand how I could survive it.

IGOR: At first they thought it was her heart. Then the X-rays showed she had an unusual pneumonia for a child. It was more like short-term tuberculosis. Within ten days, most people die.

It shocked me. The shock attacked my nervous system. My teeth dropped. It was the biggest fear of my life.

KLAVDIA: She had pneumonia for two months. Twice a day they did X-rays.

RAIMONDA: I felt like a bone was coming through my heart. And the shots, they wouldn't let me live in peace without shots. Shots in my arm I didn't feel. But others . . . when I sat down, I screamed.

Every hour they gave me a shot. Even at night, they woke me and did it to me. After all that, my muscle was so hard that they couldn't get the needle inside. But I was dying and they had to do it.

IGOR: I went to the doctors and begged for my daughter's life. I kept asking and asking. And finally, one of them who knew my reputation as a cartoonist gave us American antibiotics.

RAIMONDA: So at last I became more healthy. It was a miracle.

KLAVDIA: Raimonda was in the hospital for a long time. When she began feeling better, the doctor said to go with her out of the hospital and to sit on the bench near the hospital's big garden.

She was okay. But I noticed after sitting outside, she began to feel worse. She got very big bruises under her eyes. The air was not good outside from the radiation.

In the hospital room with the door closed and the windows closed, she began to feel better.

RAIMONDA: Finally, I got to go back home. I threw up on the way. I loved strawberries, but not wild strawberries, and Mama pushed them on me for strength. My papa almost killed her.

But I was happy to be at home.

IGOR: So, when we had to send her away from home for the second time, we knew that we could not stay in the Soviet Union. That was it. We had to move for the child.

RAIMONDA: That was when the illness began. There was a girl in our class, and she didn't come to school. We thought that she was just sick. But her mother, who was a teacher, came inside the class crying and red, and she said to my Jewish teacher: "Can I go? My daughter is sick, her hair is falling out." And my teacher hugged her and said, "Sure. Don't worry about anything. Take any time you want." She went out crying, and the teacher told us what had happened.

One day there were the usual thirty-four children in our class; the next day there were twenty. The next day there were fifteen; the next ten. The next day there were five and then two and then no one came. I left when there were only about ten left. School was empty.

We couldn't get away. We knew that the same radiation was inside the house. The officials still said, *Everything is okay.*

But we could all see there were cats and dogs without hair. It was terrible. There would be a kitten walking by in the yard, and we would see that his tail was hairless. So we didn't want to touch him anymore, to hug him as we always did.

This illness happened only in our town. When it happened, nobody told us the truth. There were thoughts that the soldiers threw out some of the chemical liquids for war. I don't know. In school, we talked about it. Some taxi driver said he saw the dumping, and he told it, and then the Party put him in the crazy house and told him that he was crazy. They thought that would make no one believe in him. We didn't know who to believe.

Everyone knew that there was radiation, and it made the children sick, and we couldn't play. Almost all of us were weak from the radiation. The kids who had blue eyes and white hair lost their hair more quickly than black-haired strong kids. Everyone was afraid that all the children would die: one morning, they had hair, and the next morning, they did not. It fell out overnight. Their nervous systems were broken, and they began to act crazy: they thought that dogs and cats were jumping over them. They imagined it.

On some streets there were more children without hair than on other streets. Every day someone's hair fell out. It was terrible. Finally, my father said: "Okay, you are leaving."

I was going to Odessa with my father's mother, Galya, to her friend's house. Our relatives did not call us, did not ask us to come. So we had to go to my grandmother's girlfriend whom she had known for forty years. At first I was very glad.

I always thought that I would be happy without my parents. But then after ten days I hated everyone else and I wanted only to go back to my parents. After ten days, it was the longest time I'd been without them.

I was walking back and forth, so angry. Then, at night, Grandmother was holding my hand, and I was crying. She said, "What do you want? Do you want to lose your hair?" And so we hugged, and all night we were friends. But in the morning we were like enemies again, fighting and fighting.

I was so nervous, I always screamed. And once I screamed at my grandmother's friend. She said, "Why are you screaming at me?" And she looked at me like I was nothing. I screamed, *"I'm not screaming at you!"* Finally, I could not even stand my grandmother, I was so angry. I hated everything. I was crying on the phone, and saying to my father, "Please, take me home. *Please.*" He said, "Okay, okay, okay." But he didn't because of the danger.

Then, just before the New Year, he said, "Okay, now you can come." We were away two or three months. For me it was a very long time. And I counted every day until we could go. Then we were leaving in only three days. I packed all my things and closed my luggage. I wanted the three days to go faster. If I had to take something out of my luggage, I had to pull it out from under the bed and open it. They were laughing at me, my grandmother and this woman, because I wanted to leave so fast.

I came home finally to Chernovtsy, and I saw my father and winter and snow and my town and everything, all my loves. I was so happy. I ran and hugged Papa. I was so glad, and I wanted to run away from my grandmother. I had been so bad, before the sickness, when I thought I wanted to leave my parents. But then, I couldn't live without them. When I saw them again, I was so happy.

IGOR: We couldn't stay in Chernovtsy, though. This sickness was just the final straw.

Glasnost had changed Jewish life. There was more and more information about Jews. It was not published in big newspapers. It was local, a feeling in the city. Big political things didn't change. But little things changed: Israel had always had a bad name. "Zionism" was the bad word. When the government said things about Israel, it was always anti-Semitic propaganda, especially in the Ukrainian newspapers. There was lots of propaganda—letters from Israel about how bad life was there, or in the United States. People read the letters and believed that there were no jobs, no good environment, lots of criminals, hot temperatures, young men killed in Palestine. It may have been true, but it was used as propaganda.

When *perestroika* began, the propaganda stopped. We began to hear Moscow radio broadcasts. When they spoke about Israel, sometimes they said good things.

Also freedom, *perestroika,* had opened the border, and a lot of Jews visited Israel and America. They visited a father or mother, sister or brother, because some hadn't seen each other for twenty years. Those first visits to the United States were big secrets. Another Jew would know something, and you would ask if you could meet with them and speak secretly about real life in the United States and Israel. There was little information about America. America was always dark.

When relatives came home to visit from the United States, one Jew told another Jew about going to an apartment to meet this visitor. There would be a big line of Jews; it grew more and more involved. But it remained secret because Jews were very afraid.

Maybe there would be a coup. People were waiting for something to happen. A coup could occur any day.

People began to compare these stories from Israel and America, and they began to consider emigration. The big question was, to emigrate or not to emigrate. And if so, when and to where? It began to feel like we lived in a big central station or airport. People lived with this thought: *Move or not move?*

The place where Jews filed documents for emigration—after they had an invitation from a relative abroad—was OVIR. You stood in line and gave papers. You filled out an application and waited. There was real competition. Some people knew more information than others. Some people didn't know where the door was. Some people paid the officials money, so it would happen more quickly. I waited only thirty days.

The synagogue and OVIR were two places where people spoke. But, to be honest, people didn't believe each other. This was Soviet life; Jews didn't believe each other. Jews never told the truth because of the Communist regime. Nobody knew who would tell the KGB. Something could go wrong.

Some Jewish activists had lost everything because they had been in prison—for nothing. Our friend Josef was one who suffered. Before *glasnost,* the KGB would break up all beginnings of real Jewish life. But they never said outright that they did it because this man was a Jew. Never. Always the newspaper said that it was because he was a thief; he stole something. But really it was politics—they didn't let Jews have freedom with Jewish life.

Now, all that seemed finished, like a window opened. Before the second war, the Jews in Chernovtsy had built three big buildings. The Soviets had since taken all the buildings for the Soviet government. There was a House of Culture with big balconies and room for dancing and a huge stage. It had been the building for Jewish community and culture. In this building in 1988, after more than forty years, Jews were allowed to come together and talk. Few Jews were Communist. And in that meeting, there was a confrontation, a struggle between Communist Jews and non-Communist Jews. Finally, the Communists got sent away from this meeting. It was in that moment that Jews understood something had changed in the Soviet Union.

Jews were working together. A friend of ours and his colleague collected money from Jews for rebuilding a very old Jewish cemetery in Chernovtsy. It was very famous and old, from the seventeenth century. The first Jews in Chernovtsy were buried there, but their relatives went out to another country and nobody cared anymore. There was a lot of green and trees; it looked like a forest. And the gravestones were broken. Anti-Semitic things were written on them. Weeds were growing on the graves. And the Jews began to have a special day together: young Jews began to clean and to fix. It was only one place, but we began to rebuild it.

Soviet life was easier. I, for example, didn't have to be afraid to go to synagogue.

RAIMONDA: With Gorbachev, it was more free for Jews. I remember the first change—it was on a Jewish holiday. It was spring. I think it was Purim. And my grandfather went to synagogue, and he was there all day. And it was the first time in my town that he was really *free* to go to synagogue, and to pray.

IGOR: It was the first time I ever saw a big crowd of Jews. It was Easter, 1989. It must have been Pesach. A big crowd was in the street, and the military was across the road, putting up barriers for protection. And suddenly I recognized that all the people in the street were Jewish, and they weren't worried about it. They weren't afraid to be in the street and show other people that they were Jews.

I recognized a lot of my friends in the city. I was surprised that young people were there, surprised to see children. A new generation grows up. I was not surprised by the old men. Old men went to synagogue all the time.

Everyone had smiles on their faces. They were greeting each other. It looked like a holiday. It seemed to me it was more civilian than religious. For me, emotionally, it was one of the bright pictures in my brain. It was the first time in my life that I recognized with pride: *Oh, I am a Jew, too.*

RAIMONDA: We were so proud, that day. It was the first time that I went inside the synagogue.

When we had driven near it in the past, my father said, "This is the synagogue." I just saw an old building, that's it. I never saw it inside, so it was the first time. The synagogue was one room and some old people. I liked it.

There were police near it, everywhere. And all Jewish people, all my friends were coming to synagogue. They weren't afraid.

KLAVDIA: Then, one day, my mother's best friend came to her. He always helps her do things. He is not Jewish, he is Ukrainian. She opened the door wearing her bathrobe, and he asked her: "Why do you have a telephone and I don't have? Why do you have this bureau and I don't have it?"

When he began to say it, she was very scared and she began to cry, and from then on she was afraid to go in the street to buy something.

RAIMONDA: In Grandmother Sofa's building, people had always tried to close themselves away from the street.

IGOR: Sometimes you forgot about real life—inside that building.

Sometimes I thought that all people around were the same as me. It was an illusion.

In this time of Gorbachev, it changed. Almost all people moved to Israel—and Klava's parents were alone in this building, as Jews. The situation changed, catastrophically changed. Usually if you live in a big building and something changes, you don't feel it. Somebody moves, somebody is born, somebody dies—you don't know. It's a big building. But inside this building, when people disappeared, life disappeared.

Sometimes I had a dream: *Oh Gorbachev, change life, and life will be better, more freedom.* It's a mistake! It's a historical moment. But it is also a break in basic life. Maybe freedom, yes. But how could my mother-in-law be happy with freedom when all her neighbors were angry, were her enemies? When all the Jewish people lived inside this building, they didn't have freedom. But they were Jewish, and inside was a real Jewish freedom—Jewish mind, Jewish thinking.

I think that Gorbachev changed life. Finished life, really finished. People who lived through it have to understand that life changed definitely. And nothing that will happen is good. Nothing.

KLAVDIA: My mother sees her country in ruins.

Still, she didn't want to go to America. We were ready. She was not. We understood that for our parents, it was too hard to start a new life. My mother worked all her life, and now she has a pension. And father is ill. They are old. And they didn't want to leave, didn't have the power inside to start again a new life. It wasn't real for them.

But when we were leaving, some Ukrainian neighbors came to me, and said, "How can you leave them when you know someone will come after them with an ax?"

THE DIARY

CHAPTER ONE

LEAVING HOME

"YOU CAN SEE YOUR NERVES SHATTER"

In the Ukraine, at bedtime, one of Raimonda's grandparents would settle next to her and draw pictures with words, pictures of the past. Her grandmothers told stories. Her grandfather sang ballads he had learned in the Second World War. Each wanted to give Raimonda something to carry with her wherever she went. They wanted Raimonda always to remember, never to forget. She was eleven years old and leaving everything she knew—the people and places of the town called Chernovtsy. She was leaving the distant mountains that ring the town, the trees growing along the streets where many families live in graceful, ancient buildings that still bear the beauty of the Austro-Hungarian Empire.

Raimonda believed then that she had been blessed with a lucky childhood. She knew friends who kept one threadbare towel all their lives, who slept every night on the same stained, thin pillow. Their parents worked in factories, while both Raimonda's parents worked as engineers: Klavdia, educated as a chemical engineer, was restoring wooden objects at the Museum of Architecture, and Igor had worked as a radio engineer. The Kopelnitskys prospered, Soviet style. They had a small blue car and a three-room apartment in a modern building. The parents slept on a pull-out couch in the living room, and the children slept in the only bedroom, where Igor had even eked a studio out of the closet. Raimonda was so accustomed to hearing his muffled radio playing as he worked that she couldn't sleep if he wasn't there. But she herself was only there intermittently; she and Simon alternated sleeping at one of the grandmothers' apartments.

The entire family spent many hours at Klavdia's parents' grand old apartment on Lenin Street, where Grandfather Adolf kept piles of newspapers and books in many languages. During the long years when he was incapacitated by his war wounds, he had read widely in Polish, German, Russian, and Yiddish. He passed his foreign newspapers along to Igor, who had studied engineering but who had always cultivated his gift for drawing political cartoons. In the late 1970s, that gift began to transcend his job. Igor sent illustrations across borders— to Poland and to Switzerland and to Germany—and won acclaim. Finally, in 1980, he stopped working as an engineer altogether. To support his freelance drawing career, he drove the family car as a taxi.

It was a comfortable life—comfortable enough to make it hard for Igor and Klavdia, both forty-three, to forsake. Their nineteen-year-old son, Simon, had long urged them to emigrate. A college student near Moscow, he had been beaten for wearing an Israeli flag insignia on his treasured denim jacket. He, more than anyone else in the family, saw the hatred of Jews—naked and fierce. In bohemian Moscow apartments with wildly painted walls, Simon and his friends smoked and mused about leaving. They told one another about letters from friends who had made it to Israel or Paris or New York.

Simon wanted what those friends had found. But his parents repeatedly spoke of their fears of being too old to start over. Simon promised to help them. He was young, he said. His English was good. He would make it easier for them. Simon's efforts were augmented by assurances of aid from one of Igor's oldest friends, Pavlik Salodnik, a physician who had been living in New York for a dozen years. Salodnik and his wife Tanya promised the legal invitation necessary for emigration. And so, haunted by Chernobyl and plagued by the increasingly flagrant hostility of their Ukrainian neighbors, the Kopelnitskys packed their fears and some belongings into a few trunks. "It is finished," Igor said of Jewish life in the Soviet Union. "And we are truly refugees."

The family did not anticipate what lay ahead: A dreamlike, expense-paid stay in a Vienna hotel was only a lulling overture to a grueling wait with some thirty-six thousand other equally anxious emigrants in Ladispoli, Italy, outside Rome. While U.S. authorities investigated each applicant for refugee status, the emigrants existed in limbo. Jewish organizations did provide education, and Raimonda studied Judaism for the first time. An eager spirituality took hold of her, and she worshipped, whether learning Hebrew or visiting the Vatican. But her exhilaration was tempered by the family's emotional tempest: Would Salodnik be able to sponsor both their family and another that sought his help as well? If they had to rely on a general sponsorship, would they be allowed to go?

While they mulled the uncertainty, they shared cramped quarters in Ladispoli with a succession of other families. Everyone suffered— and took out their mounting frustration on each other—as they watched the humiliation, and sometimes disintegration, of fellow emigrants. At the outset of the journey, eager to go to the land of Coca-Cola and chewing gum, Raimonda could not have guessed at the desolation she would feel in those agonizing months. She could not have known how often she would need a friend to comfort her when even tincture of valerian, a heartache remedy, could bring no peace.

But what she did realize just before they left Chernovtsy was that everything was about to change. That birthday, her twelfth, marked the last time her grandmothers would prepare a feast of her favorite things—the cucumber salads and knishes with savory centers. Those were the last days her grandfather would sing to her the funny song from the war—the one about the beautiful girl taking down her braids and driving the soldiers, the sailors, the tankmen wild. Slowly, the idea bloomed in Raimonda that now she would be responsible for remembering—and that now she would have her own stories to tell. She was going away forever. Nothing ever would be the same.

That's when she found Anne Frank's book and knew she would do what Anne Frank had done when the Second World War uprooted her life. Raimonda created a friend who would be there in the dark nights of Ladispoli, and ever after. She started writing a diary. This is how she began:

SEPTEMBER 2, 1989

Friday evening I met Papa on the street, where I was playing with my friends. He had a red book, and I asked him what it was. He said, "It's the greatest book by a Jewish girl." It was *The Diary of Anne Frank*. That night, I started to read it.

As soon as I had read a couple of pages, I suddenly wanted to write my own diary. That is you, my new best friend.

Now we two will share our joy and sadness.

First, I'll tell you of my life: My parents got married when they were twenty-four years old. My brother Sima was born in 1970, and I was born in 1977. Now I'm eleven years old.

We are Jews.

Right now, I live in the Soviet Union, in the city of Chernovtsy, where children and adults have started losing their hair. It is a frightening mystery. We fear the ecology is bad here. But the Party will give us no answers, even though our parents crowd around the government building and call for answers. Only silence answers. The sickness in the city is only called alopecia (the fancy word for baldness).

Since Gorbachev brought *glasnost,* there is a lot of anti-Semitism in our country, and we are certain that pogroms against the Jews will be starting soon. That's why we're emigrating to America.

Our *vyzov* [official invitation] is from Israel. But we are going instead to America. Do you wonder what kind of Jews we are that we're not going to Israel? We think we couldn't stand 48-degree Celsius temperatures. And I would have to get married when I turned seventeen to avoid the Army.

Right now we're packing our boxes and bags. Mama bought me new clothes, so big that I will grow into them slowly. I must leave behind my toys and my books. And also my grandparents. I will miss them very much.

Except for my parents, I don't have any real friends. My friends cannot keep my secrets. But you'll keep my secrets to yourself. And you'll be my only real friend.

So we're going to take a trip together, you and I. And maybe we'll see Venice.

I'll stop writing for now.

Raimonda

SEPTEMBER 3

Everything here is as usual, but it doesn't feel right to me because I know we are leaving.

I started to get very nervous—even though I didn't notice it myself. Everybody says that I talk a lot and interrupt people. Now I'm going to try to just keep quiet and give only short answers. To tell the truth, everybody's nervous. But that is understandable. We're leaving September 29. Then there'll be something to write about.

Raimonda

Today I was bitten by a wasp. It really hurt.

The Latest News

Vremya [the Soviet news broadcast called *Time*] . . . reports that the USA will not accept Soviet Jews after the new year. Is it possible we won't make it?

Raimonda

SEPTEMBER 7

I haven't written for a few days.

My papa packed the boxes, carried them out, and took them to Lvov in the car. The customhouse is there, and Papa went to Lvov with my brother. That was yesterday.

Everything went okay. But Papa packed things neatly at home, and there they just threw everything all over the place. And of course we had to pay a lot for all that.

Tonight I'm sleeping over at Grandmother Sofa's. The television over there is broken.

I got in a fight with Grandmother Galya. We haven't been getting along lately. But I think it will pass soon.

Raimonda

P.S. Grandmother bought me sunflower seeds. She changed the water four times when she washed them. But the water was black from the nitrates.

SEPTEMBER 11

I had to tear out two of your pages because there were a lot of mistakes. I offer you my apology. It's just that I want you to be beautiful.

I'm going to give you the name "Kitty"—that's what Anne Frank called her diary. She had a tragic fate. She died in a concentration camp during the war.

I read her book with tears in my eyes. I want to read another book about the Jews who died in concentration camps. I want to know everything about the Jews. When I read about them I become strong and proud that I'm a Jew.

Two girls in my class were upset, scared even, to mention their real nationality, that they are Jewish, and instead they said:

—I'm Russian.

—I'm Ukrainian.

It was probably hard for them to say that. But one of them has already left for the USA and forgotten everything.

Our class supervisor made a mistake and wrote me down in his class roster as Russian, not Jewish. I wanted to correct him. But a classmate told me it's better to stay Russian because they don't treat Jews well.

I answered my classmate rudely, and told the teacher. He soon corrected it for me. Yes, especially now, everybody in my class is an anti-Semite. They sing terrible songs about us. But I don't want to correct them. I don't want to think about the time when the students in my class sat at the teacher's desk and shouted in front of the whole class: "You're Yids." Or to remember the desk where Jewish Zhanna and I sit that had "Yid" written on it—misspelled.

All children hate. It's not their fault. It's their parents'. How can children hate unless they are told? They don't know why they hate, only that they have heard something from their parents or grandparents. It is history, and most don't care to ask for a reason. One day, my little neighbor girl didn't answer "Hi" to an older man. I asked her, "Why?" She said, "He's a Jew."

When I was in first grade, a girl ran up to me and screamed out, "Yid!" I wanted to run after her, but someone stopped me. Several years later, I walked home with this girl, and we've become friends. Not best friends, but friends after all.

My teacher that first year screamed at me: "You! You bother even my liver!" And the girl next to me repeated it with the same tone. I had only forgotten my books, just as others had. But I was the only one to get into her liver.

In fourth grade, a teacher sent me home to get my sneakers for gym; otherwise, she would give me a zero. Others had forgotten their sneakers. But she made me run home for mine—twenty minutes there and twenty back. I got back to school before the bell, but she, with her hateful smile, gave me a zero.

They don't have to call you a Jew. You can see it in their eyes and smiles. Once, a teacher in my fifth grade told the other kids: "Don't hurt them. It's not their fault." And I wanted to laugh in his face and ask him what he meant. Did he really think it was our mothers' faults? Another neighbor, an older girl, came up to me and asked me to say loud words with *r* in it, which Jews are not supposed to be able to speak correctly. How proud I was to scream out words with *r* in it—and leave her disappointed.

Enough of thinking about it. I feel pain in my heart, and I want to be alone with my joy somewhere far from here.

No! Of course I would take you with me.

You are the dearest thing that I have right now.

Raimonda

SEPTEMBER 15

On this day, twelve years ago, I was born.

It's a pity, but nothing happy has happened.

Soon I'm going to watch a detective movie on TV called *Sprut 3*. I've already seen the first and second one.

Mama and Sima are in Moscow looking for suitcases. I still don't know when they're coming back.

Tonight I'm staying over at Grandmother Sofa's.

See you soon, Kitty!

Raimonda

SEPTEMBER 17

Today was the best day in my life.

I had another birthday celebration. There was royal tort, Napoleon, fish, herring, and various salads.

I got a lot of gifts. From the other children, I got a warm nightgown, an outfit, a game, a stuffed animal, and nice little toys, and a very pretty little box. Ten rubles from Aunt Raya. Ten rubles from Aunt Roza. And from Grandmother Sofa gold earrings (little roses), a watch, "Red Moscow" perfume, and "Perfume for You." And I'm rolling in flowers from everyone.

But I don't feel good.

It's probably bronchitis.

Otherwise, I'm in a good mood.

Goodbye, Kitty
Raimonda

P.S. Voice of America broadcasts that whoever wants to emigrate to America on an Israeli *vyzov* and has the proper visa can go to Italy as of October 1, but whoever has only an Israeli *vyzov* must go only to Israel. We are lucky to have our visa. Still, we are hurrying for fear that the policy will change.

Raimonda

P.S. Papa left for Kiev to change money. Mama's coming back tomorrow at dawn.

SEPTEMBER 18

The doctor was over. He said that I was pretty. He prescribed some pills for me.

I have redness in the throat and a cold. Grandmother Sofa fixes me hot milk every hour. Mama used to put honey and butter in it when I was sick. I hated it and threw it up all the time, until she stopped putting in the honey and butter. I also get lots of hot tea with lemon and raspberry jam melted in it. I can walk around. We ate some "Debev" salad with potatoes, sausage, and peas. We also ate fish and tea with cake.

Grandmother Sofa bought some bananas. They're green, but we've never had them here in Chernovtsy.

Raimonda

SEPTEMBER 25

I was very busy today. I did the wash, ironed, and packed my suitcase. We were to leave tomorrow, but it is just as well that we are not because we still haven't taken care of everything.

Also, there were huge scenes. Papa and I went over to Grandmother Sofa's. Mama was there. We have 3,000 rubles we cannot take, and we wanted to leave it with our relatives so that they can visit us later. But Grandmother Sofa didn't trust Grandmother Galya, and Grandmother Galya didn't trust Grandmother Sofa. And Grandmother Sofa called Grandmother Galya the very worst names. She even turned on me. Me! Her favorite granddaughter. Calling me names, as if I were a black sheep! Not "fool." I'd forgive her for the word "fool," but the word she used will stick in my mind forever. And how does she know words like that? She messed up the whole house. And she kept trying to stir me up with all kinds of base and foul things against Grandmother Galya. I didn't believe her, but still she seemed hypnotized.

Afterward, Papa and I left her place. Mama, though, is two-faced and plays all kinds of dirty tricks. She has got a hand in it as well.

She had a fight with Papa. Toward morning they made up, but before that I cried a lot. Then they fought with Sima even though Mama was at fault. My bitter tears helped them all make up; they said what was bothering them and making them feel guilty about leaving. They swore that they wouldn't do anything bad and wouldn't fight. But I'm still not speaking with Grandmother Sofa.

We are scared of the future. Our apartment is beginning to be empty. We're giving our books and dishes and clothes to our grand-parents—or we are selling it. Our pasts are dying in our present. And we cannot even know what the future will bring.

Today I cleaned quince and cut my finger with a knife. I lost quite a lot of blood. I have a deep wound, it really burns. We'll prob-ably leave in September.

Uncle Felix, who is going with us, left for Lvov with our visas to buy himself and us train tickets from Bratislava, the chief city in Slovakia, to Vienna. We must go by bus from Chernovtsy to Bratis-lava. Now I'm going to Grandmother Galya's to sleep. I'll end with that.

> Goodbye!
> Raimonda

SEPTEMBER 26

Dear Kitty,

Today we filled out the forms. In the evening we'll go to Grand-mother Sofa's and make up.

> Raimonda

SEPTEMBER 28

Dear Kitty!

The ink has run out on my Japanese pen. I'm writing in black ink, but that doesn't matter.

We paid a lot of money—maybe too much—and signed the

agreement to go on the bus. We'll go by bus to Uzhgorod at four in the morning, and then to Bratislava, and then to Vienna, and then to Italy.

We had a scene. They're all so vicious, my family. Everybody is fighting. Grandfather arrived. I'm packing my things. Papa gave me a new pen.

Raimonda

SEPTEMBER 30

Dear Kitty!

At four in the morning on September 29, the bus drove up. We loaded twenty-five pieces of hand luggage. We drove through the night and part of the day.

Last evening, Papa, Mama and I went to the grandparents. We told them we were leaving, and they started to cry, all of us started to cry. Maybe I was happy—I'm leaving. Maybe I just began to cry because everyone was crying. It was like my great-grandmother's funeral, when I was a little girl and I didn't know why everyone was crying. But I felt if everyone was crying, I have to cry. Everything was happening like in smoke: Everyone was hugging me and saying, "I don't believe you are leaving me." And it was so sad for me that it was like I was sleeping and it was happening in my dream. My grandfather kissed me and hugged me, and then in this moment, I looked around in this room that I never will see again, and I really started to cry. I screamed through tears, "Grandfather, I will write to you. I love you." He cried a lot and hugged me. And when the door closed, I took my father's arm and we went downstairs in silence. We couldn't talk because everyone was thinking the same sad thing.

Then, I went to say goodbye to my friends, our downstair neighbors. They are my best adult friends, a woman and man who tried to leave for Israel. And they have a little boy, and I call him Shlomo. He is like my son. I taught him to walk, to talk, to eat, everything. And I love him very much. I started to hug him and to cry because I thought that I never will see him again. And then Shlomo hugged me and started to cry. He is so little, but he felt something. Maybe because everyone around him was crying.

And then I went upstairs, and some relatives opened our door. Everyone was smoking and talking. I had to push to go through the rooms, there were so many people—our closest friends and people I had seen only once in my life. I heard my cousin's voice and we looked for an empty place to be alone. We tried to go to the bathroom but it was busy. We tried to go to the balcony, but my brother and his friends were playing the guitar and smoking. And we found a room that did not have a lamp anymore, and there was no light, only darkness. And usually we are afraid of the dark, but this time we went in and sat and we weren't afraid. Only the moon was shining for us. She loved me and I loved her. We were not crying. We started to play, jumping like we always did. Time passed so quickly until it was two at night. People were kissing me and hugging and leaving, wishing me good luck.

My cousin and her mother and father began to leave. They were in the hallway, and my aunt jumped on my father and cried, "I will never see you again." And then my cousin jumped on my father and said, "I love you, Uncle. I love you." In this moment, my cousin understood that I am leaving. She kissed me and hugged me and called me Raimondoshka.

In the yard, we met my brother's friends saying goodbye. I didn't even see whom I kissed, but I kissed anyway.

Then everyone left, and I took my brother's hand, and we walked on a dark road with only the moon. And we felt we were really leaving.

We came to my grandmother's house, and she hugged me. My brother had to take the luggage to Mama, but I had to rest. Grandmother and I were lying on the sofa. She was telling me that she loves me and wants me to be a good girl. She said she wanted me to write to her. She was talking and talking.

I wanted to sleep. I was very tired. But I thought it was a shame for me to close my eyes because I knew this was the last time for my grandmother to talk to me like this. Finally I asked if I could sleep, and she said, "Of course. Tomorrow is a big day." At 4:00 A.M., the bus came. Grandmother woke me, and I said, "Why do I have to wake up?" And she said, "You are leaving for America."

At the bus, Father was gathering everything. I was wearing my new jeans. They are big on me. And a sweater. Everything is clean and new. I looked upstairs in my building. Only one woman was watching. I didn't like her and thought she wanted to go to America herself and that's why she was watching at 4:00 A.M. I wanted my grandmother to sit near me while we waited. But she said she wanted to sit with my father, her son.

And then we were saying goodbye to my grandparents, and we were all crying. There was a man leaving his mother and father, and he was looking through the bus window like he wanted to break it. It was raining. Grandfather told me, "It's for your luck that it rains." I didn't feel this rain, and I didn't hear the words that Grandmother was saying to me. Grandmother Sofa was hugging me and Grandfather was hugging my mother. My eyes were in smoke. Then I heard Grandmother Galya say, "Kiss me, I am your grandmother." And I just kissed everybody and went inside the bus. It was leaving. I looked outside the window and saw Grandfather crying and hugging my grandmother under the streetlamp. I said to them, "Goodbye."

I was crying and looking out the window wet from the rain. No one talked, and then everybody slept with tears on their faces. I started to sleep too, and it was the first night that I slept without dreams.

I promised to write to my grandparents every day, and I will keep that promise.

Now I'm in Uzhgorod, near to the border. We just have to go through customs. And without a bribe we'll sit here longer.

Now I'm going to sleep. There's nothing else for me to do.

Goodbye,
Raimonda

OCTOBER 1, 1989

Hello, Kitty!

On September 30 we passed through customs and were given back some Czech kopeks. And we went to Bratislava in Czechoslovakia. We arrived at three in the afternoon and reset our watches. At 12:55 Mama, Sima, and I took a walk around the city. Papa and all the others stayed behind to watch over the things. Mama bought Sima a beer and sausage with mustard and bread. She didn't buy me any because I got sick on the rabbit that Grandmother Sofa cooked without even taking out the innards or cooking it all the way through.

Papa and Sima weren't feeling well, either. Then Mama bought three smoked sausage sandwiches with little tomatoes on top and some kind of salad.

Even though it's unpleasant to write about it, I'm still going to write it all down: I had to go to the toilet. I paid two crowns—in our money, ten kopecks. I never sat in such a glistening bathroom even in my own house.

We arrived at the station at four in the afternoon. At five, the electric train came in. This is what happened: In a second, Papa, Sima, and the other men who were going with us piled one suitcase on top of another. We managed to get just one compartment.

And after that, this is what happened: Everyone began to shout, push, and look for seats, but there didn't seem to be any left.

There were eleven of us, and one old and dirty Ukrainian woman wanted to sit with us. But thank God we didn't let her; even if we did, there wasn't any place to sit down anyway. Many people had to stand.

The train started and we set out. For some reason it stopped at nearly every telephone pole. Then at the Czechoslovakian-Austrian border, the guards got on to check our visas. Finally, we pulled into Vienna. That's where everything began. We hauled out all of our baggage and the train left, and we stood waiting for a handcart. They took all our visas.

A fellow in a cap and delicate glasses took our papers, and he didn't seem to want to say what organization he was from. Papa and Sima went off to get a handcart. A man came up and told the women and children to come with him. He led us to a car.

Yes, as we rode on the train and approached the Vienna station we saw such beautiful sights: what buildings, what cars, what shining streetlamps! At twelve midnight—about two in the morning our time—cars came for us and everyone's name was called off from a list. We arrived at a hotel and stashed the suitcases in the basement. Everyone was living in the hotel, but we were led away to this apartment where I'm now lying down and writing. At first we thought that it was better in the hotel, but later it turned out that there were fifteen people in a room in the hotel and that many of them were Ukrainians.

We got separated from our friends. We were right in the middle of Vienna. My God, what a city! There's no comparing it to the Soviet Union. How clean, how much of everything there is! What shop windows! I would buy it all. But I have no money. Many people play the accordion or guitar and sing. It's too bad Sima didn't bring his guitar along. Today we saw a mime. He moved like a mannequin. He did it so gracefully that children were afraid of him. And then he started coming toward me, and I got scared and fell down in fright.

Today we had smoked sausage for dinner. The landlady of our apartment lent us money and we ate in a café. To tell the truth, the food looks very nice but it's not to my taste. The food in a fancy store downtown is very expensive. Today I found a half-kopeck of Viennese money on the ground. And the two-story buses here!

But the Austrians are anti-Semites. Today I saw someone wearing Fascist swastika earrings. It's very nice here, but it's not where I want to live.

Tomorrow they are supposed to come for Papa and he will go to the immigration offices called SAKhNUT, JOINT, and HIAS. He'll have to fill out forms and then we'll be given money. Right now I'm going to write a letter to Grandmother.

Goodbye,
Raimonda

P.S. We saw a music box in a store. When you open it, it plays sad music. And there were giant clocks half the size of the wall.

Tonight a rat ran across the cupboard. At first we thought that it was the clock ticking. Papa began to beat the top of the cupboard and the rat froze and then started creeping along on the sly, first with one paw and then the other. Then it crept out. It was very ugly, and even horrible to me.

Once, when I was younger, Mama and I were in one room and Papa was in the other. We happened to notice that a large rat was standing in the hallway next to the refrigerator. I locked myself in the room out of fear. But they killed it with a steel shovel—they just tossed the shovel and hit the rat. Then they took it out to the garbage.

That was a long time ago, though, in Chernovtsy. I am in Vienna, now. It is night outside, the street lights are shining, and empty buses are going by.

Raimonda

OCTOBER 5

We have been in Vienna for three days now. Today Papa went to SAKhNUT. They're supposed to issue our stipend. Mama and Papa have left, and Sima went to the market in the morning. I was sitting home alone. I straightened everything up. Then Sima came back with pineapples. That was the first time in my life that I'd eaten them, but I can't say they're the greatest. Sima brought potatoes, tomatoes, pickles, bananas, sausages, cold cuts, cheese, and Pepsi. I had already eaten. He bought ten pieces of gum very cheap and gave me three. I really want to go out, but I can't.

I wrote letters to my friends and my grandmother.

Yesterday we saw the mime again. But when we walked up, he just waved his hand and left.

We saw a man in a black suit and a cap. He played the street organ.

We saw a man who was dressed up like a god, a lamp was glowing on his head and he was holding a long, artificial branch. "War" was written on one of his sandals and "Peace" on the other. And in his other hand he had a poster saying, WE ARE FOR PEACE.

Everyone there was eating roasted chestnuts. Papa ate some, but he still doesn't like them, and he threw them away.

Nothing else of interest has happened. But I'm not going to say goodbye just yet, because it's only two-thirty, and Papa will be back from SAKhNUT in the evening.

Seven-thirty.

Papa has arrived.

We got 100% of our cash stipend.

Goodnight, Kitty
Raimonda

P.S. Papa and Mama have been fighting all day. I'm in a bad mood. But what can I do? I'm a zero. Twelve years old—that's nothing. What kind of independence can I have—half a kopeck's worth, which is what I found on the ground? My God! If only I were nineteen. My God, what a nightmare.

No I'm not hiding in the bush, but what was I born into this family for, with its scenes and shouting—into this nightmare that seems like it will never end? You didn't know this about me, Kitty, and I hope you won't leave me but will stay my friend forever.

How I want to pound the walls and wake up in another world instead of this greedy hell.

But if I pound the walls nothing will change and so I'll go to bed out of inner fatigue.

You, Kitty, are my second soul. I feel as if I will die and everything will disappear. Dear Kitty, you alone are innocent, even though you do hold the sins of others.

Everyone understands everything, all in silence. But the soul isn't silent. It wants to repent, but there's no one to hear. But I have you, and I can repent and relieve my pain only to you.

Suitcase
How bitterly he sighs
from its heaviness.
In him is everything that gets forgotten
and hidden from people.
And what is he carrying in life,
on his way?
His fate is condemned to be in
someone's alien hand.
In him are all the memories.
He hears every sigh.
His eyes are caressing
the burden he carries for someone else.

Mama's fighting with Sima again. He promised in Russia to take care of Mama and Papa if we would only leave. She says that he has turned away from us in this difficult time of emigration. He replied that he'll go off on his own and wants to eat separately. How boring all this is.

OCTOBER 6

Right now we're sitting at HIAS. We've had our interview. Even though they didn't ask us anything, they're supposed to give us a copy of the visas. Sima said today that he will only sleep and eat with us from now on.

The landlord lives in the next room. Last night, he heard Mama and Papa having a big argument. So Papa brought the landlord two bottles of vodka this morning and the deposit of 200 schillings. The landlord's a very decent fellow. He said, "No problem." And his wife also spoke to Mama as if it were nothing.

We received a copy of the visa. Now let's go home. That's all.

As if it were my last hour of grief.

OCTOBER 7

Today I'm in a better mood. Yesterday we bought enough groceries for two days and some gum called "Hubba Bubba." Soon the broth will be ready for lunch. We've already eaten the chicken. The chicken's wing was larger than a whole Soviet chicken.

I'm going to ask Papa if I may take English lessons. It's time for me to study, too.

The water heater is broken for showers, so we'll go take a shower at the hotel.

At four in the afternoon we met with a famous artist named Gerhardt Gepp. My God, what a luxurious house he has in comparison to our hut in the Soviet Union, even though we don't have it anymore. Mama wrote a letter to Grandmother Sofa that I'm drunk on Coca-Cola. She is never satisfied with anything. They've fixed the water heater.

Raimonda

OCTOBER 8

Dear Kitty!

Today is a very nice day, even though I haven't learned a single English word. But it'd be a shame not to see such beauty. We were at a museum. What beautiful old paintings. The most horrible picture was the head of Gorgon Medusa. Many of the pictures were from the Bible. The museum is next to a hall where there are Egyptian mummies, Greek and ancient Roman statues and decorations. For the museum we paid $6 for two—Mama and Papa. Children under ten get in for free. Since I'm short, I made it in without paying. Sima went off by himself, and was sorry later.

Near the museum there were fountains, sculpted trees, and walkways. There's a great monument to ancient warriors on horseback. And on the other side there is another museum with dinosaurs that roll their eyes and bellow as if they were real. I saw stuffed apes, some as tall as a man; a stuffed giraffe that was unbelievably tall; and stuffed elephants. There was an enormous skeleton of a whale, enormous stuffed fish, a shark, needlefish, and swordfish. Different kinds of insects and birds from all over the world. We were in the "Red House"—a castle like in a fairy tale.

Then we went to the post office and waited there for three hours. We had a conversation with some other emigrants. They were Ukrainians who pretended to believe in God. They have a guarantee from the church. They are going to Canada.

Upset, we got away from them. What's so bad about living in

the Ukraine for them—it's their own country! If it was so good for them there, then it's supposed to be better here? Anti-Semites. They believe in God in a way that makes me a slave.

Papa was ordering a call to New York so he could speak with Uncle Pavlik, but the operator said something so softly three times and then suddenly hung up, and there was such a lot of noise. Papa tried to get through five times and threw down the paper in anger, and the operator glanced at Papa as if to say: What's your problem? Papa's face showed his reply. No one was home in New York.

Then we talked with Grandmother and Grandfather for a while, and paid $8 for three minutes. The operator gave us a scathing look— he was so angry. But, at last, we heard our relatives' voices.

Papa and I accidentally got into a museum without paying. Where a ticket for children costs 20 schillings, the one for adults costs 50. So we economized by accident. We went through the exit where the register was closed. When we left it was open again. The day passed like a fairy tale.

Raimonda

OCTOBER 9

Today, I went with Papa to the hotel to stow the bags in the basement. We spent three hours there. All the other emigrants had piled their belongings on top of ours. Papa had to move them all to reach our things. And he hurt his back terribly.

When we came out to the street I was very cold; no doubt I froze in the basement. At home I didn't feel well either, and I went to sleep. I stayed home the rest of the day. Papa bought me two liters of my favorite soda. I dream about a dog every day. I want a dog so much. I'm going to sleep, it's already five after ten—past twelve Soviet time.

Goodnight, Kitty
Raimonda

OCTOBER 10

We saw the Royal Palace that has the Kaiser's room. Papa took my picture. We went to the market and bought groceries. I saved up 3 schillings and 50 groschen.

We ran into Sima for the second time in Vienna. He doesn't go out with us. Today there was a scene between Sima and my parents. When they got the stipend money, they became such greedy people. Sima has taken his money, and we've completely broken with him. He considers himself separate from us. He eats separately and walks in the city by himself. He comes home only late in the evening and leaves again early in the morning. I don't get involved at all, because I'm tired of all these scenes.

Papa went off to an interview. They took him to an expensive restaurant. He got an honorarium for pictures in a Viennese newspaper. He bought so much food he could barely carry it. Even black caviar. At ten o'clock he came back very happy. We have him to thank—he's our only provider.

Sima isn't working. Today he was at HIAS where they told him to come back any day next week. So we'll keep knocking about in Vienna.

We called Uncle Pavlik Salodnik. He left for America twelve years ago when he was young. He and Papa were friends. He was Papa's best friend. He said to write his name all over the forms. He gave us a guarantee. Now he's a millionaire doctor. When he left, I was still in a stroller. He lives in New York.

Raimonda

OCTOBER 11

Hello, Kitty!

I wrote a letter to Grandmother Sofa, Grandmother Galya, and Grandfather. They're all such nervous people. They talk and talk, oblivious of themselves.

Papa almost choked me to death, and my throat still hurts from it. He was angry. They were arguing, and I passed by like a fly. And he started to scream at me, even though I had nothing to do with it.

We brought an old painting with us to sell. This lady said that she'd help us sell it. Although we have brought it along with us, we are afraid that it will get squashed. Already there is a rumple—somebody put their suitcases on top.

I have 6 schillings.

Papa bought two very beautiful, expensive books.

I don't have anything else to write about today. I could say that today has been a happy day since someone lost some gum and I found it. Also, Papa bought me ten more pieces. Wednesday—today—is my lucky day according to astrology.

Till tomorrow, Kitty.

Goodbye,
Raimonda

OCTOBER 12

Hello, Kitty!

Since morning, it's been a typical day. We got up, washed, and ate. We still haven't been able to get used to so much food. We went hungry in the Soviet Union by comparison.

Sima went for a walk to take care of his business, alone.

Today we saw such beauty—the Belvedere Palace. We stopped inside and saw paintings from the nineteenth century—they were very pretty. And we strolled through a marvelous park right in front of the museum where there's a waterfall. I tossed in 10 groschen and made a wish that someday I'd return. It was the first time, the first place that I ever wanted to return to, so I threw a coin and I wasn't sorry.

Once I was relaxing with my grandmother on the beach in Odessa. We already had permission to emigrate, but Grandmother did not know yet. She told me to throw a coin into the sea and wish to return someday. I said I wouldn't make that wish. She asked me several times, but I didn't throw in my money with a wish. She asked me why I didn't want to throw the coin, and I answered that I didn't want to come back. Why? she asked with a smile. She didn't understand then that we'd be parting soon. Maybe she could have made it on this trip, but it would have been hard for us all.

We wanted to go to one more museum, but it was closed. We saw through the window that it wasn't very interesting.

Then we went to the market and bought grapes, tangerines, and bananas. We argued over something silly, and then made up. They bought me some ice cream. We went home. We turned off the lights and listened to nice music, and then Papa and I got up. Papa is writing a letter to Grandmother Galya, and I'm writing you what happened today.

So long, Kitty!

Raimonda

October 14

Dear Kitty!

Sima came back very late and woke up the landlord who gets up so early for work that you can't even see the hands of the clock, as Mama says. Twice the landlord said: "It is very bad."

Sima brought home a guitar. He met a girl who studied at an institute in Izmael, near Odessa. She gave him the guitar for a week. She arrived in Vienna on October 5. Sima went to their house for the guitar. He said that there were fifteen people in one room—from different families.

It's already late and we're going to sleep.

Goodnight, Kitty.

Raimonda

October 15

Hello, Kitty,

Today we went to the synagogue. JOINT invited us at ten. We had our pictures taken for German television. The crew was in Rome, and Vienna, and in two weeks they were going to the Soviet Union to photograph Jews. They photographed the emigrants today for a movie.

We took a very interesting excursion around Vienna. The tour leader was an emigrant from Romania who works at JOINT. He told us how Jews were killed in 1938; how great Jewish writers, scholars, and architects washed the sidewalks with soap and brushes. The Austrians stood over them taking pictures, and about two weeks later the Jews were shot. Now these same Fascists have built monuments to perished and humiliated Jews; now they say that they didn't kill Jews, that they were victims of Hitler, the Austrian SS, and the Austrian Gestapo.

And when the monument was built for the martyred Jews, the Austrians said that it didn't look good in the center of the city. They said it should be moved outside the city. This led to some fighting and even pogroms.

He pointed out and discussed many old places. We had been to most of them already.

We're leaving on October 29. Sima was at HIAS and found out

the date. I'm sitting home alone. My parents are coming back at eight. It's now seven. Tomorrow we're going to the museum.

Goodbye, Kitty!

Raimonda

OCTOBER 16

Dear Kitty,

Today I have a lot to write you. Sima met a Frenchman named Bruno who is twenty-five years old. He plays the guitar on the street and earns his money that way. Yesterday, Sima and he played Pink Floyd in English. Sima made $7 doing it. I'm against it and call it laziness. Even though it's better to earn money that way than lugging bricks or something like that.

Yesterday they played on the subway, and two policemen approached them and said in English very politely that they had to leave. When the policemen left, Sima and Bruno decided to stay because a lot of people give money there. Playing is allowed downtown on the square, but there they only make a little. (There is some kind of mafia. Nothing has been explained to us.) A half an hour later the policemen came back again, and then Sima and Bruno left.

Sima went to Bruno's house. He has a whole wall full of recording equipment where he records his music and songs. He was born in Paris, didn't go into the Army, and for that he spent two months in jail. He has passed through many cities and countries. He has played everywhere. He said that they give more money in Italy than in Vienna. He is a professional musician.

What am I writing about him for? He's a stranger; I've never met him.

Yesterday Sima and I went to the zoo. He hit and pinched me—it really hurt. I don't understand him. I'll ask him something or other, and he hits me and says that I'm bothering him and that he's going to go home. He was waiting for a girl he knew to come. She didn't.

I really liked it at the zoo. But it was sad to see suffering animals who are just waiting to die. A lion that was captured when he was young just paces from one corner to the other and waits to die. A panther that a child was tormenting roared out of anger and leapt, but remained in his cage out of weakness. The panther fell silent and paced from one corner to the other. There is nothing for any of them to do, and they all just sleep and whine in their tormenting laziness.

They were snatched from the wild, that is, from life. They were all like that, sleeping camels, elephants. They're all growing old and helpless. Except for the pelicans that just eat, or rather, fish for fish with their bills and swallow them right away, the birds all have clipped wings so that they don't fly away. The poor martyrs.

Today we went to JOINT. One of my teeth hurt and needs to be pulled out. We won't have to pay for it, JOINT will. It'll be pulled on Wednesday.

At JOINT there was an old man lying down who was dying of a second heart attack. They had to revive the old man. It's a good thing we didn't bring Grandfather along, all the more because he has "infectious" tuberculosis. In the subway today, some scumbag was hitting his girlfriend in the head with a stick so hard that she was wailing through the whole subway. A drunk man was walking there. He had been drinking with the girl who was being led away by her mother, and the girl and the man were still talking about meeting again, and she was so drunk that if her mother hadn't been holding her up she would have fallen.

Sima showed up. He played again and made 114 schillings.

Mama bought me a doll and I gave her my dollar. It's a very pretty doll. In Chernovtsy, I gave up playing with dolls. But here, I want them again. So do the other girls. There is too much missing in our lives.

I'll stop here.

> Goodbye, Kitty
> Raimonda

OCTOBER 19

Hello, Kitty!

Today I'll finally write you all the things that have happened over the past days. Yesterday we were at the Albertina. We were lucky.

Albert, the son-in-law of the Empress, was a strange man. In those days (in the last century), it was the fashion to collect the paintings of famous artists. Everyone was doing it—all the rich people. He, on the other hand, collected not paintings, but drafts. They've remained intact. It seemed to me that these works were better than paintings. Most of all I liked the works of Albrecht Dürer (b. 1471), Rubens, and others.

Then we ate Italian ice cream in a special shop, or rather, Café Dolce, where there were many different flavors.

At 6:00 P.M., we were waiting for Sima at the Stephansplatz— we wanted to go together with him to the Catholic church to hear the organ and boys' choir. He never came and so we didn't go. When we got home, Sima was standing in the doorway. Papa had forgotten to leave the key to the apartment for him, and the landlady had gone off somewhere. We ate and went to bed.

Today we were at the Historical Treasures of Austria Museum. We saw clothing embroidered with gold; crowns made of cut and uncut diamonds and other valuable stones; swords; boxes; and a crucifixion of Jesus Christ made of gold and relics: a tooth, little bones, cloth, and the nails like those used on Jesus Christ.

We walked around the city and dropped into expensive stores, after which we walked outside, red and hot.

Yesterday, no, the day before yesterday, I had my tooth pulled. We walked into an apartment that was made into a dental office, or rather, several offices—two for the patients, and the third for the X-ray, and the fourth as a waiting room. I was the first to be seated, in a half-lying posture, and they gave me an anesthetic injection in the gums. Part of my mouth was frozen, and in five or ten minutes my tooth was pulled so that I didn't even realize it—without any pain! It was the first time that I didn't have pain while a dentist pulled out my tooth. The dentist was an emigrant. He had emigrated with his wife many years before, and had now become rich. He's a Ukrainian. An hour and a half later when the anesthetic had worn off in that part of my mouth, it was very painful, but it passed during the night.

Today they were taking the dinosaurs out of the museum. We watched them being moved by cranes onto trucks.

There was a strange scene today in our family. I thought that I'd gone crazy. Papa gave out my secret. I told him how Sima had hit me real hard at the Belvedere. Papa began to curse—"Sima, may you die under the gate next to the drunkards." He disavowed Simon. And I said the same thing to Papa out of grief, and he said, "Go to hell." Then he said that when I'm grown up if I become a prostitute, he would disavow me too. It's too much. No one ever speaks to me like that. That exceeds everything. There's no limit to it. They'll drive me to the psychiatric hospital, and I will stay there by myself my whole life and they'll be rid of me. It's like we made up, and yet a devil is scraping my heart.

It's difficult to forget. Let him scrape, maybe he will mix up and scrape everything clean. Kitty, we'll still survive and forget everything. I'll even forget that I wrote about it. So don't be sad. But now, goodnight, Kitty!

Sad Raimonda

OCTOBER 21

Kitty, all of this is the end. I have to throw myself out the window.

We have money and are living better than anyone else; Dad has published some of his drawings here. And besides, the organization pays for everything—we don't have to pay for the apartment or for food. Yet all the emigrants are choking on Soviet canned food so that they can economize and save their unhappy money. They go to the cheap stores where most stuff is not fresh and not tasty. We went only once. But the other emigrants only look at those store windows, and we shop there. Some people really need to economize because they have no money for Italy or America. Some are just greedy.

Mama is simply a schizophrenic and still yells at me. Morally, I have completely broken with her, and Papa has too. She's breaking up the family. If she hadn't started arguing in the first place, Sima wouldn't have taken his share of the emigration money. He was the one who said that he was going to look out and care for our parents whenever they needed him. But he didn't keep his promise. Papa is hurt by this.

So now they tell me that I can't eat the liver because it was Mama's work—she brought it and cooked it. I have to leave. I will never forgive them for this—I'll always remember it.

Goodbye, my love for Papa and Mama. I'll remember this my whole life.

Now they're asking me to eat the liver. Even though I'm hungry, I'll get by without it. No, they've driven me to this point.

Now Papa is getting rid of Mama. Thank God Sima's not here.

Then Mama wanted to leave. Papa wanted to hit her. I said that we'd eat the liver, but not I myself.

If they had gone, I'd have thrown myself from the window. They're breaking my heart.

Now Mama wants to stay home and she wants us to leave. Papa hit Mama again. She promised not to fight for two weeks; she swore that she wouldn't. But she couldn't hold out for two weeks.

Mama left. Papa ate the liver. I couldn't touch it. If Sima had been here they would have blamed him, and I'm the guilty one. Even when they make up, I will be the one to apologize. I know that for sure—I'm used to it. Sima's back.

This afternoon I told Papa that we should make up. He agreed. But now everything has fallen through. I've morally broken with Mama. I don't want to do anything but keep to myself in peace and get away from this hell that has been after me for ten years. Sima earned 20 schillings. He's lucky that he's nineteen years old.

What will be will be, as long as my heart keeps beating with the help of tincture of valerian.

What a shame—I was happy that I was going to America, and now I'm discouraged and all my joy is gone.

We made up by evening. Mama is sleeping, Papa is listening to the radio. Sima is writing letters to his friends. Today he made 270 schillings.

He was playing with Bruno at the market. God, they were surrounded by such garbage, such scary people. Inga left and took her guitar and Bruno gave Sima his second guitar. For a while Sima was all red—it was very hot: 19 degrees. A drunk walked up to him and screamed out some rock and roll. But at any rate Sima earned enough money to live on for two or three days.

This afternoon Mama took a walk by herself. A lunatic brushed past her. He followed after her, but she managed to sit down between two people and he went his way. Then she sat on the bench by herself, until a man came and sat next to her. He began to say something in German. She didn't say anything, got up, and left. Looking around, she saw that he was following her. He spoke to her again in German. Mama understood the word "coffee"—he wanted to invite her to a café. Mama said in English that she didn't understand him. So then he invited her in English. And then Mama said: "I have husband, son, and daughter."

He understood Mama, but nevertheless invited her for a cup of coffee. Mama didn't accept, but he walked her all the way back home and kissed her hand. That's what happened with Mama.

Papa and I went downtown. Chileans were playing a very nice tune and suddenly a crazy woman walked up, about fifty years old, who looked as if she were thirty-five, and began to dance. She spun around and waved her hands in the air. She danced for what must have been an hour and got hot. She put her bag and jacket on the ground and went on dancing. Her eyes were insane, like a wolf's, and you could see her white teeth.

It was a beautiful melody and people wanted to dance so much that one young fellow of about eighteen couldn't resist and began to dance in a circle. This lasted a couple seconds; he danced so gracefully, so beautifully. He's probably a mountain man, a Yugoslavian in wide pants. We had a pleasant evening.

> Goodbye, Kitty
> Raimonda

OCTOBER 22

Hello, Kitty!

We got up and ate. Sima eats his own food, by himself. Mama started to ask Sima for some pieces of cheese. Twice he gave her some.

But after she ate them, she started asking for more.

SIMA: "First, twenty schillings, then you eat."

MAMA: "You promised to feed me for five years."

PAPA: "Promises. Promises. Promises."

SIMA: "Mama, give me some of the grapes for the cheese."

MAMA: "You ate two of my rolls already. Take some more."

SIMA: "Come on then."

—Silence—

Sima takes the grapes.

MAMA: "No, these grapes I'm not going to give you, only the red ones."

SIMA: "That's already enough for the cheese."

MAMA: "Tasty grapes. They were expensive, fifteen schillings."

Papa comes in and says to Sima, "I don't like this. Buy your own grapes. These are my grapes. I'm going to eat them tonight."

Enough of thinking and writing about this. I hope you've understood, Kitty, what discord and greediness for money have done! Now let's go for a walk—I won't say goodbye.

We ran into Sima, like always. Papa took our picture at the monument to the Jewish victims, and at the column with the Mogen David. Sima went off by himself. And we sat in an ice-cream shop next to the Catholic church. And suddenly up walked Lena, Anya, Sasha, Dasha, Stas, and Shiseli, our relatives.

You don't know these people. They are all relatives of ours from

Odessa who arrived a week ago. We know each other well—their mother is Aunt Dina who is my grandmother's sister; Aunt Liza is the wife of my grandmother Sofa's brother, who died many years ago. And we ran into them here. We took a walk around downtown and then went to their house. We played with Dasha. She lived in Odessa. I've seen her once a year in Russia, all my life. She wasn't my best friend, but I loved her because she is my cousin. We fought a lot.

We got home late. Sima is spending the night at Bruno's. Goodnight, Kitty. I'm in a wonderful mood. My soul rested while I played with Dasha. I already miss the children, especially Dasha.

Raimonda

October 24

Dear Kitty,

Part of my diary is finished today. You've found out a lot about me and my family. You truly keep my secrets. I've gotten used to you and have come to love you.

I'd like to offer you my apologies for the fact that I've written so messily. I can't make it out myself. I'd like to say that I haven't argued with Mama and that I'm not mad about what she's done. I love her with all my heart. She's my own mother.

I also love Papa and Sima very much.

I love all my dear relatives.

I'm very glad that I'm emigrating. I dream at night that I'm returning to the Soviet Union, and in my dream I even begin to feel cold and terrible—I'm afraid of returning.

Today we received our stipend. We went to a restaurant and ate broiled white fish, which was very tasty, and fried potatoes with pieces of lemon. We spent 60 schillings. And then Papa and Mama had coffee and each of us had a piece of cake that was very delicious: 22 schillings. Then we went to the post office. We wanted to call Grandmother Galya, but we would have had to wait five hours. So we didn't call; we just sent letters.

Love,
Raimonda

OCTOBER 25

Dear Kitty!

Today we met up with our relatives at 1:00 P.M. I played with Dasha, swung on the swings all evening.

At the cathedral there's a glass box that people throw money into for the restoration. A voice in the box says, "Thank you," in Austrian.

Mama bought food at an inexpensive store. Papa was at the library. Sima spent the second night over at Bruno's. I have 8 groschen.

Love,
Raimonda

OCTOBER 26

Dear Kitty!

Today is a marvelous day. Museums are free. Today is a holiday in Vienna to celebrate when the last Soviet soldier left Austria. I think it's funny. In Vienna there is a square. It used to be called Hitler Square, and in 1945 it was renamed Lenin Square.

Today we were at the museum of modern art. The works of Kienholz were there. Most of all I liked the hotel where there are rooms and when you push on the door a woman is crying in one room and a man and wife are talking in the other and a dog is barking. I felt bad for the woman who is crying—I even wanted to go to her and comfort her.

In another work, a young woman is sitting with her hand on a pig looking at herself in a mirror. There is a notebook with a bill she owes in front of her and a pistol lying on top of it.

Then we were at the avant-garde museum. There was a sculpture of a woman that looked as if she were alive—you could even see the veins.

We walked around downtown. Tired, but happy, we went to bed.

Goodnight, Kitty!

Raimonda

OCTOBER 27

Dear Kitty,

This morning we were at the Clock Museum. It was magnificent. There were even clocks with the Torah and a six-pointed star—Jewish clocks. All the clocks warm the soul.

We saw the city clock where at twelve o'clock figures that look like people walk out. Right now we're packing our things. Tomorrow they'll be sent off, and we'll leave the day after tomorrow. And I'll have to say, "Farewell, Vienna," just as I once said not long ago, it seems, "Farewell, Chernovtsy."

Goodnight, dear Kitty!

Raimonda

OCTOBER 28

Dear Kitty!

Hello!

Tomorrow we're going to Rome. My experiences, troubles, joys, travels—my new life—will begin.

I think that you'd be interested to know, or rather to learn or see into my life. I've come to love you and I don't think of you as a notebook but as a girl whom no one knows but me, and who has become my second soul. I have two things that are most valuable to me—that's you and my poetry. I know that if I were deprived of you and my poetry, I'd never begin to write again. I wouldn't be able to live without you both. I'd lose faith in my own future.

Raimonda

OCTOBER 29

Dear Kitty!

So the day has arrived! We must take our leave of Vienna. I'd hardly noticed the days passing and I realized only late that it wasn't a dream. It was happiness that passed by unnoticed and enchanted our wild, dark heads. And so today we're off to Rome. That's also a happy thing, not bad at all. We cannot say it's bad that we are abroad and are living for free. It's not intelligible, but pleasant as in a lovely dream.

Our things were shipped off yesterday. We'll be at the train station today at five.

Papa had a bad dream that something had happened to me.

Sima went out for a walk. He said that he won't even sell the Russian souvenirs we brought from the Soviet Union to sell in Rome. He won't help to sell them there even if there's a flea market every day. He'll earn his own money. Since he has separated from us, we don't give him money for the things we've sold here in the markets: matreshki dolls, pillowcases, sheets, nightgowns, handkerchiefs, and shawls. They are very popular. We sell them for ourselves, not Sima.

At three-thirty we're going to the station. It's only ten o'clock now. Yesterday I wrote a poem, "Farewell to Vienna."

I probably won't be able to write you again today. So goodbye, Kitty!

> Raimonda Kopelnitskaya
> *Brigand of Chernovtsy*
> (a joke)

NOVEMBER 2, 1989

Dear Kitty!

Finally I'll write you where I am. We arrived by train at a station an hour's drive from Rome.

Before we left Vienna, we went to the station with our bags. But Papa had forgotten his false tooth, and he went back for it. The landlady and the new people had cleaned up the room. As Papa was climbing the staircase, boys were carrying out garbage and returning with empty buckets. Papa thought he'd never find the tooth. But luckily it was lying in the very same place and no one had noticed it. Papa returned to us with the tooth he had had made in Chernovtsy.

We started to call Uncle Seryozha who is in Moscow so that he'd call Grandmother and tell her that we've left for Rome. But the pay phone wouldn't return 2 schillings. We called from another where we lost another schilling. But a man next to us dropped 5 schillings on the ground, and I hypnotized him not to see it. Only I had seen where it fell. After he left, I picked it up. Papa wanted to buy a magazine with the money that was left. I talked him out of it, and we bought a kilo of oranges.

We went to the train. In the darkness, the Jews all stood together, and there were many of them, but no one seemed to notice. Unhappy Jews!

We got a compartment; we were glad that the compartment was

so empty. But our joy came to an end when we brought in our suitcases and we dragged them in tired, damp, and unhappy. We laid
them out like a giant bed that we could sleep on after we ate.

We arrived at 9:20 in the morning and carried out the bags. Papa's back still hurts. I also carried bags, and my shoulder hurt. Papa
and Sima put the suitcases in the car, and Mama and I were taken
with the other women and children to a hotel. Then Papa and the
other men arrived from the train, bringing the bags. Sima and I had
to move the bags, while Mama sat with Papa and his bad back. He
couldn't carry any. The hotel was on a hill, and the luggage was at
the bottom. Many of us found handcarts to bring up the luggage; but
the hill worked against us. Simon climbed up with his luggage, and
I was following, but the handcart was stronger and it dragged me
down the hill. I almost fell. But another emigrant who was climbing,
as we all did, helped me.

When we got to our room, Sima slugged me in the head for no
reason at all. I only whispered very quietly for him to open the door.
Maybe he couldn't hear me, or maybe it was just from anger. But he
slugged me. It burned and hurt. I cried. Not because of him, but
because I was so tired and depressed. I thought it was a good enough
reason for a cry.

We were given the very worst room, without hot water, the
stove wasn't working, there were thousands of cockroaches, and dirt
and stink. Patience! We'll have to live in this apartment for three days.
Thirty people arrived and on November 6 we must go. On the first
floor some unemployed Italian families were living for free. They
wouldn't answer the door even if someone were being killed outside.

Yesterday an Italian threw peel from an orange at me. She was
smaller than me, so I picked up the peel and threw it back at her. She
clung to me and started to fight. I pushed her away from me and ran
off.

Some people here are crazy. They think we're zeros. Russian
shit. Please excuse the language, but it's true.

We are given dry rations that are also shit and it's impossible to
put them in your mouth.

When Sima hit me tonight, I cried. I'm not speaking with Sima.
Papa and Mama scolded him.

Yesterday we were in the city. We saw St. Peter's Cathedral in
the Vatican. We were at the Trevi Fountain, which is now under
reconstruction—but people throw money into it anyway to wish that
someday they'll come again, even though there's no water. We bought

ice cream. They tried to pull a fast one on us by having us pay for a big one but giving us a small one. But it didn't work. Papa angrily hit the picture of the big one, and they finally brought it to us. This is not Vienna.

Yesterday Sima went looking for an apartment for us. He also looked for a friend of his from school in Chernovtsy named Oleg. There was no apartment, and Oleg is in Ladispoli, outside Rome. Sima was upset because that is very far away. Oleg has been his friend for a long time. They even traveled together one summer, camping in the south.

Today there was a knock at the door, and it was Oleg. Everyone was happy because he said that no one gets refused entry to America now.

He has gone away for now; he'll be back after lunch. He has worked for six months already.

Yesterday I really had a fright—I almost got run over. Others would laugh at it. I had a heartache, too. It was bad at night. I thought I would die. Right now I'm very tired even though I haven't done anything.

Rome is a beautiful city. We saw the Roman ruins.

But Rome is dirty. There's garbage everywhere. And for that reason all the beauty is lost in the vast quantity of garbage. I'd like to go back to Vienna. You think it's strange, but it's true. Lovely Vienna, you are the only city in Austria that I miss. Mama said: "Raimonda, rent us an apartment." Poor Mama! Yes, emigrating is a difficult thing. Not many can endure it. And many perish.

Raimonda

NOVEMBER 4

Dear Kitty!

I got sick on some of the rations. We're all fighting. I'm sick and tired of it all. I want to go to my grandmothers and grandfather. I want home-cooked food, vareniki, a chicken's neck stuffed with meat and vegetables and served with potatoes. I don't even want ice cream; I'm repelled by the thought of it. Sima came back last night. He has rented an apartment in Ladispoli. We'll go there on Monday. Now I'm going out for a stroll.

Goodbye,
Raimonda

N O V E M B E R 5

Dear Kitty!

The first few days Rome seemed to be a city of beauty lost in the garbage. But later I started to see a lot more, and the garbage became invisible. We're going to Ladispoli tomorrow at 7:00 A.M.

We've been arguing over silly things but we've gotten over it. Mama doesn't sleep all night. We were given cheese curds and there were stickers on the container. I stuck one on you, another on my poems, and I have one untouched sticker.

Two old people died in Rome who couldn't make it. That's what emigrating is like.

Goodbye, Kitty
Raimonda

N O V E M B E R 6

I can't go on any longer. I don't want to live; I want to be left in peace.

There was another scene with Sima. Sima took the suitcases and found us an apartment. Papa says he did it all out of hate. Sima came back in the evening after he'd rented the apartment—that very day. He's got to pay $100 because the son told him about the apartment, but demanded the money before he would let Simon have it. That's it; we've got to pay a broker's fee.

Yesterday we had a scene and I cried so hard that I don't have any tears left. Papa felt that Simon was lazy and didn't want to do anything. And if Simon did help, Papa thought he did it only from spite. We were packing up our suitcases to put them in the car that would take them to our new apartment in Ladispoli. Papa said that Simon was afraid of work. Papa ran after him in the basement garbage room. Simon ran away outside, and Papa's garbage box fell on the floor and everything spilled out. A manager came out and asked, "Is everything okay?" He has probably gotten used to all these scenes. Papa was nervous, but he calmed down and said, "Yes." So we cleaned the garbage from the floor and went outside. Simon appeared and helped us get the suitcases into the car. No one said a word; we silently worked with the suitcases. Today there was another scene. Mama is crying, but I've already stopped.

All my joy is gone and I'm discouraged. I don't want to see anyone—I want everyone to leave me alone.

Mama says that Sima has wrecked the whole family. What's he dragging us to the grave for? We'll all perish on account of him. He himself is going straight to hell and is dragging us down too. I pity my parents.

Why? Why do I find myself here amid this shouting, these dirty words, in this burning hell?

Poor Mama, poor Papa—you're tired of screaming and crying.

What am I supposed to do? I can only write to you about this horror that doesn't exist in any other family.

Kitty, you don't see this; and it's not describable, but I'll remember this forever. My heart sinks when I think about it. There's terror in my soul.

Today we're taking a walk in Rome. This evening we'll go to Ladispoli. Sima left already this morning. He'll send his baggage to the new apartment.

Tomorrow I'll be signing up for school. Yesterday I wrote a poem, "The Nun."

I've been writing poetry since I was nine years old. I have two stories.

With that I'll close.

Raimonda

NOVEMBER 7

Dear Kitty,

Happy holiday! November 7 is the day of the Revolution! And here we are at home. Of course it's not our home in Chernovtsy, but this apartment is even better. Our neighbors from Chernovtsy are here, they're also waiting to go—to Canada. We have one room, and what Sima has is almost a pantry. It's clean, and there are no cockroaches or mice.

I'm in a great mood. We sat in the kitchen around a round table. Oleg told us what was going on in his life since he emigrated. He spoke about nasty scenes. He and his mother almost committed suicide. Why do we repeat the mistakes of the past? The conversation helped.

Today is the first day we've been at peace, without any discord. Mama and Sima went to the market this morning, and she cooked food at home. I just can't even look at the bag of dried beans and the cans of corn from the hotel in Rome.

Today Sima and I recorded our voices on the tape recorder. My voice was different. Sima played the guitar. He met up with Inga, who is also here waiting to emigrate, and she gave him a guitar. He sang and I did too—Pink Floyd and a song by Grebenshchikov. We played chess.

Right now I'm reading the Bible, the Old Testament. I'd already read the New Testament in Chernovtsy.

I have all the conveniences: a closet and a table. We have our own refrigerator, but the television doesn't work.

We met our relatives from Odessa again. They were put up in a different, much better hotel. Today we signed a contract with Maria. That's our landlady. She's an elderly, simple woman who owns a three-story villa.

We've already been to the sea. It's too bad we didn't come in summer and go swimming then. Children from Bukhara are studying at the school. They're dirty children and have fleas, so that the rest of us can't even walk to school without our parents worrying.

Here, the students study Ivrit [Hebrew] and about Israel, English twice a week, and math twice a week.

There's a Russian library for children.

That's all for now.

Love,
Raimonda

NOVEMBER 12

Dear Kitty!

I'll be signing up for school on Monday. I'll go from nine to twelve every day, except Saturday and Sunday. I'll walk to school.

We're eating together and not quarreling. Today we were at the sea. The weather was like ours in summer.

Radio Liberty broadcast that those who received permission before October 1 and present their visas before November 6 have the right to emigrate to America or Canada. With that I'll close.

Raimonda

NOVEMBER 14

Dear Kitty!

There was a line at school, and the classes are overcrowded. To-morrow we'll go back to sign up.

Papa went to Rome and saw some editors, but they didn't publish him—they just laughed.

Today we met an American immigration official. I didn't like the way she dealt with us. She lightly crossed out our whole story that took us a long time to write out. She blithely crossed out the main and essential facts. She's a Muscovite who now lives in the USA. Now the refusals have started again. Some people aren't making it to America.

We saw a man, a Soviet emigrant. He was a Ph.D. He got two refusals from the United States and went insane. After he went mad, his family got permission to enter the USA. His wife left for America with the children. It was clear that he had been an intelligent, cultured man. But now here he was, wearing a vegetable net on his head for protection. The poor man! HIAS and JOINT didn't even put him in the hospital. The beasts, the murderers! The poor man! I just can't get him out of my head.

Love,
Raimonda

NOVEMBER 16

Dear Kitty!

Yesterday we had our medical checkups. A fat American with glasses cheerfully called me over to him. I lifted my T-shirt, and he quickly touched me twice with a stethoscope; I didn't understand whether I was supposed to breathe or not. He did the same with Sima, Mama, and Papa, and asked them all whether they had their appendix out. Sima said he did in 1987, and the doctor took a look at the scar. We left the office.

I stayed on to wait for the family. They were having blood tests. In the meantime I read a book: *The Magician's Nephew* by C. S. Lewis. My parents had a blood test and X-rays. We took a walk around Rome. We went off to the market and bought a lot of inexpensive meat and fruit.

Today I signed up for school. There are eighteen classes at school—I'm a student in the ninth. My level is higher than nine, and on Monday I'll go to the eighteenth.

Today is a holiday that is celebrated every Saturday: *"Shalom Shabat."* We sang songs in Ivrit. Rabbi Girsh told us about the Jews, about how a Jew is someone who was born a Jew, about how Jewish women and girls have a soul in which a candle is burning, and how she passes the candle on to her child, about how every Jewish woman cooks a pie before Saturday. We, that is, Papa and I, were guests at Rabbi Girsh's.

This happened because Papa accosted an emigrant rabbi on the street who had left years before. You know that Papa has dreams that come true two days later. Papa had another of his dreams. He can feel and see dreams that show him the future. When something bad must happen, he feels it in his dreams two days before. This time he dreamed that his best friend from childhood died. It was his scariest dream of all, and he felt he should go to a rabbi about it. So the emigrant rabbi took us to Girsh. Girsh is a chief rabbi who also left ten years ago from Russia. They couldn't explain the dreams to Papa, but they explained that a demon was just scaring and laughing at Papa. And they just tried to make Papa into a believer. The rabbi's wife had six children and is expecting her seventh. She offered us pie, tea, and tangerines. We said prayers in Ivrit before we ate. Each food has its own prayer, which has to be said at the beginning just once.

At school we sang the Israeli national anthem. With that I'll close.

Love,
Raimonda

P.S. Papa came to Rome with us and stopped in at the newspaper *Repubblica.* On Sunday they'll publish his first drawing. They'll pay 150 mille for one drawing, but not cash-in-hand. Papa's got to negotiate with an agent. We all celebrated. The first money in Rome during emigration!

Love,
Raimonda

NOVEMBER 18

Dear Kitty!

Our relatives from Odessa visited us again today. I played with Dasha. Tomorrow if it doesn't rain we'll go to the big market called "Americano."

It is not like the one in the center of Ladispoli, where emigrants gather together and have a flea market to sell Soviet goods to Italians. In that little market it is impossible to sell goods for a good price. To sell, we have to beg and fight with the Italians; we all have the same goods to sell, and the Italians take advantage of it. But it is good because I have learned numbers in Italian and words like "Please" and "Thank you." With these words we beg them to buy things for a very cheap price.

But in Rome there is the famous flea market for emigrants—this is the Americano. In order to get a place there, you have to arrive at five in the morning. Then women and men run there to get a place. It's also dangerous because the Italian police are there, and they don't let emigrants sell goods there. That's why when the police come, emigrants run away. And some get caught and their goods are taken by the police. For these reasons, Papa doesn't let me go often.

Nothing else has happened.

Love,
Raimonda

NOVEMBER 20

Dear Kitty, hello!

Today I studied English in the eighteenth special class. Many of the children were from Chernovtsy. They asked me my name in English, and how old I was. I told them my name, and said that I was twenty years old. They all started laughing. The teacher tested my knowledge and then wrote down that I was on the level of the class.

Today, I got an A in Ivrit. My first A in freedom. The teacher was surprised I had learned numbers without knowing an alphabet. I was completely justified in not studying. He praised me.

The history of the Jews is taught by Lena, who is eighteen years old. She doesn't tell us anything, but just listens to anecdotes and plays songs by Rosenbaum on the guitar. But today there's a new director, and so she had to have a lesson because the director came to class. He's an American who understands Russian but speaks it poorly.

Lena told us about the king and the prophet Isaiah. The director was called out into the hallway for a minute. While he was gone, Lena sighed and loudly said a terrible curse word in front of the children—this was a shock for me. When the director returned, she went on speaking, taking off her glasses and ending every phrase in a trembling voice.

The director spoke in poor Russian and soft English:

—I'd like to ask you a question. Why was a strong and great king afraid of a prophet who was weak and not all-powerful?

I answered:

—I think that the prophet has the power to speak with God. And the king doesn't have this power. The king can say: My God, help me in this war. But he won't hear the answer. And the prophet can also see and know the future.

The director said that my answer was the answer. The prophet is a moral figure. He asked whether there was a moral figure in the Soviet Union, and I said no. He said to think for a minute.

Someone said Gorbachev. The director said Gorbachev was a political leader. Then someone said Lenin. I was about to clutch my head. How can you talk about "Grandfather Lenin" in freedom, where you're learning about God?

The director didn't hear Lenin; he said that [Andrei] Sakharov was a moral figure who spoke the truth and risked his life to reach the truth. When the director spoke English, Lena couldn't translate a lot of it and I translated for the whole class. She pretended to remember once I'd already translated. The director said, *"Shalom,"* and left. This is what Lena said: "Well, children, it's all for show, Soviet-style."

How foul and offensive that is in the free world!

Goodbye, My Dear!

NOVEMBER 21

Dear Kitty!

Hello Kitty!

Today I got my second A in Ivrit. I recited the pronouns. Lena thanked me on the side for helping her out in the last class. Today English was taught by a different teacher who emigrated to Canada.

This teacher was probably fifty years old. She doesn't like any noise or fooling around in class—she's strict, but provides good explanations and draws everyone into conversation. The other teacher only smiled but didn't explain anything. My mood is better. I just went over my English.

Goodnight, Kitty!

Raimonda

P.S. I'm going to tell you a dream I had today. I was sixteen years old and going back to Chernovtsy. It was a sleepy, sunny day and I could feel the warmth. I'm walking up to the house and in the doorway is standing my old friend Natasha, and next to her is a girl. The girl's face is covered by pimples. She is little and ugly. I say to Natasha:

—I'm Raimonda, do you recognize me?

—No, answers Natasha.

The city is warm and sunny, but it's dead. And everything around is the craziness of dreams.

I say to her:

—So where's Vova?

He was a little boy who lived on the first floor of our building. He always played in our group.

She answers softly:

—He doesn't live here anymore. He lives on the other side of the sea.

And she takes me to the ruins that surround the sea and it's impossible to get to him. And if you sit on these ruins, you'll fall through and disappear without a trace and be forgotten. We returned to the house, as my best friend Lenya was coming home from school. He walked by and didn't notice me.

I shouted: Lenya, do you recognize me?

No, he answers.

—I'm Raimonda, we were students together in the same class.

And then I left. But my best friend didn't remember me. I didn't mean anything to him. He was living a dead life. I asked, "So where's Anya?"

There, he pointed. I caught sight of an old familiar window. I said to myself—Anya will recognize me.

—I'm going to Anya's too, said Lenya.

Anya opened the door. She was not a little girl. And Lenya too wasn't my little friend. The years had flown by. And they had changed unbeknownst to themselves.

I said:

—Anya, will you recognize me?

—No, she answered in surprise.

I was choking on my tears, but then I floated off into bliss. I woke up in a field in the middle of which there was an apple tree, and next to it there was an old wooden hut. The sky was blue. The grass smelled fresh. I remembered that I had once found myself there with Mama when I was quite small. I was remembering my childhood. I wanted to sob from the betrayal. My favorite city had died and was covered in a cloud of sleep that would also die one day. My best friends who used to love me so much had forgotten me.

Suddenly out of the foliage came Vova leading his mama by the hand. He had stayed the same little boy as in our childhood. He hadn't changed. Time had stopped for him. I said to myself:

—He won't recognize me.

But Vova shouted. He turned around, let go of his mama's hand, and shouted: *Raimonda!* He recognized me, ran up to me, the only boy—he hadn't died. And I cried quietly.

Today I got another "A" in Ivrit. I've done my lessons. My parents have been off to Rome since morning. Sima left with Oleg for the library.

The day passed quickly, as usual.

Goodnight!

Raimonda

NOVEMBER 28

Dear Kitty!

Today is an important day in our emigration—I hope not the most important in my life.

Today we met with the consulate.

Poor Jewish refugees! Here too you're supposed to be humiliated in fear. Even if you know what is happening, what can you do? Nothing. You can see your nerves shatter. You can watch yourself acquiring the psyche of people who have been turned into exhausted animals.

Why are we mocked this way, frightened by the words of the consul? Poor Jews, where can you run—probably only to heaven. Refugees—without this word we wouldn't know who we are. We are persecuted, worn down, and humiliated Jews. We are Jews, the people who have been insulted and injured for centuries.

We don't have a peaceful life. We don't have a corner where we could have happy, peaceful dreams, where we could dream of the future, knowing that tomorrow will be a peaceful day.

We have to wander through the world because we are Jews.

We are poor Jews.

We are Jews, worn down. We have been chased out of our own home. Understand, we are people, not slaves; we believe in our God.

> We also love.
> We also wait.
> But we never live.
> We move like spirits, disturbing your sleep.
> For you, we are not eternal.
> For you, we are mortal
> So tell me when
> We will find freedom
> Or I will die a slave.

> Raimonda

Kitty, Today is a new day: November 29

The consulate spoke with us today!

—Raise your right hand and say that you will speak the truth and only the truth.

We repeated it.

The consul was a short, fat American man with a mustache. From his tone of voice you could tell right away that he was a strict government man.

The translator had a good command of Russian. He emigrated from the Soviet Union.

First we filled out forms. We had to sign them and write our last name out in Russian. Papa's hand was shaking, and suddenly the translator asked:

—Are you a Communist?

—No, answered Papa.

It was impossible to tell who was the consul and who the translator. They both asked questions and both spoke Russian. One of them pretended that the consul didn't know Russian.

But with every answer he nodded his head in understanding without a translation. They didn't ask Sima or me anything. They asked Papa and Mama about two questions each.

Then the consul asked Papa in Russian:

—What would you do if you were sent back to the Soviet Union?

Papa answered rudely that he'd hang himself.

Then the consul said:

—Fine. You'll get an answer in four days.

He spoke this way to each emigrant. A refusal in three or four days. But it comes out well for everyone. It all took only three minutes. I couldn't tell whether a quick answer meant positive or negative. I console myself that time will tell.

Goodbye, Kitty
Raimonda

DECEMBER 1, 1989

Dear Kitty,

Everything is as usual. I go to school and celebrate *shalom shabat*.

Today Mama and Papa were in Rome. They saw Gorbachev. They waved at him, and then started crying, probably because they spent their lives in another country and now they've forgotten it.

I don't know how to explain these tears. Only my soul understands them, but it is mute.

We'll get our stipend in Rome. They made a mistake with our address and wrote that we live in Rome. The first bit of bad luck. Papa will have to get up really early and stand in line there all day. We're supposed to get money on December 4. The day after tomorrow my parents are going to the Americano market and they don't want to bring me along.

Love,
Raimonda

DECEMBER 5

Dear Kitty,

I don't know how I'm going to write you. It'll probably be

pleasant, but it might be sad. Time flies, as do joy, grief, tears, and laughter.

I don't know whether I should be happy to be alive. Life isn't, after all, a flying angel. There's sadness too. But you have to live, both for the sadness and the tears. You have to look with torment at the crazy professor who sells pieces of paper off the ground. You have to look at old, sick people who have begun to fear each other. You have to look at people who have gotten their third refusal. But you also have to look at your own black shadow, tired and sad. You have to look at your family members, who argue with each other all day, and then talk as if nothing at all had happened. You have to look at hard life with all its suffering.

My letter has turned out sad—and I thought it would. There is no joy in emigration. Thousands go out of their minds, thousands die. I just want to cry when I think about it. No, Kitty, I'm not against the fact that we've left the Soviet Union, but it would have been better if everything had been different. My letters would then be more cheerful. But such is life, and we have to go our difficult way.

Love,
Raimonda

P.S. Kitty, today is the eighth day since the consul. So far, nothing. I think that in a couple of days we'll be able to relax.

I'm still studying at school. The teacher praises me.

Life goes on, but everything is still the same.

That's why I've not been writing you very often.

I don't know whether things could be better.

May time hurry on its way and carry with it what's been forgotten.

Love,
Raimonda

DECEMBER 7

Dear Kitty!

I don't understand what I would do without you. I've thought and thought about it many times. I feel hurt, offended, insulted, forsaken, and betrayed, even by my father. I don't know, it seems to me that I behave normally. Sometimes I only laugh. But I bother everyone. No one wants to listen to me. Everyone tries to avoid me.

I'm leaving those whom I've loved my whole life and have been with my whole life. They loved me once too. But now I've lost my childhood. Yes, Kitty, I know that much. For the last nine years it has been one scene after another. I'm leaving my parents. They've forgotten, they don't know how I drink tincture of valerian at four o'clock in the morning. What heartaches I've had at night. What tears have flowed from my eyes, what wounds and memories are weighing on my soul. It's a shame, Kitty.

There's much you don't know. I started writing you rather late in life so that I could write about this. But what's the use of upsetting you every day? I don't know whether you can feel what I'm saying, but you do help me—I can explain things only to you. I used to have a grandmother named Galya who wouldn't tell my secrets. She would console me and bring me tincture of valerian and cry. She couldn't help me with anything, but she did understand me and would cry with me. But now she's not here. I write to you, but you cannot caress and hug me like my grandmother. I can't write her all of this, because my parents would read it. And what's the use of upsetting her? She can't help me, after all.

Papa said he was sorry again—as he's done my whole life for hurting my feelings and hitting me. I should forgive him. I tell him that I'm forgiving him, and he walks away with a smile, and I keep on crying. I'm ashamed, I feel hurt that he forgot everything just like that, that he gets angry with me and doesn't think about what he says.

Where is my grandmother? Where is she? She's the only one who understands me, because she loves and believes in me. Because she's family. There were many hurts and tears in her life. She understands me. Grandmother, Grandmother, if only you knew.

Kitty, everything I've written you is the truth. But it was hollow truth. Now I imagine that you are my grandmother, that I can share myself with you. There's much I wrote you so that you'd think that I'm a simple girl with a typical life without a care, without tears. But you're mistaken. There's much you don't know. You know only bits and pieces of my childhood. The rest I wouldn't be able to tell you, there's so much. I know it all, and my soul preserves these secrets. I'd have written you this, but you wouldn't know the future. And what's the use of these sorrows to you? You think that I don't love you, but I do love you—I live through you. I don't have anyone else who could understand me. Even if someone read you, they wouldn't understand. And perhaps they wouldn't start to cry, they wouldn't feel, it would not be interesting to them—they'd just stop reading. I don't feel sorry for myself, but my soul is crying. I feel the pain. Why repeat it? I'm going to bed. Maybe I'll get some rest and be able to forget for an hour.

Love, goodnight,
Your Raimonda

DECEMBER 11

Dear Kitty!

I haven't written for a few days. The days have passed as they always do.

We were at Oleg's. We said goodbye. In two days they are leaving for Canada. We ate dinner with them and talked about Chernovtsy. They have a difficult time ahead, as we do. Today it has been two weeks since the consul. I think we can relax.

Papa and I stopped into a pet store. There was a giant cat there, a parrot, and a talking starling. He was very beautiful. He whistled quite loudly, and kept saying *"ciao"* and laughing in an old man's voice.

This afternoon Mama was in a snit and wanted to make a scene, but Papa and I just left. This evening, Mama made up with a nice dinner. Papa and I went downtown to try to sell more of our goods, but the Italians wanted everything for just a mille. We went to the exchange. But still, nothing is as simple and good as it seems after tea. Emigrating is a difficult thing. May God grant that this is the last difficulty. Because there should be something good in life, something happy and peaceful.

Raimonda

DECEMBER 15

Dear Kitty,

Sakharov died today, December 15. This is a great loss and tragedy for the Soviet Union. Sakharov was a moral leader, the only man who fought for the truth. This is the end of the Soviet Union. It'll be the end of all truth. Now Yeltsin will try to get rid of Gorbachev.

Papa went to visit some editors in Rome. He got 500 mille. We celebrated together. Sima kissed Papa, and Papa started crying. Papa bought a cake and some beer. We were very happy and had a happy celebration. Papa bought a guidebook of Rome.

There's a flood in Venice, but when it's over we'll go there. I have a new English teacher. She is very good and teaches well; she divided the class into groups.

Mama has signed up for English classes. When they tested her knowledge, she made a mistake and they put her into the first class, which is very easy for her.

Life goes on. It may be boring, but it's not too sad (today).

Till tomorrow!

Raimonda

DECEMBER 16

Dear Kitty!

Papa called Uncle Pavlik in New York from the editor's office. Uncle Pavlik said that if we're given another city besides New York we should persist, but if they insist, we should agree.

He'll give two guarantees for us and for our relatives too. Right now they're in Ladispoli. That means we're not working according to the first plan. They say you can't give two guarantees. We're out of here unless it's a rumor.

Today Papa drew a wonderful picture. Things come out better for him here than in the Soviet Union.

Mama hurt my feelings today and hit me. I fell on the floor really hard.

Sima is out with some girl.

And I've been clearing the table for everyone all day.

It's a good thing that this day is coming to an end.

Goodnight, Kitty!

Love,
Raimonda

DECEMBER 20

Dear Kitty!

I didn't write to you yesterday. Mama hurt my feelings, and I cried again.

This morning she asked me to forgive her. We made up.

I've got a bit of a cold. I haven't been to school in two days. I'll probably go tomorrow.

The new year is a few days away. We'll have a tree—or rather, I'll have one. There was a cut spruce tree lying on the ground. I cut off some large branches and put some dirt in a box. Papa tied the branches together and stuck them in the ground. We found some colorful silvery-red paper. I cut out flowers, stars, a circle, and made some sweets. Papa made a star with a hammer and sickle as a joke— now it's the topping on our tree.

Till tomorrow.

DECEMBER 21

Dear Kitty!

I didn't go to school today either; Mama's taking care of me. Every five minutes she brings hot chamomile tea and says that an hour has gone by. I have a pulmonary cough. I'm afraid of being sick again. I hope I get better as soon as possible.

Last summer, because of Chernobyl's radiation, I was sick with collapsed lungs and was near death in the hospital. American antibiotics helped me—injections. It's a good thing that it passed. My twelve years flew by like five minutes.

This year was my year (the snake), but in nine days it'll be over, and I'll have to wait another whole twelve years. Then I'll be twenty-four. A lot can happen during those years, but they'll probably fly by like five minutes too.

Kitty, the month and year will be over soon.

In the Soviet Union, in Romania, three hundred people were killed. In Chernovtsy, people have begun to lose their hair again. But that doesn't frighten us now. We know that the Soviet Union is finished. Now we're living well and eat in a way here that we didn't dream of in the Soviet Union.

Tomorrow I'm going to school, where we'll celebrate Hanukkah (a Jewish holiday). Then it's the new year. When we sing Jewish songs in Ivrit, we sing them in such friendship and freedom. Could it have been that way in the Soviet Union? No, of course, answers each of us. None of us had freedom before, and everyone feels joy in the words of a native song.

Love,
Till tomorrow, Kitty
Raimonda

DECEMBER 24

Dear Kitty! Hello!

Yesterday, December 23, we went to Rome since everyone was celebrating Christmas. The buses weren't running, and we hailed a car. An Italian man took us for fifteen minutes—when he didn't even have a reason to go to Rome. He picked us up and gave me a Barbie doll. I had been running around to all the stores looking for a cheap one, but I didn't find any—they all cost 15–20 mille—and he just reaches into his bag, pulls one out, and gives it to me.

We arrived at the square. We had tickets to the Vatican. The librarian gave them to Papa just like that, for free. At the entrance, everyone is checked with some kind of instrument to see whether they have a weapon. We went into the Vatican, past fairy-tale and ancient soldiers who stood at attention, but they had nice smiling eyes. We went inside. Our seats and row were near the main crucifix where the pope was supposed to speak. There was a little book of songs on every seat; you could say it was the program, in various languages, but not Russian. We sat down in the places pointed out to us by a policeman who kept looking to the sides. He was dressed in an expensive black suit. Nuns who were sitting in our row whispered quietly to themselves. We looked through the little books and waited. This quietness reminded us of a warm theater.

Suddenly we heard applause. Everyone stood up. The people were greeting the Father of Rome, the pope. He walked in and sat on the throne. He had a crown on his white head. He said a prayer and greeted the people for Christmas. At the same time music began, and angelic voices sang. At that moment I wasn't in a theater anymore, but heaven. The nuns sang a couplet; their voices were so lovely, even when the old nuns sang. The pope said a prayer in Italian. People understood that he was preaching kindness, and all the people began to hold each other's hand and I held hands with a nun. Everything came to a close and we awoke. Mama and Papa even cried. Why?

Because our youth and life passed by without holding hands or a warm theater.

Raimonda

DECEMBER 26

Dear Kitty,

Today everything is as usual.

Sima got a job at a construction site. He made 40 mille today. He's shoveling dirt to build a swimming pool for an Italian man. Mama is taking classes with a better group. Papa is drawing and cutting pictures out of magazines.

There is a war in Romania. Ceaucescu, the president, and his wife have been executed, like in the last century. They were murderers. The Romanian people called them animals. Now they're fighting the army that was Ceaucescu's guard. But the regular army is for the people.

Papa didn't like the star on the tree and he made an eight-pointed one.

We met the people who were also given a guarantee by Uncle Pavlik. They aren't relatives of his and they've never seen him; their parents know Pavlik's parents, who live in Israel.

Today isn't a very interesting day, but it has been quiet and cozy.

Love,
Raimonda

DECEMBER 30

Dear Kitty!

The landlord gave Sima 150 rubles—just kidding—mille.

We had an enormous argument.

I won't describe it.

I cried so hard I wanted to die, but then I decided that I do have a future. Because of my bad mood, I wrote three poems with tears in my eyes. Almost all of my poems are sad. I can't write happy ones. It's probably not right, but I can't go against my soul. You're probably bored with me, but it's the emigration. I think there'll be two or three years of suffering before we're standing on our own feet.

That's all for now,
Raimonda

JANUARY 1, 1990

Dear, beloved Kitty!

Happy New Year 1990!

We celebrated the New Year with our relatives.

Mama gave me 5 mille, and Sima gave me five pieces of gum.

The year went by unnoticed. I didn't even realize I was in Italy. The days fly by and I don't have time to think about or understand what has happened, or ever to think of my lost family and city. Maybe it just has to be that way so that the emigration will go more quickly, and we'll live in our own house with our own warm, normal life.

Love,
Raimonda

JANUARY 8

Dear Kitty!

I haven't written you for many days. I'll write you about my dream that came true.

Kitty, I was in Venice, San Marino, and Florence! Those three days will always be in my memory—I'll never forget them.

In Venice, there is a hotel where emigrant tourists stay for the night. And at night, everyone stays outside selling goods for a big, big profit. You can get 10 milles for something small for which you could get only 1 mille in Ladispoli. Some people make thousands on it; they are real businessmen. But people like us came just to visit Venice, San Marino, and Florence. We get a only a few hundred milles.

We didn't sleep all night. We went outside to sell goods with the millions of other emigrants. It was dark, but people stayed there. Many Italians bought goods from me for an expensive price. These Italians are rich. I was surprised that they gave so much money to me for something little. But then I understood that they were doing it out of pity because they saw me outside—little, poor emigrant in the dark of night. The police showed up sometimes.

Once, when I got some "big" money for selling, I rushed home to the hotel to give it to my dad, who had gone back for more goods. I had to go around to the back of the hotel to get in. While I ran, I saw young men, Italians, on a motorcycle. They called me, saying, *"Bellissima,"* which means pretty, but I didn't stop. Then they stopped the motorcycle like they wanted to run up to me. But I quickly dashed up to the hotel door which was very hard to open. But one Russian emigrant was about to come out, so I got down on my knees and I went through under that man's legs. The door closed and I rushed trembling into our room. We sold many things and went to sleep very late in the morning. But I could hear people still outside, like birds selling their nests.

Venice

Here, where old channels teem
with gliding gondolas and tenderly lapping sea water,
where pigeons play on the square,
we are surrounded by the cupolas of centuries.
The mist disappears as cold air breezes in.
The feeling whirls that we are in a fairy heaven.
Venice, goodbye, my Venice.
There is nothing more beautiful,
and I won't conceal it.

P.S. Venice is an ancient city full of tourists, buses, taxis, policemen. It's all boats; a city on water.
   Unfortunately I don't have the words to describe that beauty.

San Marino

Ancient knolls with homes,
tiny quaint town.
The world is seen from your old walls,
Smoke through your little windows.
I pass through fairy gates,
as guards slowly stretch their hands in welcome.
San Marino, you are cozy and warm.
I suddenly feel a thirst just to live,
so that smoke from my hearth
will rise past my window and look at this world.

R. K.

Florence

Your ancient comforts I cannot describe,
your sea's freshness I cannot fully know.
But your narrow cobblestone ways, endless,
take me away to foreign worlds, to dream.

To dream of a new life, kind and still unreal;
To dream of possibilities not in thrall to a power;
to understand that in life there is something I had lost
because I didn't even know that I would ever,
might ever,
see this world along your cobblestone paths
with the light far away,
where they end.

P.S. We went by bus and spent the night at a hotel. How I want to go back. When I'm grown up and rich, I'll definitely go.

Raimonda

JANUARY 15

Dear Kitty!

The days are passing. I want to write to you, but there's nothing new—everything is the same.

The family that's going with us said that they've already called Uncle Pavlik for us. Quietly everyone is calming down. There are outbursts, but you can tell that we're not in that mean and cruel emigration anymore, but in a house in Italy, in a quiet little Ladispoli where everything is our own, we're used to everything, and know that there's a store around the corner, and further on, a school on Via Bati. But at the same time you understand that soon it'll come to an end. And the difficulties will start again, emigration to America, life.

Love,
Raimonda

JANUARY 16

Dear Kitty!

I'm going to school for now. I talk, laugh, and study—a little. I'm so interested in studying, notebooks, and books in English. I want to live in a smart and clean way. Our souls will probably rest in little Ladispoli another month, and then—it's easy to guess! May God grant that our plans work out for us, that what we want works out—it's so difficult to reach.

Love,
Raimonda

JANUARY 20

[From a letter] To my grandmothers and grandfather:

I miss you so much and want to feel your caress. I look for it and hope to find it, but don't find this line in your letters: Dear mine. Even for me it's hard. I can barely contain my nerves and my heart because I can't share my thoughts with you. I can't feel your kiss. It hurts. Can't you understand me? Where is your song, Grandpa, about "Dunya," the song you used to sing to me when I was going to sleep? Don't sing it to anyone else, do you hear me, Grandpa? Do you remember? I'm crying now as I remember it. You will write to me, right? Only in a month you'll get this letter, which I will forget but you will read as today's. And I hope you'll be surprised by it, because then you will write to me.

We haven't pity left even for a minute. Here it's real life. We don't "sleep," like in Russia, where nothing is happening and you only feel like sleeping. We are moving. We don't see the time; we live. Here in this little Ladispoli, we get used to life. No one in Ladispoli can understand that he's really in Italy, emigrating. Everyone is busy in markets, stores. Everyone is living. It's too bad we don't have TV yet, but we listen to the radio every evening and that way we know what is happening in Chernovtsy. We know that there was a strike and that the government was thrown out. Wonder! How did all the people get up? What is happening in Russia? Is it *perestroika* or the end?

You know that we were in San Marino, Venice, Florence. I simply write about it, but before it was my wish, my dream. I still can't believe that I've reached it.

It is so good at school. Even though it is so little studying, you feel such unexplained happiness in it, that Jewish freedom that you always wished for. This is what the word "freedom" means. This is when you are not a slave who goes to school with feelings of hatred and fear. This is a person who says, "I'm a Jew," and gets an answer, "Me too."

Here the soul is resting, moving, but in normal life: my school, Simon's job, Mom's classes, Papa's pictures.

JANUARY 21

Dear Kitty!

I want to write you so much, but time has been set aside here only for rest.

Since morning I've been at school—on Friday we celebrate *Shabat Shalom* (Hello, Saturday).

Last Friday on the Shabat I wanted to cry. Almost everyone was leaving, and the classes were empty. Even though we've known each other for only two months, we all feel a certain Jewish family feeling. When could we ever live and study so freely in the Soviet Union? But here we can laugh about how they used to put us down. We rejoice in our freedom. And on the Shabat when we sing songs with poor, happy faces and want to cry and say to each other: "Maybe we'll meet again someday." The children with whom we sit in class, it's hard that they're leaving. We are like family. Our common great-great-great-grandmother is Sarah and our great-great-great-grandfather is Avraam, as Rabbi Girsh says.

Time has flown by unnoticed. We don't realize it's already 1990. Oh, Italy! You are like a dream that has shrouded me in memories. It's a good and warm country that will someday fly off leaving a little piece behind for my soul.

Love,
Raimonda

I read the book *Silver Chair,* by C. S. Lewis. Now I've begun to read a children's Bible.

JANUARY 31

My own Kitty!

My God, how many days I haven't written you! I was horrified to find out from Papa what the date was, and still I can't believe it. Time in little Ladispoli flies by like a sweet dream, and I check again to see whether I wrote yesterday as it seems so many days ago. It seems to me that everything that happens in the morning happened the day before yesterday.

No, it's impossible to believe that you were in Austria three months ago, and that now you've been in Italy two months, that the consul was long ago now, and today you're waiting for some sort of free guarantee from terrifying New York. The wait also turns time into a dream without winter and with spring sun in January. Everyone has calmed down; we've bought an Italian television from Russians for 20 mille. It has sixty-four channels. We watch horror movies at eight-thirty, and then we go to bed. Last Friday we called Grandmother Sofa. She cried and said: "We have to leave, but where will we get a *vyzov*?"

That's what Grandmother Sofa said. How's that? She who knew nothing but the Soviet Union, and now? No, I can't believe three months have passed, and the Soviet Union is finished. There was a bloody revolution in Romania, and now it has left the Soviet bloc. It's total war in Azerbaijan between the Azerbaijanis and the Armenians. There are thousands and thousands of victims.

In the Soviet Union there's a complete famine. Gorbachev wants to leave, the legislative Plenum is preparing. Everyone is leaving for Israel—now there's no place else, but Israel isn't sending *vyzovs*. The people are weeping. It's the end of the Soviet Union. Now, in English: It's the end of the Soviet Union.

We are refugees who managed to make a getaway, to see beauty, to relax, and eat tasty food. But many, many in the Soviet Union right now are weeping from their feebleness, saying, "We won't make it, we're late." Or, like my grandmother: "We have to leave, but where will we get a *vyzov*?" But with me, everything is as it was—I go to school, friends show up, I horse around all day. We're waiting for the guarantee. Our friends were robbed of one guarantee: All their money was taken, and silver too. There is a mafia of Soviet emigrants who take things from other emigrants by threatening people's lives at the Americano market. The mafia also steals stuff from homes. This is what happened to our friends.

A week ago, I was sick with a cold and sore throat. Papa's tooth hurt and he went to a young Italian dentist at JOINT. He didn't even take a look but gave him penicillin to gargle. Papa started to have an allergy and cough; he didn't know what it was but thought it was flu, and then he noticed spots on his body. Sometimes he gets an allergy to strawberries. It has passed, thank God. It's time to sleep.

Goodnight, Kitty! Unless the time deceives me, till tomorrow.

FEBRUARY 6, 1990

Dear Kitty,

I'll describe what has gone on even though I don't want to remember. Next to our building lives an old man who's about seventy years old. He's always blowing me kisses. At first this made me nervous and afraid, and I would shout "No" or just try not to look his way. But when he began to whistle, I told Mama and she said that he's a nice old man, that he just loves children. He himself has a wife and children and grandchildren. Later he gave candy and oranges to me and my friends from the yard.

On Friday, while it was still light out, he called me over. He was holding his little grandson in his arms, and I walked over and began to pat the little boy. But suddenly the old man started to say something to me very softly. I answered loudly, *"No capito"* (I don't understand), and then he put his finger to his mouth to say, "ssh . . ." Suddenly he tickled my knee, which I thought was an accident, but I still thought about it. That's when he started to lift my skirt. I shouted "No," but he tried to lift it again. I ran away that instant.

I can't describe to you the state I was in. My knees were shaking—I couldn't horse around or play—I ran home, told Mama, who started to hug and kiss me.

When I write now, it probably seems like a little thing, but it's not. Mama and I left for a walk to calm down, but when we returned, Papa and Sima were standing on the balcony. Then Papa shouted, "Show me where he lives." Sima had told him everything. Earlier in the day Sima wanted to go to the man's house, but I didn't tell him where it was. Papa got really angry and was swearing, and Mama was afraid to let them go because, as she said, "We're Russians, we're emigrants." But Papa didn't care; Mama's words were just air. Papa and Sima ran off, taking me along, then they rang the bell, banged on the windows, and argued with the old man and his children. Papa raised his hand against the old man, whose son-in-law almost got into the fight. We left.

My parents left for the south, to Capri, in the morning, and Sima and I stayed home with the neighbors. The sun was scorching in the afternoon, and I calmed down (today is Sunday). I wanted to go out, but Sima didn't let me. Suddenly I noticed a car and three burly men got out. The fourth was the old man's son-in-law, who pointed out our balcony and said something. You could guess what. We were scared. Sima began yelling at me, and he got frightened too. We locked ourselves in. I cried and got upset, prayed and prayed to God for Him to deliver us from the Evil One and to help our weak souls. Amen.

Now it's evening already. My parents should be back at eleven.

Goodnight, Kitty! I prayed to God for us.

FEBRUARY 10

Hello, dear Kitty!

I haven't been writing. I've forgotten everything these days, even the Soviet Union. We've been here three months and ten days already. Now and then I think of Austria. I don't love Italy anymore, this warm Italy.

It's already been a week that I haven't written a letter to my grandmothers, and I myself don't know what I want. My God, look how I'm living! My only dream is of becoming a journalist, being rich, and having a family. But where is it all? Where is my imagined dear Jewish school in America? How long will we have to stay here? All the people who arrived after us have left.

Of course there are still people left, but they're the last ones. I'm in an okay mood. I'm living, but it doesn't make any sense here. I go to school and study lessons that weren't handed out. They bought me a new Barbie doll. Now I have two. The new one is so nice; I'm sewing for her.

Our guarantor, Uncle Pavlik, still hasn't signed the guarantee.

Papa and Mama were in the south. They liked it a lot. Sima was up north. He brought back gifts for everyone, including me. He bought himself a leather jacket.

There's nothing else. That's how the days pass. That means that what fate decides; it is probably already tired of living and so time drags, like one day, like one hour, like one minute.

Nonetheless, Goodbye!

America! We will live on and raise ourselves up!

> Love,
> Italian Raimonda

p.s. Dear Kitty!
   The happiness came.
   On Tuesday they'll be signing our guarantee.
   Hurray!
   The end of emigration.
   We'll go on living!

FEBRUARY 18

Dear Kitty,

What I wrote about the guarantee has turned out to be wrong.

Papa called Uncle Pavlik. He hasn't signed our guarantee—he just signed our friends' one. Mama thinks that he won't sign it, and we'll go on a common one. Of course, that hurts.

A person wants to live for something, for a house, for study, but fate arranges things its own way, and however sad it is, a person has to battle with oneself, although Italy too has its charms.

You have to live and struggle.

Raimonda

P.S. Our school took a field trip to Rome by bus. My classmates and I were at school at eight in the morning. Everyone found a partner and talked in a friendly way. I was sitting with my girlfriend Alina.

We were put on comfortable, warm, and clean buses. On our way there, they told us the history of Rome.

Italian music was playing softly, accompanying us. Those forty minutes! How I wanted them to go on and on, to prolong that nice music, the cozy seats, the children's happy faces. And when we arrived, there opened up before us the Vatican, enchanted with antiquity.

We visited the Vatican museums. Our glances darted through the halls; we couldn't remember anything, and the children became adults and dreamed of having a house in which the richness of these walls was hidden. Finally, the long-awaited and fleeting visit to the Sistine Chapel. The weariness of the heavy walls was striking—we became children again and wanted to sleep. No one could look at the paintings anymore or the biblical ceiling. Still, we knew that this one single minute of beauty will be remembered forever. And we raised up our weary eyes, not hearing the words of our guide. It was an instant through which we passed probably in our sleep.

We went outside and ran around on the green grass surrounded by the Roman wall and ate our sandwiches. The teacher poured us sweetened water, and gave us cookies. We happily got into the bus and in a few minutes we were at a synagogue. The boys sat in the middle of the synagogue; they could see and hear everything. The girls, on the other hand, sat in separate dark tiers because we were made from the rib of a man.

Many were even insulted.

We went off to the synagogue museum and saw a Bible that had been shot through by terrorists. Once they attacked the synagogue, killed a boy, and wounded forty people. They also shot the Bible. Now the synagogue is guarded by the police.

A few minutes later we were at the Colosseum, which used to be the circus. The Colosseum was built by Jewish prisoners.

We stood around the guide and listened. An Italian man was selling a collection of postcards for a mille, but nobody bought any. He came up to us many times, and then asked in English:

—Are you Jews?

—We're all Jews, answered our teacher in English.

—*Shalom aleichem,* said the man, giving everyone cards.

Then it was time to go home. This nice man's words were a fitting end to the trip.

We got onto the bus and sat in our seats. Many of us fell asleep to the music. But many talked quietly and happily.

Who? Jews gathered us together, paid for us, and took us out. We didn't pay anything. Just because we're Jews. Before that, they told us, "Ladies and gentlemen, thank you."

"Thank you," we answered. We turned around, and went home where we talked about our great trip to Rome, enchanted, fairy-tale Rome.

Love,
Raimonda

FEBRUARY 19

Dear Kitty,

Today I straightened everything up, learned all my lessons, and got home from school a long time ago. We have new neighbors. Mama has gone off to class, and Papa's at the library. Everything is as usual. How long will things go on like this? Sima says that it will end when he's forty.

So we have to wait and hope that our dreams come true.

Goodbye,
Raimonda

FEBRUARY 20

Dear Kitty!

A boy walked me home from school today. His name is Stas. I like him. He gave me a ride on his bicycle. When I come home, I spend all my time outside with him and another boy and a girl named Yulia. She is thirteen. Stas gives me rides on his bicycle. We joke about Stalin. Stas takes a small stick that looks like Stalin's pipe, and he plays Stalin. I am the head of the Soviet secret police, Beria, and Yulia was someone whom we executed.

When it is still light outside, we play war on bicycles. We also play with neighborhood babies sometimes, and we played cards for a long time. We made friends with some Italians. We played hide-and-seek with them and learned a few Italian words, especially curses that help us communicate with each other.

Even though I left my best boyfriend in the Soviet Union, he wouldn't be enough for me here. But he left for Israel, and we probably won't see each other again.

I probably won't have any real and true girlfriend; except for my relatives, there's nobody.

Spring has begun here, but sometimes I forget and think that it's summer. I walked around all day outside. You won't catch me around the house when it's spring or summer. But now all of that is far, far from me.

> Love,
> Raimonda

FEBRUARY 21

Dear Kitty!

Papa and I are going to the movies today to watch Charlie Chaplin.

I got an A in Ivrit; we had to memorize the Israeli national anthem.

We have clean housemates now, not like those others. At first, we lived with a man, his wife, and their sixteen-year-old son. But they moved into another apartment, which they don't have to share. We have stayed friends with them. After they left, we got an old man and his wife. They were about sixty years old. But their children and grandchildren came all the time, and I think this old woman stole our salad once. And they didn't clean the kitchen after themselves much. This third family is a man, his wife, and their son of about eleven, who is in my class at school. Also, his uncle is with them. I don't like him; I don't think his own family likes him.

I can't even remember how much I've written you over the past five months. What five months? It seems like it was five days! Nothing happens, but time flies by unnoticed. That's all for now.

Love,
Raimonda

FEBRUARY 26

Dear Kitty!

I slept poorly today—I had bad dreams. Sad and horrible, I can't understand them. But the night was a long time ago. Soon it will be evening.

Mama bought me a headband at the market; a lot of candies. Whenever I want to write to you, I have nothing to say. But all the same, I know that I can talk with you, Kitty. For me, you are living my life, you laugh my laughs, you cry my tears, you have my dreams, you're frightened by my fears, you are upset by my troubles, and it becomes easier for me. I wish my grandmothers and beloved grandfather were here.

But they're not, and I have to wait.

Love,
Raimonda

MARCH 7, 1990

Dear Kitty,

We called Grandmother Galya yesterday. Everything is okay with them. We wished her a happy birthday, because it'll soon be March 9.

Sima joined up with us. He plays cards with me a lot now. He plays the guitar, and I try to sing. My parents are trying to cooperate with him.

A girl in our class was given a guarantee and transportation, and then a paper arrived from HIAS that said everything had changed.

You could lose your mind. What do they want from us?

As for us, we have neither a guarantee nor transportation. We are already here for five months and one week, waiting to go to New York. Most people who waited for New York left very quickly. But not us.

The uncle who lives with the other family in our apartment likes to tease too much, and he's a real jerk. Papa felt like he couldn't stand him anymore, so he threatened this uncle with a pan for frying eggs. I was with them in the kitchen. The uncle said: "Come on, show me!" And Papa said something like, "I don't care if I go to jail, when I get rid of you." I was scared, but I hate this uncle so much for having the nerve to curse my papa and tease him so much. My papa has never threatened anyone before, and I was surprised, and proud maybe. Then Maria came into the kitchen. She is the owner of the villa, and we pay rent to her. She was scared and my papa put his arm around her to calm her.

It may take all this time, but fine, Kitty, my childhood dream will still come true and I'll stroll through New York in the evening.

Love,
Raimonda

MARCH 9

Dear Kitty!

We celebrated Purim today at school. We all wore masks and were given Jewish cookies called "mustache of Haman," *Haman-taschen*. Many of my friends are older and like me mostly because I am still a child, while they are becoming adults. I like them a lot. Today, they put makeup on me for Purim.

We sang songs, but then it began to rain and we finished up with the Israeli national anthem.

Love,
Raimonda

MARCH 14

Dear Kitty!

Late yesterday evening there was a terrible knock on the door. It was the kind of feeling that someone is after you. How my heart was pounding. Out of fear my friend from next door, Boris, and I didn't ask who it is; we just opened the door. In walks a happy mama and she shouts out: "We got the guarantee!" My God, were we happy.

We'll forget these five or six months in a week or two, and then we'll be in New York.

God, how we celebrated! My future is awaiting me. My family is terrified at times. But we're like all Jews who emigrate to America. Kitty, congratulations! America is waiting for us!

Love,
Raimonda

MARCH 15

Dear Kitty!

There were two hundred guarantees today. The transportation will be in five to ten days. We still don't know whether it's a common or personal guarantee; probably a common one. Our neighbors got their guarantee a day after us. Papa and Uncle drank a toast. And Papa got drunk for the first time in his life. Today he doesn't feel very well.

Three people are left in our class. Those who already got their guarantee are under way. The emigration is drawing to a close.

In school, I had two girlfriends. We were always together and sat at the same desk, all three of us—that was Alina, Rita, and me. Many children had nits. They got it from children who lived in the southern part of Russia, where it is hot and they don't have water. These children don't even speak Russian. Alina was the first one to get it, the nits. Rita sat next to her, and I came next. We wanted to move away from Alina when she got nits, but we were too embarrassed. We didn't want to leave. We didn't know how to leave our friend who didn't even tell us that she had nits. But everyone knew because there was a lady (a Russian emigrant) who worked for the school and checked our head once a month. She didn't tell the class who had nits, but she whispered it to people who had it. When the whole class saw her whispering, they understood but didn't show it. Finally Alina left for America, and after that, the lady whispered into Rita's ear. I was sitting next to Rita all this time. And then she left for America. And then I sat in class alone and the lady came in. Then, the other day, the lady looked at my hair and whispered in my ear. I was about to cry. I ran up to her, but she told me not to worry because it was easy to get rid of it by using special shampoo. I got rid of it in three days. So all three of us got it, one after the other. But all three of us will go to America clean.

I've learned to ride a bicycle (a big one). My friends—Stas, who is thirteen; Dima, who is ten; and a girl named Ira—taught me to ride the bike. I fell so many times that my skin is getting blue from it. We played war on our bicycles today. Also, we played a game called "Kiss Myau." A leader has closed eyes and points his finger at someone. With his eyes closed, he can say what he wants from this person. Three answers to secret questions or a kiss. Each order had a color. When he said red, it meant a kiss; blue meant answering three questions.

To tell the truth, I don't really feel like going to school. I was behaving badly today. But now I've gotten better.

Our last days in harsh, warm Italy.

Love,
Raimonda

MARCH 22

Dear, dear Kitty!
CONGRATULATIONS!

On March 28, we're leaving—in six days. And since we have transport, I'll soon be finding myself in America. That is, after all, our longtime dream.

We left on September 29 and moved on to Rome October 29. We left Vienna on the 29th, and we'll part with Italy on the 29th at night. Right now we have guests who are marking with us this famous holiday for emigrants. Neighbors, Aunt Galya, and Uncle Sasha.

We wanted to move into their apartment, but we'll be leaving before them.

Our other friends are leaving on one guarantee on March 26. That's two days before us.

So we don't know what kind of guarantee we have. Tomorrow we'll do the wash, the ironing, the suitcases, and the purchases. For now, goodnight, dear Kitty.

Love,
Raimonda (future American)

MARCH 24

Dear Kitty!

Today we listened to the radio. There was a Jewish woman on Israeli radio talking about why she left. We cried. We cried, thinking of the neighbors', classmates', and others' taunts. Yes, we left—no, that's not true—we fled from fear for our family, from "pogroms." How that word frightened us.

But why, why aren't we like everybody else? We are better because we can't fight, because we don't love to hurt others, whereas they can't live without it. We left, and thousands have left, but that's not all; after all there still remain some whom the enemies will nag and fight to the end like dogs, and then celebrate; but why? Blood, tears. But what else?

If all of us, all of us leave, then you'll live well, the way you want to? No, you'll fight each other, because you're not even sinners, but wild beasts that can rejoice only in another's grief. If only you could burn like Sodom and Gomorrah, and if not, then rejoice: we won't bother you, and we won't look in your direction.

Raimonda

P.S. Dear Kitty, in three days we'll go to America. Italy, you're such a beautiful country, but some people here live for themselves; they're corrupt, greedy people who don't need anything. They envy their own children, but that doesn't bother me. Uncle Pavlik spoke with Papa yesterday. He didn't even know that we had transportation. Aunt Tanya, his wife, had left on vacation. We have a common guarantee, which means that the government is our sponsor and not Uncle Pavlik. So we will have to live in a hotel instead of at Uncle Pavlik's place. But the main thing is that in three days we'll be in America, and let it say to us, "Welcome to me."

CHAPTER TWO

ARRIVING IN NEW YORK

APRIL 2 TO SEPTEMBER 16, 1990

"I CAN CALL MYSELF THE HAPPIEST GIRL"

O nce, on a trip to Moscow, Igor brought home a can of Coca-Cola. The family parsed it out, sipping slowly. It was the first Coke they had ever tasted, and afterward, Raimonda kept that scarlet can on the desk where she did her homework. It symbolized America for her—a land of ever-flowing Coca-Cola and endless arrays of candy and gum. She dreamed of America, where, she had heard, Russian immigrants often became millionaires and where most of the good things in life were nearly free. When the Kopelnitskys emigrated, it was toward that dream of America that they traveled.

They arrived in March 1990, in New York City—in a welfare hotel on a rough block of 28th Street in Manhattan. Because the Kopelnitskys arrived on a general invitation, their care fell under the auspices of a Jewish organization known as NYANA, which was dealing with a two-year influx of nearly seventy thousand Soviet Jews. What the government and NYANA couldn't provide, friends did. Pavlik Salodnik, who in the end had sponsored another family's immigration to the States, welcomed them with a Chinese takeout dinner. He and his family provided a glimpse of the American good life. They were generous with gifts, including trips outside the city and the Kopelnitskys' first color television set. Congregants from an Upper East Side synagogue invited the Kopelnitskys to the celebration of their first Jewish holiday, a lavish Passover seder. One of the women they met at the seder, Carol Gold, who was working as an American liaison for the U.S. Bookstore in Moscow, helped forge Igor's path into the professional community. Carol also knew me, and thought that as a journalist I would be interested in Raimonda's story. I was charmed by Raimonda and heartbroken by her family's struggle to sort meaning out of the cacophonous rabble of New York. From that point on, my husband Andrew Rosenstein and I helped when we could, mostly by answering their questions about American banking, education, and customs.

What nobody could ease was their lingering sense of imperilment. To the Kopelnitskys, everything in the United States seemed enlarged and ominous—and, strangely, everything echoed with old fear: Raimonda tried to go away to a Jewish summer camp but panicked when what she thought was a dangerous recurrence of her radiation sickness was passed off as a cold. The subways terrified them, as did the street people; in Soviet propaganda, both had been touted as examples of the dangers in America. Dealing with the welfare system—its endless lines and questions and paperwork—reminded them of a more menacing bureaucracy. Adrift without language in this strange culture, they felt ill-equipped to understand the nuances. They sensed that every action had a consequence that they could not anticipate. They seemed constantly in jeopardy in a culture they could not translate.

Because Igor and Klavdia had only a rudimentary understanding of English, their children had to communicate for them, as well as negotiate for the three-room apartment they eventually found—and rented with NYANA's financial assistance—in the largely Italian neighborhood of Bay Ridge, Brooklyn. The apartment, in a large prewar building on a wide avenue, was even smaller than the home they had left behind in Chernovtsy. They bought three mattresses and settled in, swinging between elation at the prosperity they saw around them and depression over how far it seemed from where they were.

English lessons—and studying into the small hours—exhausted both parents. Simon tramped the streets looking for any work and battling the bureaucracy of higher education. Raimonda, who did recapture the spirit of childhood for a few more months, started public school at McKinley Junior High, a block from the apartment. But it was not at all the Hebrew school that had filled her dreams in Italy when she had glimpsed open Jewish life for the first time. As Simon observed wryly: "There is a reason your Statue of Liberty is green and her torch gold. Everything here is money."

APRIL 2, 1990

Dear Kitty!

I wasn't able to write you because you were in my suitcase. Please forgive my parents. This is already the fourth day I've been in America! It was my dream, a dream that I could never realize. But here I'm free and no one will torment me; they'll only help me, and I don't feel any envy of anything, because I'm sure that it's all mine, both the expensive house and the children's room will also be mine, although later.

We flew on Pan Am for twelve hours. A black woman in a colorful gown gave birth on the plane, and a Russian woman (a Soviet Jew) helped out. It was a girl. And now the black woman can fly for free—that's the rule with Pan Am. And we woke up in Canada! This is just pure luck! We didn't even know what it would be like. The ground was covered with snow. A Soviet plane was next to ours. Some stupid old people sat behind us saying, "Maybe we could go back before it's too late?" Cowardly and stupid people, but it was hard for them. It's a good thing that we're here, and they're here today. They won't be able to make a cowardly mistake. We were fed twice. And at the Canadian airport we reset our watches for a second time.

And then we sat at the American airport for, I think, six hours. We were the last to get our visas. It was hot inside and crowded, too. We had to find something to do, but no one could. We all waited. Some children and I got together and played for a while, but it wasn't for long. Because it was too hot, because everyone was tired, we had no interest in games.

All we could see from the big windows was a blue sky and huge airplanes flying away or just sitting there. But that wasn't what I expected to see. I wanted to go outside and see the real world.

And suddenly through the window we caught sight of Uncle Pavlik and the family he gave the guarantee to. But no one could get in to us; and we could not get out. People were trying to talk through the glass doors. I heard my parents trying to communicate with them, and I felt stronger, like all my tiredness had flown away. But we couldn't really speak with them or touch them because the people who guarded us wouldn't let us. So we went back to our seats, and I couldn't even hear my parents talking, except to say that Pavlik hadn't changed. Finally, the guards let us out. My parents kissed Pavlik, and so did Sima and I.

Then we had to walk through the airport with our suitcases until we were let out. And then I finally saw the street. It was dark, night-time, and all I could see were cars, some people and some night lamps shining brightly. My parents and Simon left me, and suddenly I understood that I hadn't heard them talking. I hadn't even seen them until now. Because even as I walked next to them, I wasn't with them. I was alone with my eyes, seeing what I could. Pavlik took me and the other family to his house in his car. I didn't talk with anyone, only looked outside the car. Everything seemed the way I wanted it to seem: streetlamps, cars, buildings, trees passed quickly in front of my eyes. Then we reached Pavlik's house. Many private houses were surrounded by trees. Inside, his house were two floors and a base-ment. I spent three nights with Uncle Pavlik, my parents two nights; Sima stayed at a hotel. I made friends with Ilona and Sasha. Ilona is Uncle Pavlik's daughter, and Sasha is her boyfriend; she's sixteen and he's seventeen. Here you can live with a boy for many years without getting married. I slept in the same room with Sasha and Ilona. We played all day.

I love the house, especially Ilona's room on the second floor where I slept. I have never seen anything like that before. Ilona's room is all in carpet, with pink walls and a white ceiling. She gave me three stuffed animals and some colored pencils. We have two normal rooms, but the bathroom doesn't have a door. It's like a passageway, so you have to warn everyone that you're going to the toilet.

The second day, we went to the supermarket. That's where my eyes couldn't see anymore—even after seeing it all in Vienna and It-aly. In the supermarket you could walk and walk, unable to find an end to all those boxes, sweets, drinks, gum, and candy.

In the evening, my parents and Simon came. We ate Chinese food for the first time. Then Simon talked with Ilona and they were smoking. I was in the room watching some tapes and listening to records. Then Pavlik's wife Tanya came home from a vacation. Also, Ilona and Sasha took me to Manhattan. We walked through the stores, and I was too excited to see the skyscrapers and stores, which made me feel little, too little to see them all. We went to a café or restau-rant, and that's where they ordered McDonald's hamburgers, which I have never eaten before. I was surprised to see Sasha picking up the whole food and eating it all together. I took everything out and ate it all separately with a fork and knife. It was my first hamburger. They tried to convince me to eat it all together, but I didn't agree. They left money on the table, and it was something new for me to see—a tip, they said. I started asking them questions about why they had left the money on the table. I kept staring at it until we left.

Sasha and I played Ping-Pong in the basement; I love to play it. The other emigrant family's son, who is about six, played with me. And we colored picture books with Mickey Mouse in them. We played cards all the time. Sasha won mostly.

Then I came with my family to the hotel. I was shocked and disappointed to see all this dirt. And I am scared to hear the noise from the street all the day and night. My parents sleep in one room, and Simon and I sleep in another, which is the kitchen. It is hot inside from the hot air that comes out in the bathroom. We can't flush the toilet. On my first night here, I was scared to death because I woke up with an alarm going off. It had nothing to do with a real fire. The batteries in the alarm weren't working, or the hot air from the bathroom made it work.

I cry at night, not knowing why. Simon tells me stories that he makes up, so I can take my mind off everything else that makes me cry. Even when he stops, I continue thinking of the rest of the story, which he saves for the next night—and then I cry again. His stories are sad, but the best I've ever heard.

This hotel is in Manhattan, on 28th Street. We live with poor people who can't afford anything else. I can see an old man in another window sometimes, and I think he must be the most unhappy, poor, and even the scariest hero in any tale at all.

We shop for food in a store on 22nd Street that is very good. Yesterday we strolled around Manhattan in the evening. The street lights were glowing, and I repeated, "I'm going nowhere else."

Nowhere Else.

Love,
Raimonda

APRIL 3

Dear Kitty!

A miracle occurred yesterday! An American Jew in a store gave us a whole bag full of candy, cookies, and matzoh. He had asked in English whether we were Jews from Russia.

—This is a gift for you.

We were so happy.

Tina came over, Sima's girlfriend who has been in New York for a while. They're eating and talking.

That's all for now. We've already gotten the forms, and today we'll go to get Social Security—it's a permit, a legal status.

Love,
Raimonda

APRIL 7

Dear Kitty!

Finally I'll be able to write you. I spent three nights at Tina's. Her fearsome grandmother didn't give me anything to eat, and only when Tina arrived from school did I get something to eat, the first time all day. But then, I did spend most of the day in the pool at the Jewish Center. I was swimming. There's probably never been such a large pool in the Soviet Union. I went to the sauna. I must have been swimming for five hours. Yes, I'd go there every day. But you have to pay $100 to join.

So far we've been living at this hotel with hundreds of cockroaches. The fire alarm goes off every night and we wake up. But we're not afraid anymore because many people have broken alarms too. Here, the terrible steam goes continually in the bathroom, and we walk around in T-shirts from the heat. It's impossible to flush the water in the toilet, and the water will go the wrong way—onto the floor. But, on the other hand, I can take a walk around "Manhattan" instead.

Today was a day full of simple charms, if not wonders! Papa saw a woman yesterday who fixes people up with volunteers. And so today a volunteer was waiting for us at one o'clock in the afternoon—a tall fellow, a clean American, twenty-one years old, who had just learned Russian. He was waiting for us, and no one else but us. He took us to the Financial Center. We went up to the 107th floor of the World Trade Center, and there we saw all of New York and the island where the Statue of Liberty is. It was snowing—snow in April.

How I rejoiced in the snow, in the freedom! Kitty, I love this all so much.

P.S. So, our family hasn't yet found an apartment. At the moment I'm going out to walk around Manhattan. How fast the days have gone by!

Love,
Raimonda

APRIL 9

Dear Kitty!

Here all the children, including me, are terrified, and want to run to their grandmothers. New York is a city where people live who drink, fight, kill people, and pick through garbage cans looking for scraps. It's a city of lunatics with bulging eyeballs who thrash their arms around in the air. Sometimes I'm terrified, but sometimes I feel sorry for them.

Maybe the only pretty, empty, quiet, and clean place is the area in Queens where Uncle Pavlik lives.

Yes, Kitty, now I want to run to my grandmothers and grandfather like little Raimonda.

I want to go to them, to my dear family, even though everyone insists that things will be better when we have an apartment.

Love,
Raimonda

Kitty, you're the only one I have in place of my grandmothers and grandfather; you're the only one, and I'll never leave you the way I did them.

Love,
Raimonda

APRIL 10

Dear Kitty!

There's never been a better day than today. Happiness at last! Happy Passover.

Today we were invited to a synagogue by some volunteers we had met named Rose and Joyce. They came for us in a taxi and took us to this synagogue. I've never seen richer people than these, or nicer ones. I've never seen such enormous tables with white tablecloths and dishes of food that make the tables sag.

What nice people these American Jews are. What a nice talk we had with them, how they kiss me when we leave, how they shake my hand and my parents' hands—and Sima's. They wish us happiness and say that I'll become a star. Many of them left me and Papa their address. We'll call them. There were very famous people there.

I've been writing to you, but you probably don't understand what about. But I can't describe it for you.

Time to sleep.

> Love, Raimonda
> Goodnight, Kitty

APRIL 11

Dear Kitty,

P.S. My parents and Sima argued over the apartment yesterday. It's a nightmare. I can't take it anymore:

They're breaking up.

They've calmed down.

We're going out again today to look for an apartment in Brooklyn. We wanted something in Queens, but it's very expensive there.

> Love,
> Raimonda

APRIL 12

Dear Kitty!

Today we were at a lawyer's office. A woman named Carol Gold who was at the synagogue yesterday invited us. She wanted to look at Papa's pictures and help him publish them. I went because Papa cannot speak English. Carol Gold is a very nice woman. And so today we went up to the twenty-third floor, where she greeted us with a friendly smile. Then she called Michael in another office. Papa showed them his pictures. We'll meet again on Wednesday. Papa will have an agent. Business moves on.

P.S. Dear Kitty!

These days have flown by like so many days. Not days but months. Vienna, Italy. And we're still looking for an apartment. It's very difficult, they're all expensive.

I've made friends with other Russian emigrant children in the hotel. They come for me every day so that we can run after each other and explore this hotel. We reached a door with a sign on it which said: "Don't ever come in or you die." There is obviously a mad man behind it. But because we were scared and curious at the same time, we stayed by his door and waited for him to come out. He never did. We also played Kiss-Kiss Myau [Spin the Bottle] to see who will kiss whom. But we stopped when we found out that everything is heard in other rooms because the walls are so thin. One girl was really embarrassed to find that out.

It's time to sleep.

Goodnight, Kitty.

And now, I'm American Raimonda

APRIL 13

Dear Kitty!

We went looking for an apartment today. We found a very good, new one-bedroom in Bay Ridge, Brooklyn, that's like a two-room in Chernovtsy, for $650.

We'll negotiate on Monday.

We've been arguing, and I'm really tired of it all. If I could only get away for a minute and rest, and forget; I'd like to get away for a month and forget. Yes, Kitty, I'm very tired of it all, however hard I try. Still, I've endured it all, all the difficulties, but now I'm tired, and I want to be far, far from here. It's just not possible.

The day is almost over, and I'm glad: It was a stupid, empty day.

I want Saturday to come, so things will be happy and everything will be forgotten.

Love,
Raimonda

APRIL 15

Hello, dear Kitty!

Today we walked around a wealthy area of Manhattan. Everyone was celebrating Easter. Everyone was so snappy and good-looking.

On every corner someone was playing instruments and someone was dancing. The black people danced so nimbly! One of them sort of swallowed a lit cigarette, and then it appeared again in his mouth.

We're all tired of living at the welfare hotel. Tomorrow we'll go to Brooklyn to talk about the apartment. This evening Uncle Pavlik, Ilona, and Sasha are coming back from a trip to Venezuela. They're supposed to call.

Someone here is coughing terribly every day—you can hear it through the whole building. And every five minutes the police sirens and fire engines are wailing. Even Papa is tired of living here.

We all want to move into an apartment.

That's all for now.

Love,
Raimonda

APRIL 20

Hello, Kitty!

We've got an apartment. Only we paid the super $200, not to mention $700 for the broker. Yesterday we bought three mattresses: one large one for my parents, and two singles for Sima and me. We're leaving tomorrow at ten in the morning. Papa and Sima are going out now to get money for the apartment and the furniture.

That's all for now.

Love,
Raimonda

APRIL 24

Hello, Kitty,

It's now the second day we've been in the new apartment. We've cleaned up the whole apartment and straightened everything up.

Now we're living like real Americans. We went to the store and bought a lot of things, a lot of different kinds of groceries. And every five minutes we open the refrigerator, take a look inside, elated by the sight. Yesterday and the day before yesterday we were at Uncle Pavlik's. They came to our place to celebrate our housewarming. We celebrated until two in the morning. Aunt Tanya, Mama, and Papa got drunk. Sima and Uncle Pavlik drank and drank but didn't get drunk. I just laughed. Charlik, their dog, bit me for taking away the garbage bag, but the next day he apologized and I petted him. At three in the morning we took the car with them to their house. The upper car window was open, music was playing, and the night lights of Manhattan were twinkling. We saw the Statue of Liberty and shouted "Hurray" to American freedom. The next day we went to the car show in Manhattan. We didn't like it. But Ilona and Sasha liked it; and so did all the Americans. We looked at them in surprise.

That's all for now. I missed you during these past few days, but I wasn't able to write.

Love,
Raimonda

P.S. I forgot to write you something. A couple of days ago Papa and I were at the office. That woman's daughter, Susie, will be Papa's agent. Another girl named Kelli will come over tomorrow for an interview about our emigration and life in the Soviet Union.

But all of that is tomorrow. Today is today, which is not very interesting—empty, happy, nasty, and nice.

Love,
Raimonda

April 25

Dear Kitty!

Today that woman, Kelli, interviewed us, and she has become our friend. I told her why I started to write you, how we used to live in the Soviet Union, and about emigration. My parents talked about their lives.

I'm in a bad mood. Kitty, I'm very tired. Help me. Rub my back, it really hurts. I can't hear voices anymore, I can't sleep, and I cry all the time.

Where are my grandmothers—my own grandmothers, my very own grandfather? I just sit and cry. The tears just flow of themselves, even though I didn't ask for them. I have no strength left. I sit holding my head in my hands. My God! Life, why are you so hard? You forget that I'm still just a girl. What a heaviness on me! I want to run away. I helped you, Mama and Papa, but you cannot understand it. You'll understand someday, but for now just leave me, don't call my name out so rudely. I'm not here, understand, I beg of you, I'm not here. Kitty, thank you for all the help you've given me—like no other friend you've listened to me and all my childish troubles. You're the only one who hasn't left me, who has understood me.

It's a shame, but these are only so many pages that I'll forget about tomorrow. Someday I'll read them but I won't understand, and I'll forget again. My heart feels only these words this instant, and only today's tears are dying from the pain.

And I hold this pain in my back, in my heart, and in my tears. I don't want to talk about the soul, about life, about fate; they can't help me, and I don't want to make amends.

What for? I'm not going to change. But at the same time I'm not going to apologize. And I'm not going to wave my hands or call on the wind to chase all this away, so that I awake with my grandmothers and you in the garden. But you mustn't be a sad and grievous and cruel notebook; you should be a happy girl who plays with me. You should be a second Raimonda, happy and cheerful. But soon I'll fall into that lovely dream. No, I should say to myself again: Struggle with life, with each day.

And I'm not going to dream that happy dream anymore. And I'll walk around sad again, and I'll wait for the night to see that dream and become happy—only at night, in a childish, happy dream.

Love,
Raimonda

APRIL 27

Hello, dear Kitty!

It's very hot today. I'm in a good mood. We bought an iron and a telephone. The telephone will be hooked up either today or Monday. Today I went to register at "Public School"—on Wednesday I'll go to school, a school like a prison, and study amidst whistles, shouting, and noise. All the windows were closed with locks like in prison. And you can't open the iron doors, except for the front one.

But yeshiva for girls costs $200–$300 per month, and we can't afford it.

Oh, I don't know anything yet. It's summertime outside, the birds are singing. I'm going to the park to the swings.

Love,
Raimonda

MAY 1, 1990

Hello, dear Kitty!

Happy May First, the Soviet holiday. I've already forgotten what it means.

I'll describe the day before yesterday. Saturday evening, Aunt

Tanya came over with Uncle Pavlik and two others from Chernov-tsy. My parents knew them, but I didn't. We sat there until two in the morning. Uncle Pavlik bought food at a Chinese restaurant. They left and we went happily off to bed.

The next morning Uncle Pavlik rang the bell. He gave us a $300 television—a Panasonic. New, fresh from the store. We all almost died of happiness. And we all went with him to Great Adventure in New Jersey. It cost Uncle Pavlik $70. We drove in. It was an open zoo. Giant ostriches came up to the car and looked in the windows. Chimps jumped around on the cars. We saw all the animals and they all came up to us. Giraffes, elephants, buffaloes, rhinoceroses, deer, bears, goats, pelicans, kangaroos—they were all there in this magical zoo.

And then there were enormous swings waiting for us and a pool with dolphins and walruses. Everyone was shouting out either in joy or fear at these fearsome swings. That's how this marvelous day went.

Papa told one of his friends that we were given a television, and he became so bent out of shape that he may never be straight again. He is jealous. He is a shitboil, in the words of a Georgian emigrant I overheard in Vienna. Yesterday we were at the welfare official's. We've got welfare. It's like a right. Today Papa has gone to another official for culture and education. He wants to find out whether I can go to a Jewish school for free; he'll be back this evening and tell me. There's one last piece of news. Our telephone has been hooked up. Now we can call Grandmother Galya, Grandmother Sofa, and Grandfather. I've already called a couple times, but it's always been busy.

God, I hope we can get through.

Today I had a dream that we were still in Italy, we had been refused, that we'd already been there many years, and that we'd die in just a few more. And I ran off and called the consulate in America, to argue, shout, and cry, and tell him everything about our situation, about emigrating—the whole truth. And when I had told him every-thing, he answered: "Gather your things, you're going to America today." And when I went out, the black figures of my parents and Sima were waiting for me and they asked: "What are you saying?" And I answered: "I'll tell you later, but maybe never. Get ready—we're going to America."

Love,
Your Raimonda

Kitty, I just spoke with Grandmother Sofa. I got through. It's too bad that Mama and Papa weren't here—we'll call again this evening. How happy I am—everything is well with them.

Love,
Raimonda

MAY 2

Dear Kitty, hello!

Last night we called Grandmother Galya. It was 4:00 A.M. over there. Everything is okay with them. They're waiting for a *vyzov*, but it's bad in the city. We watched the news yesterday. It was May 1st in Red Square. Gorbachev came out with the other ministers and started to wave happily at the people. But then all the people suddenly started waving posters and flags against the government, against the non-liberation of Lithuania. Some were even carrying flags with the hammer and sickle cut out. It's the end of the Soviet Union, the poor, tormented people—it's a good thing we left.

We were at school today. We've worked it out. Tomorrow I'm going to school. We still don't know anything, but I might be going to a summer camp.

Goodbye for now.

Love,
Raimonda

MAY 5

Dear Kitty, hello!

It's been two days already that I've been going to school—Public School: McKinley Junior High on Fort Hamilton Avenue—the seventh grade, for emigrants. I'll be there until I've learned English. There are eight Russians, many Hispanics, Chinese, Arabs, and other children in my class. The Chinese stick together, the Hispanics talk with everybody, and the Russians sit at one table but talk with everybody.

When I came, they were happy I'm Russian. I am already friends with some of the other Russian girls. The funny thing is that I keep standing up like we have to in Russia when we are asked a question. All the teachers tell me to sit down every time, and some students laugh. I'm embarrassed, but I laugh at myself too.

That's how the day goes. In forty minutes Uncle Pavlik, Aunt

Tanya, and Sasha's parents are coming. That's all for now. The day passed quietly, without any scenes, and even happily.

Love, my dear,
Your Raimonda

MAY 7

Hello, dear Kitty!

I came home from school very happy. It's a warm day today. The teacher praised me. A lot of time has passed, but it seemed like just a minute.

What a shame, but I'd never been this happy before in the Soviet Union. And it's a good thing, too, because after all we did come here, where I'm spending my entire life. And what a shame it is to think of those who are still over there, deceived and tormented. Yes, if I were to return there, I'd scream: "People, understand what sufferers you are—you don't even have bread, and the government is eating yours while they can. It's sad for me to watch you on television, but you'll not get anywhere—because you know that right now the police are on their way and they're going to beat you cruelly to death! People, people, if I could, I'd send *vyzovs* to all of you, you weak ones who have never seen well-being."

Love,
Your Raimonda

MAY 11

Hello, dear Kitty!

Today there is something to write about. Papa was published in the *Novoye Russkoye Slovo [The New Russian Word],* and he sold a picture for $100 to another magazine. He gave each of us $3. I haven't bought anything yet. A friend is supposed to bring us papers for my grandparents' *vyzov* today. We want them to come as soon as possible. They are so old.

It's not much but it's good news—except that a Russian stole my pen in class. I don't know whether or not he'll return it. But that's not important, it's just mean.

Love, my dear, until the next bit of good news—
Raimonda

MAY 14

Dear Kitty!

It's already late but I want to write you. The nicest thing is to think of my hometown where I used to live, play, and have fun. All my friends who played with me every day are now different to me, they're good and happy children. In my memories, I think of Vienna, which became my own city. I looked at the streets with different eyes, eyes that had never seen well-being.

And I still haven't forgotten Italy, those black days, which is to say, "Oh Italy!" But this half a year, which has been like one day, has given me something new that I've wanted since the first grade. And here I am, in this country of America. I don't look at the dirt, I look at the clean things. I go to school, to a class for immigrants, and study English, which I love so much.

America, when I think of it all, I feel like crying: It's like a life has passed by leaving a last trace of memory behind. And now I want to forget the tears, forget the family scenes—that is, they were for the sake of this, America, a happy life.

Raimonda

MAY 15

Dear Kitty!

They're arguing again. They—we. But I'm so tired. My God, I just can't think about it. If only I were somewhere far away—but where? Why aren't things with me like they are with other girls; why aren't they with my brother the way they are with other boys?

I had a dream today that I was strolling with my grandmother through a majestic city made of sun and gold. And there were flowers everywhere, it was summer, the sky was blue, and I didn't know the people, but they were nice and they were smiling.

But suddenly everything disappeared. And I was in another dream. My brother and I were going up into a hall for meetings and celebrations. Music was playing somewhere. I went my way, and Sima his. Children were sitting in chairs. And they were all asleep as if they had flown in from another place. And I recognized many of my friends and began to wake them up. But they kept on sleeping and wouldn't wake up.

Mama woke me up, and I went to school. Maybe the dream

cannot be understood, but I really liked it. It happened right before my eyes, and I feel like going to sleep again so I can see it.

Kitty, I just can't sleep all the time—I'm alive—what am I to do?

I'm looking out the window at the green trees that are swaying in the summer breeze. And I begin to cry without knowing why.

But I'm so tired I can't think about the shouting and crazy people. How sorry I feel for them, but that can't help anything.

> Love,
> Raimonda

MAY 19

Hello, dear Kitty!

Today is Saturday. I'm in a good mood. Yesterday I straightened up. Papa and I went to the library and I took out three English books for two weeks, including *Anne Frank*. I'm so happy. I'll read it right now. There's nothing new so far, but also nothing bad. Till there's news—good news!

> Love,
> Raimonda

I forgot—Grandmother Sofa wrote a letter that we got yesterday. She congratulated us on being here. She herself wants to get a *vyzov*. The Soviet Union is at an end. They're beating people, there's nothing there, there's just one word for it: "The End."

> Love,
> Raimonda

MAY 20

Hello, dear Kitty!

Uncle Pavlik and Aunt Tanya came over yesterday. They brought a lot of food from a Russian store, also an album and colored markers for me, paper and a notebook for Papa. We ate and drank, and then they all left together for a Russian restaurant; Sima and I stayed home. They got back at 5:00 A.M. Today everything is as usual. We saw a parade this afternoon. Everyone was carrying Norwegian and American flags. That's how the day went. We haven't been arguing, thank heavens. Till tomorrow,

> Your happy-for-the-centuries
> Raimonda

MAY 21

Hello, dear Kitty!

The days have gone by, and for me they were the first happy ones since we emigrated. It's probably because we're not arguing. I came back from school every day cheerful, tired, and happy.

Why do I love this class? Many of the boys call the teachers names, and nobody understands Russian. It's true, they treat the girls all right. Two boys have fallen in love with me; I think it's funny—I play with the girls. After lunch we chase each other around outside. In the morning we tell each other our dreams, and play like in the movies.

We write down in our notebooks every word that the teacher writes out, even if we're dead tired, but everyone repeats them to himself—it is English, after all. And that's how our school day goes.

My family and Sima have the same old conversations. Sima sadly talks about how he wasn't hired for a job. Mama talks about her courses. And Papa, when he comes back from the library, talks about something terrible or dreams aloud of a happy future. And I listen to all this, don't say anything, and hug Papa for these good dreams. And I think, Maybe it will come true.

Love,
Raimonda

TODAY IS A HAPPY DAY! MAY 23

Hello, dear Kitty!

After school today at four o'clock we arranged to meet Carol Gold and Susie in Manhattan. They took me to a store called The Gap and bought me a lot of nice things. I'm so happy. What a gigantic store, with thousands of things. Even the salesman stood on his knees and put sneakers on me. Now I'm an American girl, happy and cheerful. Today is a good day that is now coming to a close. Goodnight, Kitty. Till new good news!

Raimonda

MAY 26

Dear Kitty!

A typical day. Sima found work for cash—it's not steady—thank God it's not, because it is so awful. He gives out ads for $3 an hour.

The day before yesterday he earned $10 and brought home a whole table full of food; yesterday he earned $20 and brought pastries.

Love,
Raimonda

MAY 29

Hello, dear Kitty!

I don't know why, but I thought of the first day when I started to write to you. I still didn't understand then what would become of me. How I miss my relatives right now. But I understood that Soviet life couldn't be endured. And we cry every day when we see even for a second on the news how people are getting beaten in the Soviet Union. And it doesn't make any difference what their nationality is. They are scattered like points throughout this black country that will never change, but only keep on raging until it collapses and goes to the dogs.

And I'll never be angry with myself for being here. This is the only country where it's possible to live, even when you're surrounded by different kinds of people. And I understand that I'll miss my hometown all my life and that I'll never forget those old streets, or the house I've been away from already so long. But life arranged things its own way and has led to something better, even though it forgot to bring along my city where I lived.

I don't know what kind of life we'll find here. I think it'll be normal. But those difficult adventures have come to an end.

I don't know what this book will become—my diary—which has helped me so much and which I'll never forget, never forsake. These letters to you, Kitty, have saved me. I've always felt that you listen to me and gather up this grief. And when I'm happy, I'm happy together with you. You'll always remain my true friend, who has passed through this difficult path of tears and small joys in which I've lived.

Raimonda

MAY 30

Dear Kitty!

Unhappiness.

The back of a bed fell on Sima's head at work in the furniture store. It smashed him in the forehead. Now he's in the hospital. There's a line waiting. And he'll come back only sometime at night. My God, Simochka, where are you now? All day I've had a kind of premonition. Sima, where are you, my very own brother? Why should this have happened to you? Why?

That's what happened, Kitty. It's not bad luck; fate is simply mocking us.

Raimonda

JUNE 1, 1990

Hello, dear Kitty!

Sima got back at one in the morning. He got seven stitches. What horrors he told us about. But the day has already ended.

It's Sima's birthday in two days. We went to a Russian store today and bought sausage, herring, caviar, and pastry. Now I'm going to bed.

Love,
Raimonda

JUNE 2

Hello, Kitty!

Tomorrow is Sima's birthday. We were at the library. I already have my own card. I took out a lot of books. *Mary Poppins, Sweet Valley Twins, Alice in Wonderland.* Mama and Sima argued. Mama's nerves are completely shot. Today we got some tables. They were left behind in the apartment house by people who moved out. My mood has been ruined. I'm going to read now.

Love,
Raimonda

JUNE 3

Hello, my dear!

I'm in a wonderful mood. We celebrated Sima's birthday. I gave him $1; it was all I had. I wrote poems for him and drew everything in them like postcards. Uncle Pavlik and Aunt Tanya came over. They gave Sima $75.

We had such a good time, drank, snacked, talked, laughed, and joked until two or three in the morning.

Today is Sunday. Everything is the same with us. Sima bought two Pink Floyd tapes. They're my favorite group. Tomorrow he's going to buy a guitar.

Love,
Raimonda

JUNE 7

Dear Kitty!
Hello!
School is over in twenty days. We've already sent a *vyzov* to my grandmothers and grandfather. We called them a little while ago. We get letters very often; they want to come over here—the Soviet Union is finished. We've been here three months already.

Life goes on. Sima and I already have beds, tables, curtains, and an armchair. Papa has a table, television, curtains, and a mattress.

Love,
Raimonda

JUNE 8

Dear Kitty, hello,
I got home from school, which I hate. Alas. School, where Russian boys study and make fun of Lisa, Ira, Marina, Natasha, and me. They call us names that I've never heard before, and we can't call them names back, and if we say one simple word to them they answer with a hundred, and not simple ones either.

My nerves are shot. We can only think of how to annihilate them. How I want to go to a yeshiva, how I dreamed of one in Italy, how I thought that a free Jewish school was waiting for me. But there's no such school, alas—it costs money. And I have to sit here, and when I recite a text by heart, a Russian boy begins to babble loudly and I make a mistake. But I got a 100 and a 99 anyway, whereas when they read you want to stop up your ears.

So that's the kind of school it is—where the teacher doesn't understand the Russian boys, and the girls go home in a rotten mood.

Raimonda

JUNE 14

Hello, dear Kitty!

I'm going to describe for you what happened to me in school.

After lunch, Natasha and I went out to the playground at school as always. Suddenly a black girl walked up and lifted Natasha's skirt; I was wearing pants. At a loss, Natasha asked in English: "Why?" She answered: "I'm showing what the boys do." When she walked over to her friends, she started to laugh. "It is not your business," I said to her. She ran up to me and hit me in the head. I ran away from her, but she chased me and grabbed me by the hair and began to hit me incredibly hard. She was fourteen or fifteen years old.

I ran away and burst into tears from the pain and insult. She left. Lisa and Natasha went over to the guard or school chief and told him everything that had happened. He came over to me, and there were a lot of children following behind him asking what had happened.

I looked at every black girl who looked like the one who did it, but all of their faces became friendlier-looking, or so it seemed to me. But suddenly at the staircase I caught sight of the one with the laughing face. The teacher walked up to her—she knew everything already. But she didn't manage to ask her anything before the girl vanished off somewhere. I wrote down my family name and went back to class with my classmates. I decided that she wouldn't be found anywhere and that everything would end with that. But in the second-to-last class we were studying in the hallway and suddenly I spotted her going into the bathroom. I recognized her easily. When she came out she saw us and, mumbling something, went into the "Din," a detention room where this kind of incident is investigated, with a piece of paper summoning her there. I was called in, and the black girl started to lie right in my face that I had called her a "bitch." But I told the truth and they believed me. Then the black girl said with a smile, "I'm sorry," as if she'd hit me in the head again. She went out laughing. And I left too. But five minutes later I was called in again into Din. I told the story to the teacher who works there and she said: "Thank you. I'll take care of it."

Sometimes it seems to me that the teachers themselves are afraid of her, because in the hallway the teacher smiled at her, even though I told her how the girl was behaving. And I left. Then there was class, where I managed to cut my finger and my head hurt. I can only say that it was an unhappy day.

Love,
Raimonda

JUNE 16

Dear Kitty!

Today is Saturday, a marvelous day. A woman named Joyce from a synagogue came over. She is helping us. Most likely I'll be going to camp, she says. My God, what nice, marvelous Jewish people. Sometimes I can't understand why Russian Jews don't want to help Russian Jews but only want to wish them the worst. But the American Jews are marvelous, cheerful, good people. Joyce gave me two chains with a little heart and a bird, charms, and a bracelet. Mama got a box and a bag and a chain. Papa got a pen. Sima got a chain with the letters of God and life, a notebook, and a poster.

We are happy.

We ate, drank, sang songs, and talked. It was very cheerful.

Right now Joyce is helping Sima with work.

A marvelous day.

And today I understood that every Jew should help another Jew.

Love,
Raimonda

JUNE 18

Dear Kitty,

Hello Kitty! Papa's having an exhibit on June 21 in Manhattan.

Papa was published in the *Novoye Russkoye Slovo* and *The New York Times*. The first steps, as Papa says.

I'm in a good mood. I read a story called "The Flying Class." And I cried—it was about children from a boarding school.

So that's how today ended.

Love,
Raimonda

JUNE 20

Dear Kitty,

Hello—Only nice things happened today. First I received a letter from Zhanna. She's my friend from the Soviet Union. The second is we got a letter from Grandmother Galya. The third thing is that the people across from us are moving, and we got a nice writing desk from them. We've been polishing it up since then. Sima and I were arguing the whole time. I'm sure that tomorrow we'll fight over who gets what shelves in the desk. They're the same neighbors we got that first little black and white television from. The fourth thing is that Joyce helped us with the camp. I hope that I'll be going. And the fifth I couldn't describe in twelve hours. Today was a marvelous day. Till tomorrow, Kitty.

Love,
Raimonda

JUNE 21

Dear Kitty!
Hello!

There was a concert at school today. The eighth graders danced so gracefully and beautifully that everyone had fallen in love right away.

Today is a good day. I wrote two poems. And right now I'm sitting at the writing desk. I wrote a letter to Zhanna. Today we received a letter from NYANA saying that we couldn't go on welfare because there were so many emigrants. Again a problem. But not for me today.

Love,
Raimonda

JUNE 22

Dear Kitty!
Hello.

Today is Mama's birthday. Sima and I gave her a magazine filled with pictures we drew. We wrote it: I put in a poem, and we made up a lot of jokes. I'm very sleepy; it's already late.

Today is an important day, but I just can't sit and write any longer. I'll be able to describe everything to you all day tomorrow.

Goodnight, Kitty.

Raimonda

JUNE 23

Hello, Kitty!

It's late. But I want to write to you. All the thoughts haunting me are just sad dreams.

JUNE 24

Hello, dear Kitty!

Papa took you away last night and said it was time to sleep.

But today I have forgotten what I was going to write about. I've probably gone out of my mind.

I remember that my mood wasn't so great. We were at the synagogue yesterday. Then we went to Uncle Gera. He studied with Papa in the university. He's a hero. He decided to run away from the Soviet Union and to emigrate to America. So he went to Yugoslavia as a tourist and there he tried to cross the border. Yugoslavian soldiers caught him and sent him back to the Soviet Union. They didn't put him in prison, just let him go to America with an Israeli visa—if he promised not to complain.

We got home late, very tired.

I didn't like it at the synagogue. It wasn't at all like it was before, even though it was the same place. Joyce invited us. She wanted to help me with camp and Papa with his exhibit, but no one has helped us. Everyone just smiles at us, and it was even offensive to me. They behaved—I don't know how to describe it—in a rotten way. The rabbi acted like a salesboy. The people who discussed the Torah didn't discuss—they sat around doing nothing, yawning, many of them sleeping. There was a little table where people got food and ate. Mama also brought salad. We didn't get a chance to try it, even though it was only so-so. If I had known English, I would have read the Torah, I would have spoken with that lively rabbi who kept looking at his watch.

And then, like dogs, they flung themselves at the food. There were grapes and bread, and they gave me some. Then with a rotten smile they said, " 'Bye," and that was it. After our Passover here, I was surprised to see this at the same synagogue.

Joyce wanted us to go to the synagogue, but she said that Simon had to cut his hair so he would look more intelligent. She made it sound like coming to the synagogue was very important, like we would get some help with jobs. So Simon cut his hair. And when we arrived, there was nothing special about this synagogue. No one cared. People were lazy and sleeping. After Simon saw all this, he was really upset and he just stood outside and smoked.

Life is very strange, very difficult to understand. Sima said that I was the prettiest girl there, and he was the only one who looked into the book and heard what the rabbi said.

But today is today.

And I'm living my own life because I'm tired of remembering.

But I really love you, Kitty! And you live my life; even my brother doesn't live my life.

And I'll never leave you. You won't be my memory, you'll be my life.

Raimonda

JUNE 25

We're arguing again. My God, what's with Mama? Why was I born? It would be better to be dead; what's the use of living? My heart is breaking right now. I can't take anymore. I'm not going to write you any more of this. This book is only about feelings.

That's all.

Raimonda

JUNE 27

Hello, dear Kitty!

I haven't written you for several days. But today I'll write you. My mood has gotten a little better.

My parents have broken with Sima. Sima says that he comes home from work in a bad mood and tired. I feel really sorry for him. My parents are constantly badgering him—and shouting at me. But when it's time to straighten things up, they don't shout. Mama lies around all day doing nothing. I don't know what happened. Everyone is on edge and in a foul mood.

In twenty days I'm going to camp, from July 17 to August 5.

Mary helped us. I'm going to a camp in the mountains of New Jersey.

It's very hot. School is out. That's all for now.

Love,
Raimonda

JUNE 29

A Happy Day
Hello, dear Kitty!

No one has ever had such a blissful mood as mine today. Today I can in complete honesty congratulate myself, that is, call myself the happiest girl. Starting at nine in the morning, Joyce and I spent the whole day in Manhattan until 10:00 P.M. Where weren't we! We went to the movies—*Dick Tracy*—and had a snack there. Then we rested at her house. Then we went to a restaurant where a nice Jewish couple, ninety-three years old, served us a giant dinner. I was sure they were only seventy to seventy-seven years old.

Then we were at the synagogue. How many nice words I heard. I forgot my Russian and spoke English without thinking too hard. And only then did she take me home by car. Tomorrow I'll go out with Joyce again.

Even though I've given a very brief description—because I'm really tired, my eyes are closing—today was the happiest day.

Love, love, love,
Yours forever,
Raimonda

A Happy Day
Today we've been in America three months.

JULY 1, 1990

Hello, dear Kitty!

Now I have time to write to you. Yesterday, Joyce and I were at the zoo. It was really hard to look at the animals because it was so hot. Joyce bought me a Panama hat. It was a happy day.

This morning we called Grandfather in the Soviet Union. Grandmother Sofa is in the hospital because of her eyes.

Love,
Raimonda

JULY 3

Dear Kitty!

Hello.

Today is a strange day. It's the second day my parents have been going to classes. The area is terrible, but the courses are good.

Sima got back from work today at eleven o'clock. He always gets back at seven. We were very worried—we didn't know what had happened to him. No one was at work, and he didn't call before eleven to say that he was coming home. Papa wanted to go find him and call the police. But then here he was. He was working moving sofas and doing dirty work. When he told us what horrible things happened during the course of the day with his boss, who is a businessman, we laughed even though we probably should have cried.

I got a letter from Annushka. I'm happy she hasn't forgotten me. But last night I was crying thinking of her. I'm going to the camp in fourteen days.

Mary has found out about a school. We have an appointment on Thursday.

Maybe I'll be going to a private Jewish school. But all of that is still ahead.

Now I'll say goodbye.

> Love, your Raimonda
> Till tomorrow

JULY 4

Hello, dear Kitty,

Today is July Fourth, America's birthday. We walked along the shore watching the fireworks display. It was really frightening—like a war.

We couldn't see the fireworks from the Statue of Liberty island because they were on the other side. There were many Russians on the shore. They were all talking about their English courses; but it wasn't interesting. They were all setting off fireworks with bored faces. But people were running and jumping and talking, and then they left. A Russian girl got a piece of firecracker in her eye. Then a firework fell in the bay with a terrible explosion. It was deafening, and my teeth hurt.

Then two ambulances came; it seems another firecracker fell on someone. Everyone left in a downcast mood. The Statue of Liberty was still standing, though, surrounded by rockets. But it was far away from us, and there was space on our side.

Right now we're back home, and it's already almost twelve midnight. I'm going to bed, but I won't be able to sleep today, like yesterday, because of the heat. Sima wants to go north; I feel like going to the pool. I'll say goodbye for now. Till tomorrow.

Goodnight, Kitty!

You can still hear stupid people setting off firecrackers outside my window.

Love,
Raimonda

JULY 5

Hello, Kitty!

I'm very tired today.

We went to a private Jewish school. We'll get an answer on July 30 whether I'll be going or not. It's an Orthodox school. Most likely I'll go there in September.

For the meantime the government will pay for me. But in five months Papa would pay $100 per month.

I'm going to camp in twelve days. If you only knew what the heat was like, you'd collapse and die.

We found a fan in the basement of our house.

Today I bought a lot of things for school. A notebook, pen and ink, and an eraser.

Love,
Kitty

JULY 7

Hello, dear Kitty!

Yesterday afternoon we got a letter from Grandmother Galya and another from Grandfather. Grandmother Galya writes about how Grandmother Sofa and Grandfather have insulted her. They even sent their letter and immigration forms separately.

We made a scene after we got the letters. I was angry at Grandmother Sofa and wanted Mama to write her a letter saying to stop all these rumors and arguments. Mama hit me and I went out into the hall, but didn't cry—what is there to cry about? I just think my grandparents should all come together; otherwise the whole family will be crushed—here and there. We made up in the evening. But today I did cry.

Mama is writing in a letter and saying that I'm bad. But it's not true. I just don't understand why Mama won't give me her letters to read. And then Grandfather opens his letters with the words, "Hello dear Klavochka," and forgets completely about me. I cried so hard and wrote my grandparents the whole truth, and Papa did too.

Mama doesn't love me even though I do everything. But enough of this.

I'm not going to go to a private Jewish school. It's very far away in a bad neighborhood. I'd have to change trains three times. Joyce will be coming over today.

Dear Kitty, I've been writing you nine months now, and I'll never part with you. Even though we're not going anywhere again, emigration has left its mark. I learned how to write you only in Italy. In the Soviet Union and Vienna I wasn't able to describe each day for you as it happened. And every page in this diary describes only my feelings that I'll forget forever, leaving them in these pages. So much time has passed and I've forgotten everything. When I close you, I forget everything.

I've tried many times to read through you, but I've forgotten everything page by page and I don't know why. Simple books I can remember. But my own life, each day, I forget; I almost never remember it. And in truth there is a lot I want to forget. But when I cry, the memories come flooding back to me, and I see it all like at the movies. But today I don't want to write about it. I'll forget that too, after all.

And I know that there's no friend like you. You don't have to be consoled—you just take all this in. So I'll never think of those tears and sighs of those days.

Thank you.

Till tomorrow, Kitty.

Raimonda

P.S. Joyce was over today. We spent the whole day together. First there was supper, then Russian music and dancing. I sat thinking of our yard, friends, and house far away. And then I danced like never before. And Mama never danced like that before, and Papa and Sima danced. Then we went to the ocean. I played with a girlfriend of mine. We got home late in the evening. The grown-ups talked about welfare. Joyce asked, Shouldn't my parents be standing on their own two feet at the age of forty? They already started once, and had to stop. And now they have to start again. Why is it so difficult to live? Simply because it's life.

Maybe Joyce will find a bus to take me to school after all. Uncle Sasha called us today. Our relatives, they live in Colorado. They were given four separate apartments, furniture, money, and food. Now they have a car, they're working, and going to college.

We made up after the letter and forgot everything.

Papa is reading, Sima is listening to music. It's very late.

> Goodnight, Kitty
> Raimonda

> You came,
> grieved with sadness,
> full of tears, insult,
> and cruel memory.
> But I will help and calm you.
> And you, as a child,
> will forget soon.
> Your tea glass will empty
> and you'll hurriedly leave.
> I'll be left alone,
> silent and sleepy.
> The memory will come to me.
> It'll become sad and painful.
> Tears will call for you,
> But you'll never come
> to console me.

JULY 14

Dear Kitty!

It's already been a week that I haven't written you. It's because Sima bought a video with his money and we've been watching it every night.

My parents bought a lot of food yesterday for cheap, even knishes and pickled tomatoes from a jar.

Nothing's happening. Nothing good, nothing bad—like in the Soviet Union.

Raimonda

P.S. Uncle Pavlik gave me a flower in a pot. I'm growing his "violets."

We watch videos every night. We have many cassettes. They were given to us by Uncle Pavlik and by a Polish man in Papa's English class.

Please forgive me, Kitty, that I haven't written you very often, but I've been very busy with problems with NYANA and the house. But now I'm going to go back again. I'll write you later.

Love,
Raimonda

JULY 16

Dear Kitty!

I'm going to camp tomorrow at noon. I think it'll be good. I don't know whether Papa will let me bring you along. Of course I would want to, but you'd only be safe here. But I do know for sure that if I don't take you I'll bring another notebook and I'll write!

I don't know who will take care of the house, who'll clean up. But I do know that when I come back, everything will be as it was before—clean and warm. And of course I'll miss everything in a week at most. I remember when I went to Odessa with my grandmother, and I was so glad to leave everything and get a rest. But the whole time I counted on my fingers the days till I came home. That's what kind of person I am. I did the wash because my parents are in class.

Something new awaits me. Now I'll really learn English right— I'll be with children.

I hope I'll make friends with them. But all this is tomorrow.

Love,
I'll definitely write you.
Your Raimonda

JULY 25

Hello, dear Kitty,

I don't know whether I'll be able to write you all that happened today. But I can tell you this about my adventures this month.

On July 17, we left home and went to Manhattan. It was still early, and everyone was standing around the synagogue. At about one o'clock everyone gathered. I met a girl named Yulia. We said goodbye to our parents. Everyone got on the bus. We drove for two hours; the time passed quickly. When we arrived, we were surrounded by lush nature, a lake, a river, and barracks. For a while, I thought that geese lived in the barracks. But no. We were led into one of them. It was a wooden cabin without windows, with mosquito netting, beds, and bedside tables. I made the bed and arranged my things, helped Yulia, and then wanted to call home. But they told me that there was no calling from the camp. We didn't get to eat before evening. It's an enormous hall with tables and chairs, also open. I didn't like the food. That's how the first day went.

On the second day, I got to know the girls. We went swimming at 3:15 in the afternoon. We swam very little. They corrected how we swam. I know how to swim, but I didn't want to swim in the deep water, so I swam in the pool, which is part of the same lake. It's just separated by some boards. We had breakfast at 7:45, lunch at 11:45, and supper at 5:45.

On the third day, the girls started calling us names. I didn't pay any attention. I thought it would stop. Yulia's personality changed— she showed her true face. We went swimming again. Then I washed off in the shower. The bathroom was very dirty. I had an upset stomach.

The fourth day. The girls hated us. They pushed us around and called us names. They didn't understand us, and we didn't understand them. They have had a different life. They kiss boys, even in bed. They were putting on a show that night for themselves. But I got under the covers and slept.

The counselor named Bee—that's her nickname—gathered us together. She said: "It's your choice: either you ignore each other, or you become friends." Each one of us said what was on her mind. After that, the girls hugged Yulia and me and asked us to forgive them.

The fifth day. At first everything was as usual. We went to the beach and swam for a long time. In the evening we sang songs. But suddenly a boy shouted, "Help!" A counselor was carrying him and he was gasping. He had been looking for a stick for the fire. He found a big one, and used all his power to break it and apparently, from what I could tell, he had pulled something loose inside him. Many of the children stopped singing, but many kept on singing. You could hear the boy shouting for help over the singing. I couldn't believe everyone could just go on singing. But finally everyone went off to sleep. No one wanted to sing anymore, and I didn't feel too well. The boy's sister is in my bunk. She went with him to the hospital and got back very late. She said he was very bad, that his face looked like stone, but that they helped him.

On the sixth day, I saw him back at the camp in the morning and I was very surprised that he came back to the camp after being in the hospital. A little later I got sick. I went to the medical station. I had a fever of 39 [102 degrees F.]. I slept in my bunk. The next day I had a temperature again—38.5. I had tonsillitis. I lay there all day, and no one gave me pills or even anything to drink. I rushed off, saying I was going for my pillow. I made it to Bee, and told her that I wasn't being helped at all. It was the same with her. She was sick and nobody was giving her anything. She was lying in her bunk. I played a game with everyone outside. A boy grabs a sock from a girl and they go get married, or the reverse.

Later, they came from the medical station for me. Yulia went with me. As a joke she told the doctor that she was sick—but it turned out to be true: Her temperature was 39.

Night. No one was sleeping. No one brought us bedding. At 2:30 A.M. I went off to ask why not. Bee was sitting on the table and the other counselors were all sick. They were giving oxygen to one of them and taking him to the hospital. Bee was crying. They brought us pillows. I had the same old dream for the thousandth time—I call home, pack my things, and leave.

The seventh day. I called home. Everything I said was like in a dream. It cost me a lot of tears to call home. But the doctor woman, who kept hugging me and asking me not to leave her, told me not to say that I was sick. But I was telling the complete truth. It seemed to me that a virus had broken out at camp. Everyone had gotten sick. Everyone had at least a 39-degree temperature. Everyone was feverish and had a sore throat. Some people didn't even know they had a virus. That's what happened. Papa said that he'd pick me up that day.

I ran out of the hospital while the doctor was talking on the telephone. I gathered all my things in a second. They caught up with me
again, but I escaped again. Bee and another girl also escaped. We sat
there cursing the camp. Bee was crying. She was feeling bad for the
third day, and no one was helping her. She gets very little money
and wants to study at college in September, but there's not enough
money from working at the camp.

Then I wanted to get Yulia. But Yulia disappeared somewhere.
I ran off, but Yulia stayed. A minute later she ran up to me—she was
also on the run. No one wanted to lie in bed all day with all the sick
children and without medicine. Some people from the office came for
me. But I wasn't afraid. I had called home and Papa said he was
coming for me. Then Kelli called and said they'd pick me up at 6:30
P.M. It was 11:30 A.M. The time flew by unnoticed. They wouldn't
let Yulia go. I said goodbye to everyone. And I was happy. Children
with bored faces waved at me, but soon it would be all over. I'm
going to forget the whole thing.

Love,
Raimonda

JULY 27

Dear Kitty!

Today is a typical day. I straightened everything up. Now I'm
going to watch a movie. My parents are tired after their classes. Sima
is out with a girl. I've wanted to eat constantly since camp. I'm feeling better.

Love,
Your Raimonda

AUGUST 7, 1990

Dear Kitty!

I haven't written for a couple of days—because the days were
empty, typical. Today is, too. I'm mad at my parents: They won't
let me call Grandmother Galya even though today is Sunday. You
can always call Grandmother Sofa. They're always finding fault with
me, even for loving McDonald's.

Mama tells me that I'm a pig; Sima laughs at me; and Papa has
sold out again against me.

At this moment I'll begin to think of my friends and grandmother. I've never cried with them. I don't write about America; it was my dream, and I love America very much. I believe that I'll have a difficult time ahead in America. I don't think of the Soviet Union, I think of people close to me, whereas I see my relatives as enemies this time; there's malice boiling inside of me. My feelings are hurt about Grandmother, and my sense of fairness that I am always laughed at and insulted is hiding inside of me and wants to get out again. But I don't let it. I know that it's senseless.

How I want to spit on the clean floor, on everything—so that they'd understand that I'm the one who does everything and that they need me. And I say to them—go on the way you are, but I'm not going to clean up. Let them understand that I have some need in me, even if they are unable to love.

And as soon as Sima came home, Mama gave him and Papa something to eat, but not me. I forced them to give me something too, and now I'm sorry I did, because I could have been stronger.

So my list of complaints is winding up very sadly.

Everyone had gone to bed in peace and even happily, while I'm starting to remember and think, saying to myself, "Oh, how I want to call my dear Grandmother Galya."

Love,
Raimonda

AUGUST 13

Hello, dear Kitty!

Yesterday we had guests for Papa's birthday, and they left late. Papa now has $200. We called Grandmother Galya yesterday. She was crying and wanted to come here. We've already sent the forms off to Washington. A woman from the *Voice of Village* is coming over today to take our pictures for an article about our family. 'Bye! I'll write you some more today.

Raimonda

AUGUST 14

Hello, dear Kitty!

Everything is as usual. I have a headache today. Mama and I went to the playground on Shore Road near the ocean. We go there every day because the weather is hot. It's a little cooler there, by the water.

Mama and Papa can't speak English anymore. The good courses are over, and they don't get asked any questions in these new ones. The teacher is not interested in listening to Papa try to say something but fail—so she doesn't call on him. She calls on the other Russians who can speak quickly and are beginning to speak at a twenty-minute stretch. But Papa's only able to sleep. They want her to be fair, but who should he ask—the lazy American teacher, or the insolent people who speak all the time? No, there's no fairness in this life.

LATER—

Dear Kitty,

I'm going to write you about my mood; I know that there are many unhappy people in this world. Today it seemed to me that we are the unhappiest people—tired and accustomed to emigrating, people who want a lot of things but cannot afford them, who cannot be proud, like other unhappy people. And I want to cry out what an unhappy girl I am, how I want a dog but cannot buy one because there's no money even for meat, no room in the apartment, and a lot more is lacking. And no one is working.

It seemed to me that my parents are poor, without language, without money, and no one will help them.

But I came home and shouted this the whole way in front of the house. Mama walked on ahead. I was silent, and she was dear and unhappy for me again. And it would have gone on like this forever, except that Papa told us about our friends and about a good, smart, upright man whose wife left him. Emigrating had shattered their nerves. And they are upright people who love each other but have to part. Their brother who is nineteen years old got married in the Soviet Union, but the wife's parents wouldn't let her leave.

The brother worked hard in order to buy a ticket to go to the Soviet Union and to bring his wife here. His nose was bleeding from the stress; he slept with adults in the same room because he feared retribution; and his wife fought with the government. But she got tired. And when he called her, he got this answer: "Forget about her. She's already with someone else."

After hearing that I didn't become happier, but I did understand that there are many unhappy people in the world, and many unhappier than I.

Raimonda

AUGUST 15

Dear Kitty!

Sima is happy. He's already working at a steady job, for $5 an hour. He has two days off, on Saturday and Sunday. Work begins at 10:00 A.M. and ends at 7:30 P.M. He's at work now.

AUGUST 16

Dear Kitty!

A friend called us the day before yesterday. She knows of an organization that gives out and delivers furniture for free. She works there. She gave us the address of the organization. Yesterday she called us from this organization to say they'll bring us some furniture on Tuesday. We'll have to hide the television and video. Now I'll write you about the newspaper called *Voice of Village*. This is a newspaper for writers and poets. After our meeting at the synagogue, they were interested in you, Kitty. I decided to tell it all.

But they've been thinking about it for a month already. Kelli, the writer, came over and interviewed us, and took some pages from you. She said they'd be published in the newspaper. I didn't believe it. But I was wrong. Next Wednesday it'll be in the paper. I'll be famous. Even though that is not the main thing in life, it is a great joy.

Love,
Raimonda

AUGUST 21

Hello, dear Kitty!

Today is a happy day. A week ago some friends of ours called. They work at a Jewish organization that provides assistance to immigrants. We were put down for Tuesday. They brought us two beds, an armchair, two lamps, bed sheets, towels, quilts, and dishes at eleven this morning. At one they brought us a table and four chairs from a store. They're new and beautiful.

Papa and I cleaned, fixed things up, and moved things around all day. Mama didn't do anything. Sima got home from work in the evening. Then we had supper at the new table, with the new dishes.

Now our place is clean and beautiful.

I got two toys and Papa got bookshelves. The best gift was two silver cups for the sabbath.

When they gave us all these things, Papa began to cry and sob. Mama kept saying that the Jews haven't been forgotten. Sima was also very happy. How nice it is to eat from new plates!

There's one other piece of news. Our shipped luggage has arrived. Now we have to pay, and then they'll bring our bags. Papa said that this was the last connection with the Soviet Union and emigration.

That's how the day went. I'm very happy and cheerful.

Love,
Your Raimonda

AUGUST 22

Hello, dear Kitty!

There has never been such happiness before. I've been published in *The Village Voice,* and now people are talking of nothing but that. The article is four pages long, and includes our photograph. My picture is on the first page. It's called "The Diary of a Young Girl." It's a miracle! Everyone is talking about it. We called the woman from NYANA who helped us in the Hotel Latham, where we first stayed in New York. She was full of praise and said that they were crying— that only the Jews understand what emigrating means. There are eight pages of my diary in the article, and it's all about us.

Dear Kitty, my dear, what happiness, how long I dreamed of being published, but I was expecting to publish something when I was grown up, not now. No, I'll go out of my mind.

Dear Kitty, my own dear one, my dear happiness.

Love,
Raimonda

AUGUST 23

Hello, dear Kitty,

Since yesterday was such a happy day, I didn't want to write anything bad. Papa's diploma was snatched away and stolen, together with documents and money from his gift. He wanted to buy books. Papa says there were $50 there; Mama says it was $100. Poor Papa, how happy he was about buying the books!

After their classes today, Mama and Papa went to renew their documents. Papa called to say that the food stamps have already been issued. They'll arrive soon.

P.S. Early this morning, Mama and Sima stopped talking. Of course it'll be hard for Sima to eat and cook after work. But I would have broken away long ago if I were in his place. I'm always on his side. With that I'll close.

Love,
Raimonda

AUGUST 26

Hello, dear Kitty!

Yesterday Sima came home from work and told us what he did with his friends. They went to a bar where young people play the guitar and black people shine your shoes for 25¢. Then a director started talking about a new movie. He was an anti-Semite and was talking about the Jews, and everybody was laughing. Sima and his friends left right away and they shouted, "Fuck you," at him.

Love,
Raimonda

P.S. On August 25, yesterday, we walked around Manhattan, ate at McDonald's: french fries and Coca-Cola.

P.S. We'll be going to Manhattan again tomorrow at eleven in the morning to meet people who really liked the article and who want to get to know us.

AUGUST 28

Hello, dear Kitty,

Yesterday was a marvelous day. Mama and I met a woman and her son in Manhattan as we had agreed. She's a Jewish woman named Tova, and her son is Dov. We went to a Jewish restaurant and talked about the article, Jewry, and anti-Semitism in the Soviet Union. Then we walked a bit and went to an art museum. It was a very good museum. She—Tova—is from San Francisco. She lived in Israel with her children for ten years. She has a house. Her son lives and works in Boston. He's a lawyer—twenty-five years old. Her daughter is in

San Francisco, and her other son is a lawyer in Europe. They bought me sneakers. Her son Dov is a real Schwarzenegger, even his teeth are the same. He met Schwarzenegger; they're the same height and their muscles are the same, and you can't tell their faces apart. I liked him a lot.

After the museum he bought me a watch. I closed my eyes and he put the watch on my wrist. And in the afternoon he also bought a large clock with an alarm: a little hammer beats little bells.

Then they led us to the subway and we said goodbye.

They said they'd help and call later. Tomorrow Tova is going home and Dov to Boston. But they will call from there. It was a good day. On the subway a man told us where to switch trains onto the R. He was holding *The Village Voice*. And Mama showed me to him. He said: "I cannot believe it; it's one case in a million." And he smiled to himself when he looked at the magazine.

That's how yesterday went. I hope I have many more days like that.

> Love,
> Raimonda

AUGUST 31–SEPTEMBER 1, 1990

Dear Kitty!

Hello! Uncle Pavlik and Aunt Tanya came over today. We ate, drank, and talked. They usually bring Chinese food, sometimes Russian. And we toast for any reason we can find—anything good that happened during the week. Tonight Uncle Pavlik, Papa, Mama, and Sima went out to a restaurant and heard some music. Aunt Tanya and I stayed home. Tanya talked of Russia, her friends and her life as a doctor. She finished, as she always does, by reciting the poems of Pushkin. She knows them all by heart. Everyone else came back at six in the morning, and we all went to bed.

> Love,
> Raimonda

SEPTEMBER 2

I began to write you exactly a year ago. How quickly the time has passed. The Soviet Union, Vienna, Italy, and now finally America.

In one year our life has changed. We've begun to live over again. And I know that we'll remain friends to the end. My dear Kitty! Today is your birthday, my best friend's day.

Love,
Your Raimonda

SEPTEMBER 5

Hello, dear Kitty,

We agreed to meet a woman journalist this morning in Manhattan. She's thirty years old. I didn't like her. Well, she's Jewish, has a family, lives in Israel, makes movies, and wants to do a film about me. It was understood that she doesn't have any money, and we'd have to fight for every dollar. We called Kelli to get her opinion. So far we haven't said yes.

Love,
Raimonda

SEPTEMBER 6

Hello, Kitty!

How I'd like to be Tom Sawyer right now and look for new adventures!

Love,
Raimonda

SEPTEMBER 9

Hello, dear Kitty!

We agreed to meet with a woman today at the museum in Manhattan. We met up with her at one o'clock at the Metropolitan. She found out about us in *The Village Voice*. She's an American Jew, very poor. We looked through the museum. I liked the paintings a lot. We ate fish, tomatoes, and cornflakes instead of bread! She invited us and paid for the museum, and we ate together. She is poor, but she invited us.

We had a good day. Only Papa and I went.

A lunatic or crook got on the No. 4 train, kicked the doors with his feet, and yelled terribly at our backs: "Get Off Now!" We ran off in fright right away, scared out of our wits. My heart was pounding, and even my feet were wobbly. Tomorrow I'm going to school.

Raimonda

SEPTEMBER 16

Dear Kitty!

I didn't manage to write yesterday, on my birthday. Uncle Pavlik, Aunt Tanya, Uncle Lyosha, Aunt Sveta, and Ilona and Sasha came over. Uncle Pavlik gave me a camera, shorts, shirt, a sweater, a bag, and candy. Aunt Tanya—$50. Uncle Lyosha—a sweater and a sports outfit, but it's too big even for Mama. We sat down and drank and laughed and talked.

Uncle Pavlik and Aunt Tanya stayed the night. We went to bed at 3:00 A.M. Sima gave me $10. The next morning we ate breakfast, and Uncle Pavlik and Aunt Tanya left. Then at two Lena and Liza came over for my birthday.

We played, watched a horror movie, and danced. At six the girls went home, and Kelli and Andrew arrived. We ate and drank. I had an allergy from the wine—I tried a little. They gave me a sweater, socks, *The Diary of Anne Frank* (which I dreamed of owning—it's a big, beautiful book), $300 from *The Village Voice,* and a chocolate cake that Kelli made. We put candles in it. Papa took our picture. I blew out twelve of the candles right away, but the thirteenth stayed lit, and I blew that one out, too. It's the first time I've managed to blow them all out.

They brought Sima a guitar and a book. Sima played for us. When Kelli and Andrew left, I cleaned up and washed the dishes. Uncle Pavlik said that on Thursday morning we'd go to see America by car and return on Monday. We'll go to Cape Cod and Martha's Vineyard, an island. That'll be a trip! Right now I'm going to call Grandmother.

Love,
Raimonda

P.S. Papa and I went to buy a lottery ticket for my birthday. I still didn't know what we were paying for. Papa paid for me and got a receipt that shows what numbers I picked. I didn't know anything about it.

When Papa came over to me, he showed me the lottery receipt. I looked at the check and saw that the two numbers were the same, and I started to look really hard at the lottery ticket and the receipt. I saw that all the numbers were the same. And at that moment I probably could have passed out; I stepped backward and almost fell down, but Papa grabbed me. And he asked what happened. I showed him the receipt and said that the numbers were the same. Papa started to laugh.

I had thought that this piece of paper showed the numbers you had to pick. But they were my numbers—it showed that I had written them in. I started to laugh and Papa did too; as soon as I looked at the check I thought it was so funny, and I doubled up with laughter. We laughed like that for about five minutes, and then we went home happy, even though I didn't win anything that evening. And now that piece of paper—that had my 100 million dollars printed on it—is lying somewhere, just trash.

CHAPTER THREE

SETTLING IN

OCTOBER 13, 1990, TO OCTOBER 11, 1991

"OUR MEMORIES WANDER SO FAR"

S till leading a life in translation, the Kopelnitskys nevertheless
were finding more reason to be hopeful. Raimonda was making
friends and excelling scholastically in a special class for immigrants at
McKinley Junior High, and as she moved on to high school, she was
amazed at Brooklyn's Fort Hamilton High. Here, behind the bars and
security systems of this relatively tame urban high school, was a freedom unlike any she could have imagined. Her father, who had long
suffered from poor dental care, now began to get proper attention for
his teeth. He was also working steadily as a freelance illustrator for
The New York Times, though he fretted a great deal between jobs.
Klavdia, a relentless and able student of English, was reading Danielle
Steel romances and *The New York Post* because they suited her reading level, if not her taste. Restless, she longed to work, but instead
watched the fevered comings and goings of her family. Simon, though
he would continue to be plagued by bureaucratic glitches as he tried
to start college, was working steadily at a music and electronics store
in lower Manhattan. The discount he got on electronics thrilled the
family because it meant they could at last have fine electronics—as
opposed to the twenty-year-old black and white television set they
left behind in Chernovtsy. Soon, the family had two stereos, a VCR,
and a couple of Walkmans.

The Kopelnitskys were avidly curious about American ways. They
accepted their first Halloween pumpkin and an invitation to partake

of Thanksgiving turkey and all the trimmings. They remained wary, though. Clearly the events they most enjoyed were those that echoed earlier times in the Soviet Union: Raimonda loved trips to Jones or Robert Moses Beach because they reminded her of riding the waves of the Black Sea. She loved ice skating because her childhood had been filled with it. She asked for a green tree for New Year's, and when she got it, the Kopelnitskys unwrapped the carefully stowed ornaments their family had treasured for generations of New Years.

As much as they clung to the remembered comforts of home in the Ukraine, they also knew that home was no place to be just then. Raimonda's grandparents sent tales of woe—beatings, long lines for less food, continued illness. They begged their children for passage to New York. Klavdia spent hours preparing documents that would clear the way for her parents and Igor's mother to immigrate. The coup in August 1991 jolted the family. They feared that the Soviet Union was on the brink of dissolving into rival factions motivated by hatred. "It is finished," each of them said again and again. Suddenly, the Kopelnitskys didn't know the contours of any place. Home had become in some ways as foreign as New York.

For Raimonda, even as she appeared to be settling into New York, the dissolution of the Soviet state intensified an identity crisis. The fading memories she cherished from her homeland no longer corresponded to recent reports from that part of the map. Always before she could at least say where she was from, if not who she was now. Even as she reveled in having a job—distributing promotional fliers— to earn the money to buy black jeans from The Gap, she despaired of Russian friends who rebuked their shared past. Some refused even to speak their native language. Others were becoming embarrassing parodies of Americans, with their big cars, fur coats, frosted hair, manicured nails, and large diamonds. Her immigrant friends were her last link with the Soviet Union. They had shared her experience. And who would she be when *they* forgot where they had all come from?

OCTOBER 13, 1990

Hi, dear Kitty!

Today is Monday and I was given a lot of homework to do, but I did it all already. Simon bought a huge music system with everything. Andrew helped him set it up, and then we ate supper.

Today is a happy day. We joked a lot, moved our furniture. I've never seen a music system like that in my entire life. A Russian man would go crazy from jealousy.

Lisa stayed in my class. Many others, almost everyone, left for Russian class. The teacher speaks Russian only once in a while—when she can't explain in English. Okay. I'll stop on that. Kiss 'n love.

Raimonda

OCTOBER 14

Hi, dear Kitty!

It's just a regular day. Our room seems smaller and strange. Parents are watching the news, then we're going to go eat. Mom and I were in the park and came back just now.

Today when Mama and Papa went to English classes, they were giving away free clothing. Papa took a white sweater and pants for me; they didn't have time to take something else. After he went into the classroom and showed that he took those clothes, all the other Russians started to show their snobbish fastidiousness. But when Mama went to the bathroom, where some more free clothing hung, Russians who had just shown their fastidiousness started to fight for that clothing. They screamed and cursed at each other. One screamed, "May you wear these clothes for the rest of your life." Another screamed, "Eat it, I won't take it for myself."

We got a letter from Grandma.

Raimonda

OCTOBER 17

Hi, dear Kitty!

I broke up with Lisa. I didn't know who she really was. I gave Mama my first present to her—$30. Mama wants to buy a skirt.

Simon is being kind, and can't get away from his music system. He loves it. Uncle Pavlik might bring over Charlik, his dog. I love dogs, but not Charlik. He bit me two times; he's angry too.

Papa has a friend who is always changing his voice to make it sound like another friend. His voice sounds just like the other friend's voice and you start talking to that other friend. Tonight it happened: At first he called and I thought that he was Ilona's Sasha. He even talked that way. Then he asked for Papa and started to talk to him, not joking anymore. On the other hand, his name is also Sasha. Maybe I just misunderstood.

Then Papa called him because an old friend named Tanya arrived in America for a visit and was staying with Sasha. She's also from Chernovtsy. So Dad thought that he was talking to her, but it wasn't her, it was Sasha again.

Raimonda

OCTOBER 18

Hi, dear Kitty!

Today is Saturday. Yesterday I cleaned everything and did my homework. Today is a free day. Mom is going to go to Brighton Beach to buy food. Papa is still asleep. Charlik is living with us. It's the second day already. Yesterday my girlfriend, Natasha, came. She kissed and hugged him. He was happy, but then he almost bit her. Then we stayed on the bed. We thought that he wanted to eat us. I came to the kitchen by walking on the beds, but Natasha was too late. Charlik struck. But later she made it too. We wanted to open a can for him. I was holding a can and Natasha was trying to open it with a knife. Suddenly by mistake she didn't cut into the can but into my finger, with all her power. I thought that I had lost half of my finger. Natasha said that I got pale. She started to scream, "Please Raimondoshka, forgive me!" On my finger I had just a scratch and a little blood. I started to laugh, and she did too. Even our stomachs began to hurt, and my tears were running so quick. I didn't understand why since I didn't need to cry. It could be out of fear. I don't know. Then Mama and Papa came. Natasha, Charlik, and I went out for a walk. So passed yesterday. In my entire life I never laughed so much or cried either.

Raimonda

OCTOBER 20

Hi, dear Kitty!

I just watched a movie, *The Diary of Anne Frank*. How I cried. It's the best film I've ever seen. No, I will never forgive those Fascists. Never, never. So many people died. Why? Why did the Nazis burn my great-grandmother in fire? Why have I seen the black tree that still stands at the killing scene of Babi-Yar? The Nazis weren't people, they were beasts. And let anyone try to tell me that everything is over but I will still hate what they did. My mama never saw her grandma, and my grandpa left for the front and never saw his mama again.

Kitty, you do so much for me. When I'm angry, I start screaming. So everyone thinks that I'm an angry person, but I'm not. I'm trying to fight this anger, but I can't. But everything is okay now, and we are in peace. We didn't fight, nor make up.

It's hard for most people, but when you know how it is in Russia, it gets easier. Because Russia doesn't need war, or peace. Everything has ended forever. How scary it is that people are hungry. There are no more sellers and the store shelves are drying, having been washed after being empty for so long.

Everyone knows that it is an end and that there will be no beginning anymore. I pity those people, but not all of them. Many *are* the end; some are running from it.

It gets easier for us, easier because we live.

Kitty, if I hadn't started to write to you, I don't know how I would be. Empty and closed. But I'm with you.

> Yours,
> Raimonda

OCTOBER 22

Hi, dear Kitty!

I'm very tired. I left school at one o'clock today after lunch. I asked for permission to go home. They said that Papa has to come for me. It's a rule. However, they were just lazy and kept repeating to me, "It's a rule." I just sneaked away from school. The school yard was empty, and I even got frightened. I knew that the door— once it closed behind me—wouldn't open again. I was walking through the yard and got out through open gates. All the people seemed different; the cars didn't want to stop; the children were all at school.

We met Kelli, our friend from *The Village Voice,* in Manhattan, and together we went to an agent who is interested in getting the diary published. First we must translate thirty pages. Then we met Pavlik, who took us to some lawyers in a building made from glass with thirty-one floors. We got up on the elevator. The lawyers were nice, clean and clever. Papa said they are angels. They will "rule the business" with the diary.

Later, Pavlik showed me an open skating rink right next to a golden fountain. I wanted to cry. I wanted to go there so much. Pavlik promised that Ilona will take me when she goes.

Tomorrow I'm gonna get a zero in math because I couldn't open my locker where I left my math book. Well, it's okay—for the first time. In the evening Simon and I were listening to what we recorded in Italy. Simon and Oleg recorded songs when Oleg was leaving. It's too late now. I'm tired and I'm going to sleep. The end of this happy day. Oh yes, I made up with Lisa a long time ago.

Raimonda

OCTOBER 26

Hi, dear Kitty!

On Monday I'm going to a new class. I was in a mixed class with seventh and eighth grades together, but I will go to the eighth now. That means Lisa won't be in my class because she's in the seventh.

Mama has begun to speak English very fast. I cleaned everything and invented a new plan—25 cents from everyone who messes up the apartment. I got 50 cents from Mama already. This way I will get a lot of money and everything will be clean.

It is Pavlik and Tanya's birthdays tomorrow. They'll call us. I wrote a letter to my grandparents. I will rest now because it's Friday. We got letters from Grandmother and Grandfather.

We don't fight too bad because for each rude word and scream I get 25 cents too. Why didn't I think of that in Vienna? I would have a million dollars now. Simon is writing letters to Grandpa. I will watch a movie or read.

Love,
Raimonda

OCTOBER 28

Hi, dear Kitty!

It's so hot in our apartment. It gets you to sleep. But it's like winter outside. Pavlik went to some other place to celebrate his birthday, and he didn't call us. Papa was waiting for his call. Papa prepared a present for Pavlik—one of Papa's drawings. He bought a frame and made a funny birthday card. I wrote a poem. Mama and I were cooking the whole day, then went to the store for ice cream and foods. But they never came. It's only seven-thirty, but I'm going to sleep.

Raimonda

OCTOBER 29

Hi, dear Kitty!

Tomorrow comes a day I've long desired. Our luggage will arrive. Papa paid for it already. I did my homework fast today. The apartment is clear. Papa came. He was with his friends from Russia and their son in Manhattan. Papa said that they were arguing all the time. There was a fire where they walked, and the fire trucks were driving along so they couldn't hear themselves arguing.

It's not the first time that I was surprised by seeing how weak people are, how fast their masks fall off, and everyone becomes someone else because the harshness comes, the harshness which we aren't used to. One of my friends told me that her father almost strangled her mother while they were fighting over nothing.

I want to go to Manhattan a lot. We might go on Saturday.

Raimonda

OCTOBER 30

Hi, dear Kitty!

It is a happy day. There are things everywhere: our luggage came. I did my homework and we started to gather up all our stuff. There's a carpet in our room now. We have a new blanket and pillow. Finally, I met my favorite toys, my favorite books, and poems of Aleksandr Pushkin. We had time to clean up just our room. Tomorrow we'll clean the other room, kitchen and bathroom. Our luggage is intact. All our things are safe. It's like I put them in the box just now. I am in a high mood. Simon turned the music on. Tomorrow is Halloween and I still need to go to school, even though it's not safe. Only tomorrow I go to my new class.

Goodnight.

Raimonda

NOVEMBER 1, 1990

Hi, dear Kitty!

It's Friday. I cleaned everything after school and Uncle Pavlik and Aunt Tanya came. We were eating, and Aunt Tanya was telling an interesting story.

I got a letter from Ann today in Chernovtsy. She's my best girl-friend. She's going to Israel on December 31. They are very glad to leave. It's almost a war in Russia; on the other hand, it's even worse than a war. In Moldavia, six Russians were killed.

Grandma Galya called today. She thinks that Mama doesn't want her to come. She wanted to talk only with Papa. When I took the phone, I said that it's me. Grandma said, "I know." Then I asked her how she is. She said, "Okay," and didn't want to speak to me any-more. I gave the phone to Papa. At that moment I remembered that there's something I don't like in my grandparents, but I have forgot-ten all that. It's hard for me to remember because it's been a year and I've changed. I have different thoughts, different friends. Everything has changed in one year. And now I like only this country for every-thing, I love it. I don't remember my country, I forgot my home-town, but I don't pity myself. Everything is changing. Hometown, country, time . . .

Simon is playing the guitar and singing a sad song. That's prob-ably why I'm writing this way.

Yesterday I played chess with Papa. Even though I don't know all the secrets of the game, Papa said that I'm playing very well. He was even surprised we didn't finish the game, but I knew I was losing anyway. However, it's nice to hear him say it.

Sometimes I want to write stories—become a writer with a seat next to a table—but then I see myself as a doctor. It's hard to be a writer in life because there are so many geniuses in this country and many of them are writing. Being a doctor, I have to study and then I'll have a normal but interesting life. I'm just thirteen, so I don't have to think about it now.

Simon is playing, and I still want to write to you. It's so empty to finish when you are writing about life. Maybe I am the only one who needs it. When I'm at school, I see crazy students, and tired teachers. It seems to me that I'm tired, and I look at them from an-other side. But then it seems that I'm also getting crazy. I wrote a strange letter today, but it's "private," as Americans say.

Raimonda

NOVEMBER 5

Hi, dear Kitty!

Today is a bad and crazy day. After school, I swung on the swings with the girls as always. Then I did my homework and cleaned. Tomorrow is a holiday and I don't go to school. We got food stamps.

Papa fought with Mama because Mama just felt like fighting. Anger is feeding itself with anger, that's for sure. After all this, Papa's heart hurt, and Mama started to pretend that her heart hurt too. Papa said, "Forgive me because I can die." Mama said, "I forgive you."

Second part of the bad day.

The black part of my body woke up. That's what I call it. When I am writing poems or in my diary, I'm in a good, thoughtful mood, and I am always fine. But sometimes my nerves start shaking and I can't stop them anymore—because it's not me.

And now it's not even daylight.

I'm laughing with Simon. Now I am going to read *Alice in Wonderland*. I don't know why, but this book seemed to pull me to read it.

The end of a good, bad, and crazy day.

Raimonda

NOVEMBER 6

Hi, dear Kitty!

It's a marvelous day. We got furniture from a Jewish organization. Bookshelves up to the ceiling where we can put our books; two night tables, where we can put our clothing; an iron bookcase for papers and notes; and a writing table.

Papa wasn't at home. Simon brought everything in by himself.

Papa came home from the dentist. His tooth got pulled out because it was rotten and hurt; he didn't get his teeth filled in the Soviet Union. He came home, and his lips and face became lazy and curled because of the anesthesia. We laughed so much. Then we thought for three hours where to put all this furniture, but we could think of nothing. While Papa was thinking, he fell asleep.

Mama came in the evening, and only then without agreement we started to do everything. Everyone got tired. After we were finished, I cleaned the room and Papa cleaned his. Our room has become easy and nice. Papa's room has become "capitalistic." That's what I called it because he used to have only boards for shelves; now he has bookshelves, a bookcase, and a writing table. But Papa has much more to clean, still. Mama is asleep. Simon is lying on the bed, he's very tired. It's his day off today; however, he didn't rest. But still I'm very happy. I'm going to listen to the music now and go to sleep. Tomorrow is school.

Raimonda

NOVEMBER 7

Hi, dear Kitty!

I don't even know what kind of mood I'm in. At school everything is as usual. Until eight o'clock tonight, I was home alone. At first I watched cartoons, did my homework, and cleaned the kitchen. Sima came. Then at nine, my parents came and we had a scene again. We fought because someone wants to make a non-fiction movie where I am going to play myself for $5,000. Papa wanted to do it, but Simon and Mama started to scream and argue, saying that $5,000 is very little money, that they just want to buy us. I kept silent, but Papa screamed at me and I was hysterical. Even Sima stayed on my side to defend me.

Papa said that I have to keep silent, that I am an angel, but it's a sin to talk, and I have to keep silent otherwise I am going to have an unhappy life.

It is they who are unhappy! Unhappy and weak! That's what. As soon as there is an obstacle, some kind of difficulty, Papa starts looking for something easy, and Mama looks for something difficult but worth fighting for. The scandal starts, and I am as always a fly on which they can show their nerves and scream, driving me to tears and craziness. What am I doing? I clean everything, and where is their thanks? Oh yes, I forgot that I talk. I won't see them for the whole day! That's what.

It's they who are unhappy! And I asked them to buy me a Nestlé's Crunch bar—that's my favorite candy bar—but they forgot for the second time, and I didn't forget to clean the house. I won't clean anymore, I won't do anything at all. It's close to midnight and I'm going to sleep late again. Papa kissed my hand, he understands that he is wrong. But it's too late, everything is annoying. Everything!

Raimonda

NOVEMBER 8

Hi, dear Kitty,

Today I cleaned everything, even though nobody asked me. But it's my character. I can't stand to see dirt. At eight, my parents came. My parents brought me a Crunch bar and we made up. Mama said that I'm an angel.

                              Raimonda

NOVEMBER 9

Hi, dear Kitty!

Today we had an amusing evening. Uncle Pavlik and Aunt Tanya came. We ate, drank, and joked. After they left, I called Grandma Sofa and Grandpa. Grandpa had a heartache and he was taken to the hospital. They suspected an infarction (heart attack). Everyone cried. Mama cried. My grandma, my own grandpa. Why do I remember only the moments when I said goodbye to you? When I went outside your well-known door, you hugged me and cried, and I was so little. I couldn't describe it, I didn't understand.

I remember that rain, when you stayed under the streetlamp, hugging each other and crying. No one felt that rain. And your song, Grandpa, about Dunya. How I love it. You hugged me and I fell asleep and you sang. This song is from the war. I don't know why I love it, maybe because it's Grandpa's.

                              Raimonda

NOVEMBER 16

Hi, dear Kitty,

At first the whole day was really boring, but at 8:00 P.M. Papa came home with his friend from the university, from twenty years ago. Uncle Borya arrived for three days. At first I didn't like him. I thought he was too critical, but he was only joking.

He's telling us about emigration, about his life in San Francisco and his job there. All of it is sad, but he tells it and jokes so we laugh and there is no seriousness or sadness. He tells about emigration in Italy; we had the same experiences. He tells about his job as a computer engineer, how hard he worked without even knowing the language, and then how he lost his job because the company didn't have enough orders from other companies. Hearing those stories you should cry, but we laugh because he tells them as jokes.

All Papa's friends call Papa by a nickname, Michael, because when Papa was young he called himself that after a Jack London story. My father was Michael and his friend was named after another character, Jerry. Most don't even know Papa's real name now.

Tomorrow we are going to Manhattan to walk around till the evening.

Everyone is going to sleep. I am in a good mood. Goodnight.

Yours,
Raimonda

NOVEMBER 18

Hi, dear Kitty,

Today Uncle Borya, Papa, and I were in Manhattan. How I love Manhattan! We went there at ten o'clock in the morning and came home at 8:00 P.M.—we spent the whole day showing the city to Uncle Borya. It was cold. We ate at McDonald's. I don't like it as much as I used to. At first, I was eating McDonald's because in Russia it represented America. I had never eaten it, so I wanted it all the time. Now I realize there is nothing special about it. In the evening we drank coffee and hot cocoa and ate pastries. Then Papa went to the bathroom because his stomach ached. When we got to the subway, I had a stomachache, too. I was dying from pain, and after several stations, I was running to the toilet.

We came home tired and happy. Mama cooked us a supper. Simon is playing his guitar.

On Thursday and Friday, I don't go to school. It's Thanksgiving Day. Kelli invited us on Thursday at two o'clock.

Now I am going to read. My Sunday ended, a wonderful Sunday.

Yours,
Raimonda

NOVEMBER 22

Hi, dear Kitty,

I wasn't writing to you for several days. I didn't have time even to read. I did my homework, cleaned, took a shower, and went to sleep.

Uncle Borya left three days ago, and that day my parents were on the boat to Ellis Island. NYANA arranged it. The island was where immigrants were coming when they first arrived years ago. They were checked. Mama told me about it, about how rich people could buy a ticket on a ship, the best class, and just go through without checking into America. But the poor people had to go through immigration. And if they were asked, "Are you a Communist?" (just like now), and if they didn't even know what it was and answered, "Yes," they were sent back. Sick people were also sent back. They even separated children from parents. Now it's a museum. Papa said that they showed a movie about it, and the whole room was crying. "It was a moment when I felt that I really came here," Papa said. Their pictures were taken, and the next day I saw the picture in the *Daily News,* a newspaper. It was Mama and Papa.

Today is a great holiday in America, Thanksgiving Day. Some organizations give food to the homeless and the people sick with AIDS. It is a happy day even for them.

Kelli and Andrew invited us to celebrate Thanksgiving at their house. Before, it used to be a one-family house, and the people who lived there ate on the first floor, studied on the second, slept on the third. It was before the Revolution (just a joke). Now, four families live there.

Andrew's parents and sister came. His sister is twenty-three years old, and she studies Spanish. We ate special foods for Thanksgiving: turkey, parsnips, sweet potato soup. It's really different from Russian food. We didn't like it and swore to cook only Russian food from now on.

Kelli gave me a newspaper from San Francisco. I opened it up and there I saw an entire page with my picture on it. There I was with the open diary. It is the same story from *The Village Voice,* a reprint. I still don't understand that it's my picture, that it is me.

I cleaned everything, and Papa is watching the news. Uncle Pavlik and Tanya came yesterday. We spent a nice evening. We got two days off from school. Our teacher said, Thanks to Thanksgiving.

I have three days to rest at home.

Yours,
Raimonda

NOVEMBER 24

I was reading a sad book by Mark Twain, *The Prince and the Pauper,* and crying from it. I wanted to calm down and went to take something to eat. The refrigerator was empty, except for Simon's shelf. I asked him to give me something to eat. He got mad and hit me on the hand. It never hurts and it didn't hurt this time either, but after the sadness of the book, I started to howl. He thought my hand hurt and gave me ice cream. I didn't explain to him that it didn't hurt. I just fell asleep.

NOVEMBER 26

Hi, dear Kitty,

It was a usual day at school. After lunch, the boys were running after us outside. Then we got a lot of homework, and I walked home with the girls. I did my homework and at 5:00 P.M. Mama's English teacher came with her boyfriend, Greg. He's a poet and a very smart man. We ate, they talked, and I watched a movie.

Now, Mama is thinking about Grandpa and Grandma. Simon is listening to music. Papa is drawing. I am waiting for Wednesday. This way there'll be only four days left to wait until Kelli, Andrew, and I are going to the skating rink. I never think ahead about something good because it might not happen, but I can't help thinking about skating rinks all my life.

Yours,
Raimonda

NOVEMBER 27

Hi, dear Kitty,

Mama came to sleep in our room because Papa had to draw for The New York Times. I went to the kitchen and suddenly heard, "Pig!" Mama screamed it at me because the light was on in the kitchen— even though she was covered by blankets and couldn't see it. Then I went back to my room and listened to Michael Jackson on the Walkman. And again, Mama screamed at me for sleeping with the Walkman. I kept silent and couldn't even answer from offense and surprise. I came to Papa, but he didn't want to listen and screamed out, "Go to sleep!"

I went back to sleep. Mama was still calling me names, probably because Papa was on her side. The hard night passed.

Yours,
Raimonda

NOVEMBER 28

Hi, dear Kitty,

I didn't talk to Mama, but made up with Papa because it wasn't his fault. Mama said that she won't make up because I was the one who called her names. I was in shock. I was laughing for a second. Then I cried. Then I howled from offense and ran away to school.

Afterward, I didn't clean. I did my homework, and then I listened to the Walkman with pride. Mama came home and said, "I expected everything to be clean." I said that I will never clean again.

Two hours passed. I was walking next to the couch where Mama sat. She started to cry and asked me to kiss her. She said she was sorry. We made up.

I cleaned the kitchen, even though it was late. Then I listened to music and went to sleep.

Yours,
Raimonda

NOVEMBER 29

Hi, dear Kitty,

After school, I walked home with the girls as usual. I opened the top lock, but then I realized I had forgotten the key for the bottom lock. I was afraid that my parents didn't have keys either, so I stayed and waited for them from four o'clock till eight. This is when I finally saw them coming in. My parents were worried because I looked very pale. My side hurt, too.

I went to sleep and everyone went to kiss me. I probably looked like a corpse.

I always like these moments. Everyone is worrying and caring for you. I felt like a queen.

Yours,
Raimonda

DECEMBER I, 1990

Hi, dear Kitty,

Today is the happiest day in my life, and I waited for it for two years. At twelve-thirty, Kelli, Andrew, and I drove in Brooklyn to a big skating rink. Music was playing and green trees surrounded us.

Kelli took pictures of us while Andrew and I skated. At first I was scared that I had forgotten how to skate, so I held on to Andrew. But then I could skate quickly as I used to in Russia. I didn't forget.

We fell several times. Then they cleaned the skating rink. It was icy and you could see through it. We were skating for three hours.

My dream came true. I love America because the dreams can come true here. It takes so little to cheer me up.

Yours,
Raimonda

DECEMBER 3

Hi, dear Kitty,

Everything is as usual. We watched a cartoon called *An American Tail*. It's about us. The cartoons are immigrants who come here full of dreams and fantasies. But when they finally come, they don't find their dreams come true—until later, and only if they fight for it. We are just like the mice who thought that there were not any cats in America. I thought that America was a crystal kingdom and found a real world.

You always wait in America.

Yours,
Raimonda

DECEMBER 7

Hi, dear Kitty,

Friday passed. I waited for it and don't even know why. I like this school better and better. I am getting used to the people and the atmosphere. You joke, you laugh, you feel free.

I cleaned everything. Mama meant to give me five food stamps for it, but she didn't see that she really gave me ten. I was happy and so was Papa, but I did feel guilty for not telling her about the extra money.

Well, I am still in a good mood anyway. I am almost asleep, just waiting for someone to say in my dream, "Ask for a thousand wishes and all of them will come true."

Happy dreams.

Raimonda

DECEMBER 8

Hi, dear Kitty,

After all, Mama found out that five food stamps were missing. She was about to cry. So we told her the truth. She left them to us, but we had to buy food with it in any case.

Raimonda

DECEMBER 9

On Sunday morning, we woke up early and went to Manhattan to meet my mother's English teacher and her boyfriend. They invited us.

For the first time in my life, I cooked and ate Mexican food. It's a thin pancake—Papa thought it was a piece of paper. On top of that pancake were haricot beans, cooked rice, and eggs that were fried in water. Some grass (vegetables) went on top of that. After all that, I can say this: "I am never eating Mexican food again."

Then we climbed on the roof. This house and its view from the roof and the balcony reminded us of Chernovtsy. It even smelled that way, and if it weren't for hearing English, which brought me back to reality, I would have seen myself in the yard, playing with my friends and stealing apples from the garden.

We walked around Chinatown on Canal Street. It was very cold and we went back home.

Raimonda

DECEMBER 12

Hi, dear Kitty,
Happy Hanukkah!

Yesterday my parents were at a concert with Uncle Pavlik and Tanya, but they didn't tell us anything about it.

I read a book called *Foreigner* by [Sergei] Dovlatov. I liked it a lot.

After school, I did my homework and we went to Manhattan to celebrate Hanukkah. NYANA invited all Russian immigrants. It was on the third floor. Some food, like doughnuts and potato chips, was there. Then the rabbi was telling about Hanukkah—why it is that we are celebrating this holiday and what wonder happened on this day.

Then we lighted the candles and sang the prayers. We were listening to the concert of Soviet-Jewish emigrants. We were at another of their concerts in Chernovtsy—after *glasnost*. We had a nice time.

Raimonda

DECEMBER 14

It's Friday. I usually love to call it a happy day. But this time it was unhappy. I fainted today.

At lunch, I was waiting in line as always. Suddenly I saw something falling. Then I heard laughter and a question, "Are you all right?" My head hurt and I understood that a five-meter stick, which is used to open and close the school windows, had fallen and hit me on the head.

I didn't understand how it had happened. Everyone started to tell me that some boys wanted a laugh so they dropped the stick on my head. But I fainted and that's why I didn't even see their faces.

At that moment, I just wanted to cry. But I held myself. But when I finally sat on the table, I started to cry. My head hurt, and everything was moving around in front of my eyes.

Someone just needed a laugh. I didn't go to the Din office. I didn't go anywhere. I didn't know who did it anyway. Someone saw the boys who did it, but wouldn't tell me their names. I asked him to tell them that I'll kill them. That's all I could say. And he was laughing too, telling how I staggered.

I came home and only in the evening told my parents what had happened. Simon came later, and I told him too. He gave me a Walkman and said that he's going to kill the guys who did it.

I was watching a movie, *The Kid Who Loves Christmas,* and crying. Today I was crying the whole day and now too. That's how my Friday went. At least now I know what it means to faint.

Raimonda

P.S. I wanted to write to you about school. When I first came I probably hated school, but now I've gotten used to it. I understand the freedom which is given in school, too. I have friends—Russians, Chinese, Korean, Hispanics. Most Americans are too far away and too alien for me, still.

This freedom prepares you for the future, but for some it's too hard to take or too easy. Using this freedom makes it easier to go down, to drop out rather than to keep up.

Teachers teach you. If you want, you can learn. You don't have to if you don't want to. No one stops you. You are free.

In Russia, you are just like everybody else. You go in the same line. You have to learn to be an actor if you are in society. You usually get there by acting, by being the same.

I remember watching a movie in Russia about Soviet emigrants living in America. I didn't understand their lives or what they said. A man in the movie said: "Freedom everywhere, all around you, and maybe it's too much." I think I understand him now.

Raimonda

DECEMBER 16

Hi, dear Kitty,

Today Mama and I went to Manhattan. We met Rose, the woman who first took us to the synagogue when we were still living in the hotel. We hadn't heard from her in a while. We walked in the city and saw the windows of stores where dolls move. Then we went to Rockefeller Center. There was a big green tree and it was beautiful. There was also an orchestra of five hundred people that was playing American Christmas songs.

In that moment, I was trying to remember the Soviet New Year. All the members of our family and our closest friends gathered together. We made a big table of food. We ate from ten till six in the morning. We had a green tree that would stick its top to the ceiling. Then at midnight our president would show up on TV and tell about the year, its problems and his wishes for the next year. Then the Soviet hymn would play and everyone would stand up to meet the New Year. After that, the TV was on the whole night with New Year's jokes, concerts, and music. I knew all those songs, the music, the people. I stopped remembering.

Now, I don't know these American Christmas songs that sound so beautiful, nor these people. It's a pity, or maybe not. There'll be a day when I forget my past, and music from the past, and people. There'll be a day when I know these American songs and these people. At least both of these cultures will always celebrate New Year's with me. There will always be a new year, and it will always be celebrated. So even if I don't know American songs or will someday forget Russian songs, the sentiments will still mean the same thing.

Raimonda

DECEMBER 17

Hi, dear Kitty,

It could have been a happy day, but we listened to the news. A Jewish girl who was thirteen years old was thrown off a bridge in Williamsburg and burned in fire. Her body was found under the bridge. It's terrible.

Raimonda

P.S. Kelli and Andrew came. They bought us a green tree. It's big and beautiful. I wanted to have one so much, and we do have one this year too, in America. We decorated it with some toys that we brought from Russia. There aren't many, but we love them. They are our favorite toys that were given to us by our great-grandmother.

Andrew made a cake. It is made of cookies and cream. It's a house with people and snow. We drank tea and ate it.

Then we moved the table to the other side so the green tree would stay there. It looks very nice there. Simon got a present. It's a book and a tape.

We put our toys and the toys that Kelli and Andrew gave us on the tree. I can't stop looking at it.

Raimonda

DECEMBER 20

Hi, dear Kitty,

I didn't write for two days. But there is nothing to write. Life is boring. I mean, it's even more fun at school than home. In school you talk to friends, study, and time goes fast. At home you don't talk, you study, clean, read books, watch TV, sleep, etc. Time passes slowly. Today it was impossible to study at school. Everyone gets crazy before holidays. We are happy and congratulate each other with Happy Christmas, like it's coming this second and not five days later.

Today one angry Korean guy writes to me: "Happy Holidays. I hope your wish can be accomplished and don't be stupid."

I answered: "Happy Christmas and New Year. I wish you happiness and don't be stupid either."

However, he didn't get my joke and still thinks that I'm stupid. But that's what I think he is.

I prepared cards for the other kids. Tomorrow at school we are just going to play games and fool around. Even our teacher says that it's impossible to study.

My mood is perfect, mostly because there was no homework and tomorrow is the last day.

Raimonda

DECEMBER 22

Hi, dear Kitty,

It was fun in school. We didn't study, but fooled around. When I came home, my friend Luba, who is eleven and came here from Vilna, was waiting for me, and then my best friend, Natasha, came crying. Someone stole her $50 jacket in school and it was raining outside, so she was all wet. But we calmed her down, and she changed her clothes and drank tea. Her father came to pick her up.

There was a concert in school for eighth graders. They played rock and roll and a teacher asked another teacher to dance. They were beautiful. Then he kissed her and everyone applauded. They are different from my old teachers. They are free and they enjoy this freedom, which can be so warm and beautiful. On the other hand, my ex-teachers would never dance like that and will never enjoy those moments, not only physically but in their minds too. They'd stay there straight and cruel or—wait! I forgot. There would *never* be rock and roll playing!

Raimonda

DECEMBER 23

Hi, dear Kitty,

It's night outside, keeping its last moments of day. I did nothing today but laugh. I went to the movies with some kids of my mother's friend. We watched *Home Alone*. It was very funny. Then we watched another comedy with Mama and Papa at our house, *Fat and Thin*. Papa was dying from laughter, and Mama screams loudly at first and only then does she laugh.

Grandma Sofa called us. She asked: "On whose money am I going to live?"

To tell you the truth, I don't know myself.

NYANA?

Raimonda

DECEMBER 25

Hi, dear Kitty!

I got tired today.

First, in the morning, we watched a movie, *The Road*. We cried. After that the whole day was sad and harsh. I got bored so I called my girlfriends. They said, "Let's walk." But where to? On the street back and forth, and talk about something empty or keep silent. It was cold. I wanted to play, to fool around like I used to, but they just laughed. So we talked. One of the girls said that in Russia her parents used to give her 10 rubles a day, and she didn't even know what to spend it on or what to do with it. Here they don't give her the same because it would be $10 now! We all left to go home.

Then Simon called. Oleg, whom we have not seen since Italy, came from Canada to visit New York with his girlfriend and with Liana. She used to be Simon's girlfriend, but they broke up. They wanted to look like grown-ups, but they were just acting. They looked boring to me, and they couldn't even talk. I could see through them. They played the guitar and then I asked them to play my favorite song, but no! They started to play others and mix it with mine. What did they want me to do? Scream, beg, cry? Big deal!

I feel like going to school now. Time goes fast there. I don't have real friends yet. I mean I have friends, but not the kind I want to. One of them is smart but too cunning. Another one is very kind but not smart. The third one is closed. I think she's smart and everything, but is afraid to open up. That's why we never talk about money, our parents, work or business. I don't care, but if you ask, they'll lie and won't talk the whole way. Why is that so secret? I don't know, maybe they are just scared of something.

I remember when we came to Vienna and many emigrant families waited to fill in the most important document—the one to write where they wanted to go, Israel or America. We all were there and I stayed next to Papa. There were little kids about four or five years old playing around. Of course, they were from Russia going to

America, but Papa and I just wanted to talk to them. So Papa asked, Where are you from and where are you going? And then it started! Some kids said they were from Israel going to Russia or from America going to Israel! We laughed. Poor kids, they heard so many things from their parents and tried to memorize it, but mixed it up! Or maybe their parents wanted them to mix up everything?

Our grandma's and grandpa's birthdays are today, and we aren't with them. That's why it's a sad day. I remember how Grandma used to cook my favorite meals. And then she would invite us and some of her neighbors or friends. The table would almost be crushed from all these beautiful dishes. And my grandma and grandpa would grow older one year right before my eyes. But the only thing I would think about is how two people, a husband and wife, can have a birthday on the same day. I would walk after Grandma back and forth, getting in her way and asking her to show me her documents and Grandpa's too. However, she would laugh and walk ahead, never showing me any proof of their birthdays.

Grandma, we called you and you cried. Grandpa didn't, but he said, "Thank you that you don't forget us."

Where are you now? I am sure that you didn't make that dinner this year and you never wanted to, except for us. I don't care if you were born at the same date, but to see you again!

I am in Papa's room now. I love it. It's so mysterious and magic. Papa is as always working with his pencils and pens. The music is quiet and fast. I see a man looking at me from the picture. I have a pillow under my head and I look outside the window. I see a street-lamp, but there are no stars tonight. I dream again. Grandma, Grandpa, I still don't believe you that two people, a husband and wife, could be born on the same day. Come! Come to prove, to make me believe! Come!

I am reading a book. It is full of adventures and happiness, but the author needed to finish this book, so the hero died. I cried again. Then I read another story, by the same author. It's about a grown man who was a teacher and whose parents died. He had just one dream, to become little again. Suddenly a dwarf comes and makes him little again, so he became just a student and his parents were alive and young again.

Goodnight for now!

Maybe a dwarf will come to me too. I have a lot of dreams.

Raimonda

DECEMBER 27

Hi, dear Kitty,

Today was the happiest day! The first snow!

Yesterday, Simon gave me $20 for New Year's, and I bought him cigarettes, the ones he wanted, for $15, and gave them to him today. I gave Simon $70 and he bought a tape recorder in his store, which really cost $90, but he got a discount price. Almost everyone has this recorder here. But in Russia it cost 2,000 rubles and Papa was able to buy it only when he was forty. I'm only thirteen.

But the most important thing is the snow. I love it. I waited for it and we played snowballs today. It's night already, but I'm still looking out the window, gazing at the first snow.

Raimonda

DECEMBER 30

Hi, dear Kitty,

All this time we've spent watching movies because Uncle Slavik from Russia came and he knows good movies. I don't have time to go for a walk because of this. However, yesterday, Lisa and I played snowballs and built a snowman. Lisa is my girlfriend who emigrated from Leningrad. I met her when I first got to school because we are together in a special class for immigrants who don't yet know English well.

Tomorrow is New Year's. We are already nine months in America. We left Russia in 1989. Tomorrow is 1991. How fast time goes! There'll be a day when I'm old and have grandchildren, and every New Year I will gather them and tell them: "In 1990, I came to America. It was a beautiful day!"

Raimonda

DECEMBER 31

Hi, dear Kitty,

Mama fought with Papa. She just needed a reason to run away from cooking, cleaning, and so she did. She was at her friend's house and came back only in the evening when everything was ready for the celebration, which means I cleaned, and then Papa and I cooked.

We turned on the radio at about 5:00 P.M. Papa can catch Soviet

Radio, Moscow. It was almost twelve there and as always I heard: "Speaks Moscow." Then the president congratulates the New Year, and the Soviet hymn is on and Moscow's clock loudly beats twelve.

Maybe there was nothing special in it, but I used to hear it every year somewhere in my childhood, somewhere I lived.

Suddenly I feel tears on my face.

Raimonda

JANUARY 1, 1991

Hi, dear Kitty,

Papa and I went to ice skate in Manhattan. The rink is in Central Park. Poor Papa had to stay there for the whole day, while I had so much fun skating. The time flew so fast. It was almost dark when we left. Those huge skyscrapers were shining with different colors and people seemed so tiny compared to them. But the view was beautiful.

Raimonda

JANUARY 7

Hi, dear Kitty,

Today is Monday. I did my homework already. I cleaned and read. We got a package from Grandmother Galya with our pictures and the cards I used to collect. It was my hobby to collect cards, especially with actors on them. I was surprised to see that I had already forgotten their names and faces. Just a few seemed familiar. Most just escaped from my memory. I put them away. Maybe she shouldn't have sent them?

Raimonda

JANUARY 10

Hi, dear Kitty,

It's already nine months and ten days we have been here. I've never been so happy in my life. Happy because I live here and not because I watch terrible movies of Russia where nothing is made for life. But I've never wanted to go to school like I do here. There, I didn't feel like going, and there was a feeling that time stopped. Now, I can get away from home, from those fights. Now my class is my friend. None of the students are my "real" friends, but friends. With them I joke and laugh. This way, time goes fast. I go outside and walk on the street. I enjoy every house. I enjoy even the air.

Most children wanted to go to America because of gum and candy. I wanted to go because I wanted to have my own skyscraper just like from the movies. I wanted a refrigerator with Coca-Cola and a red Rolls-Royce with glass that wouldn't break. I was sure that America is crystal, that even the earth is crystal.

I came here. I understood that I can have much gum and candy, but not a skyscraper. At least I can walk in every one of them. But I will never have enough money to buy one. God, what childish dreams I had. America is no crystal, but I love it. It's for people, for life, for happiness. You just don't get it all the time.

Raimonda

JANUARY 14

Hi, dear Kitty,

On Friday, Uncle Pavlik came to pick us up. I took my home-work and we went to Pavlik's house in Queens. On Friday we ate Russian food—salads, sausages, cheese, bread, vareniki—and watched TV. Also, I did my homework, walked Charlik the dog, and built a snowman. Today we came home. My parents are watching news again. Somehow they feel that the louder the TV is, the faster they will learn English. It's funny.

Raimonda

JANUARY 16

We got two letters from Grandma Galya. A seventy-year-old man asked to marry her so that they could come to America together. I don't believe him. He has no love for her. Come on. He's seventy years old! He just wants to use her to come to America. Grandma is scared of being alone. She asked us what she should do. We wrote to her. Poor Grandma, it's hard for her to move when she's alone—so she thinks that he will help her.

After all, this man is not the first admirer. She always asked for my advice. That's why whenever someone came to her house to court her, we agreed that I would find a reason to come and look at him. I usually came saying that I forgot a doll because Grandmother kept a lot of my old dolls. So I, as a respectful granddaughter, would come to greet him. Just by looking at him and listening to Grandmother talk about his life later in the evening, I would know all about him. None of them were good for her. I never said no, but I advised her in that direction. I knew that one of them was afraid to be old and wanted someone to take care of him. Another one wanted to give his apartment to his children and this way he could live with Grandmother. Poor people, they all had to leave. They all got a kind but negative answer. But they didn't go with crushed hearts because the real love—or love of any kind—had died in them long, long before.

The end comes to Russia. Food is burned. Milk is poured away. People are angry. There's nothing to eat. They don't know who is guilty. They've got freedom to speak, but they don't know how to use it. They think freedom is calling a Jew a Yid, looking for a guilty one.

Yesterday our teacher was teaching a history lesson. A Russian man came in. He was in a rush and talked rudely. Then he apologized and said that his country taught him that. What should I say? I don't believe him.

Raimonda

JANUARY 17

Yesterday war started between Iraq and the Americans. Saddam Hussein is using chemical weapons. Today he sent a rocket to Tel Aviv. Houses are destroyed. In Israel, people wear gasmasks.

War, this scary word. How many people might die? Who will win? Arabs don't surrender. They believe in Allah and say that they will fight in bloody war. The whole day we listened. It gets worse and worse.

Raimonda

JANUARY 18

War is still on. Saddam Hussein is throwing bombs on Israel. The Israeli houses are destroyed. People are injured. No one knows when it is going to end.

Raimonda

P.S. Life goes on. I got the best mark on English midterm. It's 96. Everyone else got less than that. Some applauded. The Koreans were jealous. It seems like Koreans and Russians have a silent war to be better or best. Others (the Spanish and Arabs) don't care.

I am really happy because of the test. So Dad and I went to the store and bought the folder I dreamed of having.

> 'Bye,
> Raimonda

JANUARY 24

Hi, dear Kitty,

One of Simon's friends was beaten up on the subway and robbed.

Sima came home from registering at college. They made Russian students come only on the last day to sign in. Sima couldn't choose the subjects he needed and wanted because everything was full already, even math. He doesn't work today. That's why he's kinder and happier today. He will go to college from ten to eleven, in English as a Second Language. And then, only at two o'clock, he will study radio and TV, which he doesn't need. I think that he's a great man. But his fate isn't easy enough.

Mama is becoming an unhappy girl sometimes, a girl who can't walk ahead because she sees no future and has no hope. And I want to help her. English is hard for her, but she tries so hard that words just jump out.

Papa doesn't pay much attention to his English. Sometimes he brags about his English, and sometimes he falls into a depression for a long time. He never had depression like this in the Soviet Union. First of all, it's because he wasn't thinking about tomorrow's future. Whereas here you have to think about it, because you aren't sure about it. It's kind of a hard life. You feel lonely and helpless. He knew in Russia that nothing was gonna happen. That's why you had no hopes. Whereas here you think every day of the future. When he first came, he had culture shock because people were different and he didn't understand the culture or the language. Now, he has a depression, like an economic depression because he doesn't get many jobs. His depression comes very unexpectedly. Sometimes it lasts for just a day or half a day, but sometimes even for three days. It might come because the weather is changing or because he doesn't get a job for a long period of time. When he is really depressed, he's kind of separated from the world and he sees no happiness or no luck and he's in a bad mood.

> Raimonda

JANUARY 25

Hi, dear Kitty,

Today is Friday. I passed all of my midterm tests. Many failed.

Papa got a job for *The New York Times*.

Sima is upset because of college.

Mama is learning English and tomorrow at five in the morning, the light will be on in the kitchen. That's how early she starts to learn.

Sima is going to work tomorrow. Papa will work all night. And tomorrow is Saturday.

                                        Raimonda

JANUARY 27

Hi, dear Kitty,

The war is still on. People are dying. Saddam H. continues to bomb Israel. Sometimes I feel that America shouldn't have gone to war because maybe all of this will end with an atomic bomb. And if Saddam Hussein built a city underground, he will live after the atomic bomb and have all the world for himself. But there will be no one else to kill. He will be unable to rule.

Here, it's unbelievable that war is on, that American soldiers are risking their lives—or maybe it's too late even to risk them.

Tanya's parents and relatives are in Israel. They wear masks to protect against the gas.

No one knows what will happen. People only want to live and they want peace.

                                        Raimonda

JANUARY 30

Hi, dear Kitty,

I want to go for a walk, jump and run just like in Russia. But where and with whom? And will I be able to do it now? Will I be the same?

Simon came back from college. He has to pay his own money for it, and he doesn't have a grant yet. That's why he's leaving again, to go to work. In September, he might go to another college.

Simon doesn't have much luck lately. I pity him.

                                        Raimonda

JANUARY 31

Hi, dear Kitty,

Today in school a teacher comes in and he has a magazine published for new immigrants called *US Express Journal*. Then I hear everyone calling my name, and saying that I was published there. And it's true. The article comes reprinted from *The Village Voice*, only a little shorter with some words written that I didn't write. But maybe they are from a tape.

Mama got sick, but it's not really a sickness. She just pretends. She stays in her bed and screams. But when everyone is busy, she's quiet.

With Simon, I fight all day, but only as a joke. However, we use fists. That's why it hurts.

I used to be sick every week in Russia. But not here. There I was afraid to drink cold water for fear of catching cold, and I barely ate ice cream, only in the summer. It's a pity that I'm not sick here because I like it sometimes. You feel like a queen and everyone cares for you. I didn't even have to play a trick with the thermometer like some kids did. I was sick anyway.

Raimonda

FEBRUARY 2, 1991

Hi, dear Kitty,

Tomorrow all Russians from our class will gather to play *"Kazasky Razboyniky,"* which is a game where you run after each other and hide too until you catch someone and put him in your prison, where you ask for their team's secret code. For instance, Black Cat. You also have to make up your team's own secret code (maybe Red Rose), write it down, and hide it someplace between Fourth and Fifth Avenues.

We just watched a scary movie and my mood went down. But a movie is only a set of pictures.

Raimonda

FEBRUARY 3

Hi, dear Kitty,

Today we gathered outside next to my building and waited for the guys to start playing.

I put on black sunglasses, but when Papa came outside, I took them off. But he smiled and loudly asked me, "Why did you put on glasses?" Then he laughed and passed by. There were five girls. I was the leader, then Lisa, Luba, Natasha, and Julia.

The boys came, and we started the game. We started to run after them, caught them, and didn't know how to torture them in order to find out their secret code. They wouldn't tell anyway. In Russia, we were little kids. That's why it was easy to make someone talk; you could tickle, or click on someone's head, or pinch someone to make him or her talk. But because now we are grown up, we couldn't use these tricks anymore. No one was afraid of it.

We stopped the game and bought ice cream. The game couldn't go on because everyone ran away and didn't listen. Luba ran away home and everyone wanted to do the same thing. Our mood had been spoiled again. Then we went to Luba to calm her down. The game didn't go as we planned, which means the way we used to play it in Russia. The boys changed; they aren't the same anymore. There's no big yard with trees and garages to climb on. Just the noisy street and cars.

After all, Lisa came home with me and we played cards. We were tired and I was surprised to see that both of us wanted to lose. When Lisa went home, I went to sleep. Then we ate. I read and later listened to the music. I couldn't sleep more so I only imagined that I was somewhere far, far away on the stars. Far, far away, where there's always happiness.

Raimonda

FEBRUARY 4

Hi, dear Kitty,

And again, Friday. I always think that in America, everyone is waiting for Friday. I am waiting for Friday because I won't have to clean on Saturday. I can sleep a lot, rest, and forget everything.

My parents are waiting for Friday because they won't have to go to Manhattan for English lessons. And then again it will be Monday.

It's summer outside in February. In Moscow, the snow is up to your knees.

I am about to sleep. My alarm clock won't work, but I can wake up without it. I got used to it.

Raimonda

FEBRUARY 6

Hi, dear Kitty,

It was a boring day, and I forgot all about it except for some funny moments.

Papa said, "I am thinking of eating something." Mama screams, "Are you stupid?" Then Simon screams, "Danger!" And I jumped away, just as a big flat board was falling on me. My parents caught it with a scared look on their faces, and Papa said, "Why do I keep it?" It is a door he found in the garbage and wanted to make a table from. He didn't, but he just couldn't throw it away, so he kept it in the hall, leaning against the wall.

The saddest thing is that Papa threw away a notebook with my short novel in it. It was a pity, and I started to scream that it was a genius work. Well, it's not true. Papa said that he's going to look for it, then continued, "In Manhattan's garbage."

That's all.

Raimonda

FEBRUARY 10

Hi, dear Kitty,

And again I am thinking of life. I don't have to go to school, and I could have slept late, but I was awakened a long time ago. I could have been joyful, but I cry now.

Why do they fight again?

They think I'm asleep, but I lie and cry.

Why did someone steal a car from Natasha's father? He just bought it seven days ago on borrowed money. And now he talks sadly, like he laughs at himself. He says: "A car is nothing, just metal. The most important thing in life is health." Then he smiles again.

At school, there is a boy. He seems to be happy. But at home, every day, his family fights so loudly that Natasha can hear it through the wall. Then the boy comes out the next morning with his sister's hand in his. He asks her, "Why do I need to wear a hat, when no one else wears one?"

Why? I ask myself. Why do I cry? Is it just because my parents fought and woke me? Or is it because someone's car was stolen? Or is it because of the hat?

Raimonda

FEBRUARY 13

Hi, dear Kitty,

There's a feeling of sadness all the time. No one wants to remember the past. We hide it deep inside because something is sad about it. It's not pity, but sadness. This is the way we all live in the present. I like to speak of the future with friends. It's a joy to imagine about happiness that doesn't become sadness.

Goodbye, past.

Raimonda

FEBRUARY 15

Friday
Hi, dear Kitty,

Today in school we got our report cards. My grades are 90, 90, 80, 90, 95, 95, and a yellow card, which means that the overall grade is around 90. It's a nice day.

Raimonda

FEBRUARY 16

Hi, dear Kitty,

My parents fought again. It's a funny thing, but I was laughing this time. They are in their room cursing each other. This time Papa picks up "real curses"! Usually, he uses normal curses, like bitch. But these are worse than that. Simon and I are laughing. What a curse!

One minute I want to say that I hate them. I want to have my own room or put all the dressers and bookcases next to my bed so I won't see them. But then in another minute it seems that I love them. And all of it seems funny to me for the first time, the way they fight. That's it.

That's how my Saturday went, and even after I laughed I still call it an unhappy day.

Raimonda

FEBRUARY 17

Hi, dear Kitty,

It's already ten months and eighteen days that we have been in

America. We had forgotten about emigration a long time ago. Some-times I even think that nothing had happened and we always lived here. I like this school and my class. But I want to do so much more. I wonder if I have changed? When my parents are fighting, I think that I hate them, but in reality I love them all. When they fight, I try to calm down and say, "I just don't care," but somehow I can't build quiet in myself.

Do I like this apartment? It's clean, new, white, but it's too small for us. I want to be alone so often, where I could write poems and at night I could watch the stars. Now I dream of it. But will I have a room? I'm thinking of the future. Before, I used to think only of dolls. For now, I must be bored from cleaning or watching TV. I want to travel and see new life.

But "now" stays the same. It seems that I'm always waiting for a Friday to come and change my world. But then Monday comes again, so hurriedly and quietly, to remind me that nothing has changed.

Raimonda

FEBRUARY 20

Hi, dear Kitty,

It's Wednesday again, a normal day. But I am okay. In fact, I enjoy walking with Papa to the library, talking to him. He tells me some funny and wild stories which he never ends, and I just laugh. And when I think of what I might want now, I find that there's nothing I want.

I watched a movie, *Amadeus*. I was overwhelmed by it. So, Si-mon and I taped some songs that Mozart played. But it just wasn't good. I can't hear the music and can't even play a rhythm with pen-cils on a book, like a drum. Somehow the voice inside of me seems nice, but not on the outside.

Raimonda

FEBRUARY 23

Hi, dear Kitty,

We woke up early and went to Manhattan to take fingerprints again for the green card. We wanted to stay in Manhattan, but it was too cold to walk. So we went home. The weather changes here every day. It was warm yesterday, like in summer, but it's as cold as winter today. Life is changing here so fast. Every day I see a new store open. Later, some will go out of business. In Russia, nothing changes so soon; there'll be the same stores for years. Sometimes I think that if I go back, I'll see nothing changed. Time stopped there. Whereas I don't remember yesterday here, they will remember each minute of it there.

Raimonda

P.S. The war is still on, but if not for TV news, I would even forget about it. It's so far away that crimes that happen in New York every day seem to be much more close. Bush says that if Saddam Hussein's army won't leave in forty-eight hours, the war will continue. Saddam Hussein himself wants to end the war. He understood that he lost.

FEBRUARY 27

Hi, dear Kitty,

I had a lot of homework today. Mama came home and she's really angry today. She screamed at me, but I just said that she will pity that tomorrow when the house is dirty.

We talked and somehow Papa said, "When I die . . . " And he said it so sadly and truthfully that I started to cry and hugged him, and he cried himself. So then we laughed. And Mama came up to kiss us, and we made up.

Simon and I talked till midnight. When we start talking, we usually talk of the past. But because he has more stories, he goes first. We both start to remember our grandparents and even more often our great-grandmother, who has been dead for a long time. I don't know why our memories wander so far.

Tonight, Simon read me a story he wrote, and I cried because of it. Then I read him one of my stories and my new poem, too. He suddenly remembered our great-grandparents and told me of his childhood. (I know everything about him and all his girlfriends, even when he didn't tell me or they lived miles away in Odessa. I was a spy!) Once when he was about ten, he was in camp. There was a girl who liked him and fainted after she confessed that she loved him— because he just jumped on the bed, laughed, and fell down. He says that when he was nineteen, he was walking on the main street of Chernovtsy and there he saw a young woman about nineteen walking with someone else. Their eyes met, and he says that he suddenly remembered her. And he was sure that she remembered him too, but neither of them stopped. Just walked ahead, leaving their childhood behind.

The war has ended. America won, and now it's peace. This is the happiest news of all.

Raimonda

FEBRUARY 28

Hi, dear Kitty,

The last day of February, and tomorrow is the first day of Soviet spring. We will get cable tomorrow; it's free for a month, and $23 after.

Soon we'll have tests again. I'm nervous about the lab test. Ms. Ricarrelo reads real fast and gives only a few seconds to answer the question. When I first came, I scored only 6 percent, but I need 40 percent. I will go to high school no matter the score, but if I get less than 40 percent, I will attend ESL [English as a Second Language] classes.

On the news, they showed how the Arabs tortured soldiers from Kuwait. It was horrible, and Papa didn't let me watch it.

I did my homework, and I will read now. So many things happen in the world, but nothing to me. Happy Purim.

Raimonda

MARCH 1, 1991

Hi, dear Kitty,

We got cable, but Papa doesn't let me watch more than one movie anyway.

Goodnight,

Raimonda

MARCH 2

Hi, dear Kitty,

We got a letter from Grandmother Galya: "Our life in this country is harsh. *It's good that you aren't here.* Fight through your problems strongly."

I can't believe my grandmother wrote that.

Raimonda

MARCH 6

Hi, dear Kitty,

Simon is acting strange today. He smokes and reads. He hasn't even done his homework yet.

Kelli came. As we talked, I remembered some stories of the past. But it was so far away from me now. It was funny to realize that so much is behind me. And here I was talking in English, to an American friend. It seemed funny.

Raimonda

MARCH 9

Hi, dear Kitty,

Yesterday, Pavlik and Tanya came. We ate, drank, and listened to a tape of KVN, which is like a Russian concert of jokes. Two groups of young people—one group of students from Odessa and another from Moscow or someplace—come together to joke. There is a leader, a famous man who used to be in prison. He makes a competition of jokes. Whoever can make you laugh better wins. It's not just clown stuff. It's adult jokes, most of it about politics, economy, and food—all the major problems. We laughed because the jokes were free and truthful. I was surprised that they've come to that. In the past, they couldn't speak so freely. We laughed, but the feeling of it was unpleasant, like pity for myself because I missed something, like I could have been there. When we were there, they wouldn't joke that way. Now, they're free and I'm not there anymore.

I feel kind of sad. I miss Grandmother Galya. It's her birthday today!

Raimonda

MARCH 10

I have no desire to write to you of today, but only of yesterday. Kelli, Andrew, and I went to a pizza restaurant, and we saw shining Manhattan from Brooklyn's side. It was beautiful. We talked and ate pizza. I wish I had that Saturday back.

Raimonda

MARCH 18

Hi, dear Kitty,

It's been a long time since I wrote poems. Sometimes it seems that I have forgotten the Russian language. But at the same time I don't know English. But then it's impossible to know and not to know two languages at the same time.

From March 29 until April 8, I have a spring vacation.

Raimonda

MARCH 19

Hi, dear Kitty,

On 77th Street, a Russian store is going to open in several days. It's just two blocks from us, so now we won't have to go all the way to Brighton Beach for Russian food.

Simon came back from college. He didn't come home after the concert yesterday and slept over at his friends' house. He was angry today. Everyone is asleep now, except for me and Papa, who is doing a picture for *The New York Times*. He has to have it ready for tomorrow morning. I like it already, even before it's done.

I broke up with Luba, and I haven't talked to her for a week and four days. I don't really understand why we fight. It's nothing, but I have never broken up with anyone for so long.

I wish I could travel, see the world, because it's getting boring to live a usual life. But for all that you need money and the green cards, which we will soon get.

A woman is passing by with her dog dressed in a colored shirt. The American flag is waving on the top of Lincoln Bank, so proud and lovely; it spreads out freedom into the sky.

Night, and I am asleep, still trying to see something beautiful in my dream, something that you can't see in life.

Raimonda

MARCH 20

Hi, dear Kitty,

I made up with Luba, but nothing has changed. She spoke against Natasha again, but I didn't care this time. And when Natasha came up, Luba was smiling and talking with her. I am annoyed by it. Lisa kept silent the whole way, and I just didn't listen to any of them.

Raimonda

MARCH 24

Hi, dear Kitty,

Sunday is almost over! Everyone is angry and crazy today. They are watching a movie, but didn't let me watch with them. Papa screams because Mama said that I have to go to camp. This team is closed— I'm not going.

I am listening to music and looking at cards with my hometown on them. I forgot, but still remember. Where am I? It's sad, and I want to come back just for a day. I dreamed of my old apartment, met my old friends, but spoke in English. No, I don't want to go back.

Probably everyone hates me now. Simon is sitting on the couch so angrily and screams out "No!" to whatever I say. Mama is smiling, but at whom? Maybe at me, but I can't smile back. Papa is sitting at the table, surrounded with papers.

The music is sad.

My mood was better when I was at Luba's house, and we talked of childhood memories. I know we lied to each other, to make those memories even more colorful and happy. But we liked it because those stories were fantasies of happiness. And now I am left alone, even if Simon is here and the music is on.

Raimonda

MARCH 28

Hi, dear Kitty,

Today was the last day in school before spring vacation. We had a party and everyone brought foods from their countries. There was a lot of food, but I was scared to try it all. Mostly, the Korean food seemed funny and scary to eat. Everyone was anxious for 3:00 P.M. to arrive, as usual. No one could study. We just joked and laughed. I walked home with the girls. Everyone was in a great mood.

Raimonda

MARCH 29

Hi, dear Kitty,

Today is an important day in our lives. A year ago we came to the country of our dreams, to the big village. We'll have a special supper tonight.

In April, we will get our green cards. And even if we won't be citizens yet, at least we won't be refugees anymore!

Raimonda

P.S. It was the happiest day ever!

We celebrated our first year in America. We listened to Russian records, ate, danced, and played cards. We laughed the whole time. We were together, together laughing.

Raimonda

APRIL 2, 1991

Hi, dear Kitty,

In five days, my vacation is over. These days pass away just as fast as they all do. We went to Manhattan and left Papa's portfolio at some office for a "drop-in." It was great to walk on those streets, watching strange and unusual people. Then I got jeans at The Gap. Later, we picked up the portfolio and went on 43rd Street, where Papa had an appointment. After the library, we went back home, pretty tired. Papa, Simon, and I are reading.

Mama is asleep, but will be up at six in the morning, ready to wake everyone for no reason at all.

Raimonda

APRIL 4

Hi, dear Kitty,

We went to Manhattan again. We had an appointment at NYANA, and afterward we went to the Modern Art Museum. We spent an hour there. In the subway, I fell asleep. Then we ate and watched a movie. Simon is talking on the phone with his friend, and you can start counting the word "fuck," which he is using a lot as he talks.

Papa has a picture to do for *The New York Times*. And this day is over!

Raimonda

APRIL 5

Hi, dear Kitty,

It's Friday, and I was with Lisa and her mother at the Aquarium. We saw fish, sharks, and whales. It was raining and cold, but still fun to watch the hungry and wet penguins walking around.

Yesterday, Simon and I were writing stories till one o'clock at night. I wrote six stories and my parents liked all of them. Mama is sleeping in our room. That's why the light must be off. Papa is nervous because he didn't do his picture yet. Simon is in the bathroom reading, where else?

Raimonda

APRIL 9

Hi, dear Kitty,

It's four days since my last letter. But it seems like one short day. I don't even remember what was happening during these days.

Zhanna and her father called us several days ago. They liked the article from *The Village Voice*.

It's already two days that I've been back in school. I have lots of homework and new books in English and science. Even though nothing is happening, I still don't have time to get bored.

Time goes so fast. Winter is dying, and hot summer awakens.

Raimonda

APRIL 12

Hi, dear Kitty,

Friday the 12th. It's a pity that it's not the 13th, like in the movie. On Monday we have a half day in school, from 8:35 till 12. We'll get our report cards. I am very tired because I cleaned. Before that, I took a walk with Natasha. She is a kind girl, but she doesn't understand life.

Raimonda

APRIL 13

Hi, dear Kitty,

It's Saturday. I went to Natasha's house. We were watching a movie and decided to eat some popcorn. We put some popcorn in the iron plate and put it in the microwave. Eventually, I saw that the popcorn was on fire. I screamed out, "Fire!" Natasha turned off the light, and I unplugged the line. Then we poured water on the black popcorn. We were scared, but while we did all of it we were laughing. Then we cleaned everything, laughed and joked, feeling so proud.

When it began to darken outside, I came home. I told the story to everybody, but didn't get much attention from them. Anyway, we were proud. Maybe because we weren't confused at that moment or because we acted like grown-ups.

Raimonda

APRIL 20

Hi, dear Kitty,

It's more than a week since I've written—for no reason at all. But a week seems like one day. And at the same time, I am bored and tired of many things. I want to travel and see all of America. I miss my yard and my friends. There's no yard here and not even friends, really. Luba is younger by two years, and we don't communicate much anyway. Natasha is dressed like a slut. At first, only the Russians noticed it, but now even the Americans do. She's always trying to find a protection in me. But she does things her way anyway. Russian girls laugh at her, and Americans are probably jealous. I don't care, but it's embarrassing sometimes. Lisa is the first girl I have met who thinks the same way I do, who dreams the same way.

Kelli and Andrew came today. Kelli talked with me, while Andrew trained Papa to drive in their car. Papa is training to drive in New York, so he can get a driving license.

I got a letter from Zhanna Lehtman. She was my Jewish friend who lived across the balcony from my grandmother Sofa's apartment. Before I left, I promised to write to her. She said that many people make that promise, but when they get to America, they don't write anymore. I laughed at her words, and said that I would write. However, I didn't. And she was right. And now I have her letter from 1990, when it's 1991 now. I still think that I won't answer. Is it too far away, were we separated for too long? Or is it just me?

Raimonda

APRIL 24

Hi, dear Kitty,

It's Wednesday again. I cleaned, did my homework, and watched *Jaws*. Zhanna Rosenberg called from Detroit. It's her birthday today. I'm not going to school tomorrow because we are going to get our green cards, which give us the right to travel to other cities and countries. We aren't immigrants anymore. But who are we?

Raimonda

APRIL 26

Hi, dear Kitty,

On Thursday we woke up at seven-thirty in the morning. We went to Manhattan to get a green card. There were a lot of Russians in that building and many of them we have met before, probably in Italy. Most children wanted to show off their Americanness. They listened to Walkmans, chewed gum, and were dressed in American style. But I could recognize Russia in them anyway.

After we did fingerprints, everyone stayed in line to have an interview. We got to know a Russian emigrant from Odessa, who was a very funny and intelligent man with spoiled teeth. His teeth were worse than Papa's and he showed them to me, too. I exploded to show my reaction in some way, and he smiled. We saw him before in the hotel in Italy, where we went when we just arrived.

We met Aunt Lilya and her family, the people that Uncle Pavlik provided the guarantee for. They are leaving New York, because Uncle Grisha, her husband, got a job in Connecticut.

Then the officials called us, and we walked through a long white hall, following a man who looked like a soldier. We went into his office and put our hands on our hearts, saying, "I swear to tell truth and only truth." The first thing I heard was a question to Simon that made me angrier than it made him. That soldier said: "You just came to America and became a hippie so soon." Sima answered, "Yes." I don't know why he answered that way. He doesn't really have anything to do with it except for long hair. "Do you take drugs?" asked that official, fast. "No," answered Simon. The official kept silent for a long moment. I looked at Simon, then at the official, and barely stopped myself from asking, "Do *you* take drugs?" The official suddenly stopped his silence and loudly asked, "Are you Communists?"

"No," we answered.

At that moment, I remembered Russia, emigration, and the fact that it's the second time we have been asked this very same question. I remembered that in Russia I lived for twelve years and was born there. And here I am just an immigrant who slept and forgot who she really was, forgot that she was Soviet before. I remembered, woke up from my memories, and became sad. I was angry at that man who reminded me of it and who awoke me from my thoughts now, asking us simple questions. I was angry at him because he awoke me and made me feel alien, unneeded by anyone, immigrant.

Now, I awoke and sat up strongly on my chair. I was nervous inside, but fought with myself on the outside. I wanted revenge by looking at him. He started interrogating Sima, then Mama and Papa. I was still sitting there and looking around his room. I heard voices from another room. One of the officials said to a Russian baby, "Tell me, 'bye, or I am gonna send you back to Russia." How easily she said it, and I got mad and offended for myself, for that little child who told her " 'Bye" anyway, after all.

Our official asked me questions now, and he was impressed by my grades. He asked me who I wanted to become, and maybe he saw a good future for me in America when I answered that I want to be a doctor. But I didn't need his opinion. I knew that I will fight for my future, not as an immigrant only. Mama stared at the table still as the Statue of Liberty, but without triumph. The official was silent and wrote down our documents. Then he gave us these little papers with our pictures on them called green cards.

We went outside on the noisy street of New York. The sun was shining. It was warm outside, and I smiled. I enjoyed walking like everyone else and looking around at windows, which always kept a sign: SALE. Papa and Mama kissed, then they kissed me and congratulated me on the green card. I was joyful because now we could travel, but the most important: I wasn't an immigrant anymore. Papa put our green cards in his pocket and we walked happily, glancing at windows on the noisy streets of New York.

Raimonda

APRIL 27

Hi, dear Kitty,

In the morning at seven, Mama and I went to the Jewish Center's pool. But it was closed and we had to wait about one hour for it to open.

During this hour, we decided to go to the supermarket and buy food. We knew that it was somewhere near, but decided to ask. The woman we stopped was Russian, about sixty years old. She didn't answer our question at first, but started to tell us of her life. Why us, strangers? She told us all of her life and the life of her relatives too in about ten minutes. Life is so long, but how short it is in words. Her story was sad at first, and she said, "At first I just cried for three months." Then she calmed herself down. She didn't need to know Mama's life and certainly not mine. But she needed someone to listen, just to listen about her life. She knew that we would forget and so we did. But she didn't care. Then she told us where the supermarket was, just a block from where we stood. I wonder if she calmed herself down after she told her life to the air, to the wind, to us—strangers.

How short life is in words!

Raimonda

APRIL 28

Hi, dear Kitty,

I hadn't written poems for some time. Sometimes I think I don't know Russian, that poetic Russian, that I used to know and learn from poems and stories in school. But then I think that I don't know English either. I can't feel it. Not when I read, or even when I talk. My teacher said that I am a good student, but I have a Russian accent. I know that. I didn't even try to change it. It could be from laziness or like my brother said, "I don't have ears." Many Russians want to change it, and it's easier for little kids about four or six. They even forget Russian. Will I be able to change mine in several years? I don't know, but it doesn't really bother me much if I can't.

Raimonda

APRIL 29

Hi, dear Kitty,

Yesterday we went to the circus with Uncle Pavlik and his family. There was a big difference here. First of all there were three arenas and all three were demonstrating something. My eyes were running about, and I couldn't concentrate. In Russia we had just one arena.

Then clowns came out, but there weren't one or two, but zillions of them. I couldn't keep up with any one of them. And elephants used the arena as a toilet. That's why workers had to run about picking up the heavy stuff elephants left behind while dancing.

We had fun, and I liked the elephants most.

Raimonda

APRIL 30

Hi, dear Kitty,

Today, Joan from NYANA agreed to meet with me. At four, we met. She and I came to a synagogue where I was invited to talk to Jewish-American teenagers about emigration.

I recognized the synagogue. It was the first synagogue we went to, where I met Carol Gold and where I talked of my diary, not even imagining that it might be published in a newspaper. The synagogue was where it all started.

We went to the second floor. There were children thirteen years old. All of them were pretty and rich and American. We talked for two hours about emigration and NYANA. One girl took my phone number, and I knew that she would never call, but it was nice. Adults that gathered those children were praising me. The children left, and there was a feeling that they came just to eat pizza. Joan said that this is a reason they come, but they usually leave much earlier or sleep or talk rudely. But this time they didn't; they asked questions and listened. They were interested.

I will wait till I have American accent, till they can't see that I am Russian and then, only in this way, I'll try to get to know American teenagers, because I don't now. However, it's good to know many languages and understand movies where someone speaks in Russian and for Americans those are just sounds. I always thought that English is prettier, and people are smarter. But now I understand. The languages have the same meanings and people have the same thoughts, even if they are spelled differently.

Raimonda

MAY 1, 1991

Hi, dear Kitty,

An old friend called from Detroit. She found out my phone number from someone. It was nice to hear a voice from my childhood. My past. She asked me if I knew something from anyone at our school, but I didn't. I wrote two letters to my classmates, but never got the answer. If I really wanted to, I could have reached them somehow. I could have written many letters. But I didn't want to. We were too far away and too different now. We would just keep up with my memories if I were to write to them. And even if I got their letters and they would write it in the present about their school life today, now, it would still have to keep up with my memories because I wouldn't be able to live in their present with them. So I left them. I left them in my past, my childhood, my memories, which I won't wake up for a long time. This is the second time I say goodbye to the past.

Raimonda

MAY 2

Hi, dear Kitty,

My girlfriends from Italy don't call me anymore. They live in Brooklyn, but we never met again. They called me at first and we usually spoke of Russia. One of the girls described to me her riches, that mean nothing here. First of all, she doesn't have them anymore. But then things got better in her life and in mine, too. We found friends here, and even though we live just forty minutes from each other, it seems like a world away.

Emigration is over, not just in our lives, but in our memories too, and what could seem sad and terrible to me then seems funny and maybe beautiful now. I have forgotten everything, but the beautiful places of Rome, Venice, Florence, and San Marino. I have forgotten everything, except for only some happy moments from my hometown and my favorite street. I don't remember my room that I left behind, or my toys, books, and furniture. Some other family lives there, another girl maybe with her own toys, books, and thoughts. That is a Russian girl, who will go to Russian kindergarten, school, and college. Who will know Russian culture and Russian friends only.

I cry, but not out of pity and not out of jealousy. I cry because I do remember! I try to kill my memories, hide them deep inside, but I remember each book on my shelf and each toy on my bed.

My memory lives, but I try to kill it.

I got a letter from Grandmother Galya. She reminded me of some memories. I am different now, but I don't notice it. In reality, all my life has changed. Not only pieces of it or the feeling that you are moving to another apartment, but everything—language, friends, holidays, history.

I looked at the flower on my windowsill and suddenly I remembered that once I was in the hospital with pneumonia and I a wrote letter to my grandmother. I asked Papa to draw a flower on it and so he did. But my grandmother didn't know that he did it and couldn't stop praising me. Somehow I never told her the truth.

Sometimes I have dreams where I come back to my hometown, but instead of Russian, I speak English. Even my dream makes it much easier to wake up in reality.

Raimonda

MAY 3

Hi, dear Kitty,

I just want to tell you a funny story that happened today. I walked with Simon in Brooklyn. As we walked, I saw a girl with her grandfather, who embraced her and was probably telling her a story or a fairy tale. I looked at her. She was different. She was ill, and I pitied her. I even wanted to smile at her. Our eyes met and her wide mouth opened and she whispered, "Fuck you." When she was far away from me, I looked back. She was still walking with her grandfather, who was telling her of something kind.

Raimonda

MAY 5

Hi, dear Kitty,

Mama left with Aunt Tanya to go to Houston. They just called from a hotel. I am jealous but still have the power to tell Papa that we will travel around the world, see every city and travel by ship until we are tired. And only then we'll stay in New York.

We bought tennis rackets, one for Papa and one for me. We spent $90. But I am happy; I need nothing else. It feels that we finally started a real life.

Raimonda

MAY 8

Hi, dear Kitty,

Mama came back, and she didn't bring any presents. She tells stories of Houston, but she can't speak quickly. That's why I have no patience to listen. Only Papa has the patience to listen.

Raimonda

MAY 23

Hi, dear Kitty,

Today is the happiest day of my life. I mean it's not the first time I start that way, but each time I write that, the day has something special.

However, it started very normally. I came home from school, did my homework, and cleaned. In the evening at seven-thirty, Papa and I went to the meeting at school where awards were given out. At first everyone stood up and sang an American hymn. Then the awards began. Papa was talking with Russians; I sat with girls from my class. They got awards before me, but stayed to wait for me. When I was called, I got up like in a dream and came up to our principal and director, who gave out the awards. They gave me an envelope with something like all the others before me got and shook my hand. It had a deed in it. But when I opened mine, it had a white box with a medal in it called "American Legion." And in another envelope was a $50 bonus.

Papa was busy writing a letter to Grandma. He missed when I came out. Some teachers looked at me and smiled.

We left, and I showed my award to Papa. He cried from happiness and said, "It's God." He said something about being proud. In America, he said, they always see who is better. In Russia, everyone goes in the same line, and no one gets anywhere. There is no point to life in Russia. You're going to struggle the same way and end up at the same point—nowhere.

We went outside and I also wanted to cry because I was in America, because I had an American Legion award and $50, and because we ate supper and everything was clean and celebrated, and because I am here enjoying this happiness.

Raimonda

MAY 27

Hi, dear Kitty,

It's so hot. I can't sleep all night. School is almost over and we all wait for the last day, even the teachers. We went to the beach—Brighton Beach, of course. We bought Russian food. Simon is working again in the same store, but as a salesman now.

Twenty-six days left till summer vacation.

Raimonda

JUNE 4, 1991

Hi, dear Kitty,

Sima had a birthday and I gave him $5 and wrote a poem. Our parents gave him $21. And Uncle Pavlik with Aunt Tanya gave him $75. We celebrated till night. Simon was tired from work because the air conditioner doesn't work there, and it's hot.

Raimonda

JUNE 8

Hi, dear Kitty,

I loved today. Kelli, Andrew, and I went to the beach and stayed till seven. The water was cold, but then it got warmer. We ate ice cream and Andrew's car broke down because of the heat.

We put on this cream for sunblock, but I hate it because we never used it before. However, then my legs hurt because I forgot to put the cream on them.

Papa went to Washington with Uncle Pavlik, and I miss him already. I had a great time. Simon is going to the beach with his friends, and of course he'll never take me.

Raimonda

JUNE 18

Hi, dear Kitty,

School is almost over and so is my last year in junior high school. I'll be in high school next year, and I'll be fourteen. We won't study anymore this year, and our books were already taken up.

Papa bought an air conditioner. Mama is translating an article from *The New York Times*. Then Papa will draw a picture to go with it.

I want to go to sleep. What am I gonna do when school is over? I can't wait till that, anyway.

Raimonda

JUNE 21

Hi, dear Kitty,
Today is Graduation Day.

In the morning, I was angry at Papa because he didn't go with me and Mama. He was on deadline with a drawing.

Graduation was very joyful and triumphant. I got one of the biggest awards. The problem is that I had no idea that I would get one and missed all the things the director talked of before calling my name. I just heard something like "big progress," and I am not sure about that, either.

I said goodbye to my friends, and it was sad in a way, but joyful too. I got used to and maybe even loved this school, these friends and teachers. Goodbye, McKinley.

Everything is ahead. That's why you can't stop, especially when you have freedom to become either a doctor or a McDonald's worker. I already picked the first choice. On Monday, we go to school for the last time, to pick up diplomas.

Papa is of course happy and kind again. The award did it. We went to eat ice cream.

Raimonda

JUNE 28

Hi, dear Kitty,

On Monday, I came to school and picked up my diploma and report card. I said goodbye to my classmates again and shook hands with a Korean boy I was friends with. I walked out very easily, fast and joyfully. I met with my friends and we walked the same way for the last time. Lisa and Natasha have one year still to go; they'll go to eighth grade next year. Luba has two more years to go.

It's already the sixth day that I am on vacation. It's 100 degrees outside. That's why I am not going outside. Joyce hadn't called us for one year. It's strange, but she called yesterday and reminded me of camp, which I happily forgot a year ago. During this year, many things have changed. We have furniture and our apartment isn't as empty as it used to be a year ago, though it's still tiny.

It's summer again.

Raimonda

July 1, 1991

Hi, dear Kitty,

It's so hot outside! Who would ever think that I am in bed, sick. I read American books all day without the dictionary. It gets easier. After all, I read three hundred pages a day in English. I am resting now, if you can call it a rest. School starts September 5.

Papa just screamed at me for being sick. Mama fell asleep a long time ago. I won't even check. I am sure of it.

Raimonda

July 8

Hi, dear Kitty,

I was working on Saturday for $3.50 an hour, distributing fliers. I got $25.

Yesterday a woman called who met us a year ago in the Metropolitan Museum. It's strange that people so easily call after a year has passed. Joyce came on Saturday. We talked and bought food in the supermarket—ice cream and stuff. She changed. She was kind of joking, but she said that I should be baby-sitting. We said we don't have anyone to baby-sit. She said that maybe she would have a baby.

Raimonda

JULY 11

Hi, dear Kitty,

The most important news is that my grandparents are already in the emigration computer. That means they'll be here in half a year.

Papa had work for *The New York Times* the whole week.

Raimonda

JULY 15

Hi, dear Kitty,

I worked yesterday and got so tired that I couldn't do anything else. You won't believe that I want to go to school already. But I do.

Raimonda

JULY 21

Hi, dear Kitty,

I know it's Monday, but I barely remember the date. It is 102 degrees, one of those tropical American summers. I want to go somewhere just to leave all that surrounds me, even this apartment, to leave not only things and places but memories and thoughts, too.

Simon is home earlier for the first time. He is always out with a Japanese girl named Yoko. We haven't seen her. They met where Simon works. He used to laugh at the way she opens up her mouth when she gets surprised.

Now it's raining. Nothing is happening and I wait for adventures, but they died a long time ago, just like the yard from my childhood. I don't pity or miss it. I just wait.

Raimonda

JULY 30

Hi, dear Kitty,

You know that I don't like to keep money for long, count it and hide it, like my mother does. That's why when I'm rich, I'll give her the money to keep.

Sometimes my parents disapprove when I waste money, but I usually answer, "I spend my money to enjoy my childhood while it's not gone yet." But I really mean I do it because I am afraid that eventually I'll have to throw them away, these dollars, or like my grandma said, "to glue them on a wall," worthless. That's what my mom had to do when we were leaving the Soviet Union, just throw them away, spending on some sweaters, blankets, pillows, which meant nothing to her. I pitied her.

So I bought a mini-music system, "Panasonic"! I listened to music for the whole day and Papa gave me all of his records he collected in Russia. If someone would come in our room now, he'd think that he came into a crazy house where two music systems are standing opposite to each other. Everyone laughs when they hear that Sima doesn't let me use his system, but I am the only one who thinks he's right. Because I wouldn't let him either if I were to have a system like his, which costs about $1,000.

Dad is going to Manhattan tomorrow. He has a picture to do for *The New York Times*. He's going to show a draft today and pick up an article. Mom is going with him.

Simon's girlfriend is coming tomorrow, and I want to see her. Maybe Simon will get married. I can feel how annoyed he is at this tiny apartment. And I do wish to see the wedding! That's something I've never seen before. Lisa and I are probably the only people on earth who haven't been to a wedding.

And I am annoyed by all this, too. There is just a month and six days before my vacation ends. And then comes my birthday. I already feel it coming, my favorite holiday just because I get older and get presents.

Suddenly, I remember Venice, my Venice that I've seen, after all. I have to end this letter because there's nothing to write about. Always when I have nothing to write about, I remember emigration. But why? Everything is written, and if not all, then in my memory all is kept.

Raimonda

AUGUST 1, 1991

Hi, dear Kitty,

Simon's girlfriend came, so he cooked and I cleaned everything. She's a lovely nice girl from Japan named Yoko. She's twenty-two now, but I thought she was sixteen. Dad is listening to music on my system. I'm so happy about it. It sounds so great. Mama is sleeping already, as always. Everything is clean and peaceful. We talked English the whole day. I wanted to call Kelli and Andrew but they have been gone from New York all week.

Raimonda

AUGUST 6

Hi, dear Kitty,

Simon broke up with us. He even called me "shit," after all I've done for him. After I always loved him. And after all, I'm his sister. It all began when Yoko started to live with us for three days. Simon started to think only of her and he stopped respecting us, especially me. At first we broke up. We haven't made up, but we have stopped fussing. But I still remember about "shit." And I'm gonna make him remember that too.

Yoko was living with us for three days. I like her. We played cards and chess all the time. I could easily win with Yoko, but never with my papa. In the evening, he drank cognac and told me that he's drunk and that I'll win this time. But he lied. He wasn't drunk, but remained as smart as he always is. For the first time I wished he could be drunk so I would win.

I am reading a book now called *I Know Why the Caged Bird Sings*. I like it. Papa is watching the news. In Russia, they usually showed about a good harvest on farms. I usually never watched it because I was bored and there was nothing better on than harvests and farms. And here there are so many interesting places and entertainments, but what I usually hear is "murder, killed, shot, AIDS, cancer, died." Maybe that's why I usually never watch the news here too.

Raimonda

AUGUST 7

Hi, dear Kitty,

It was a great day. Papa and I went to Manhattan and walked on those dirty but amazing streets, surrounded by skyscrapers.

Papa gave his new picture for *Inx,* a syndicate. He got $100. We ate breakfast with Papa's publisher in *Inx,* and he paid. We went in every bookstore that was on our way. I saw books, adventurous books, that I loved but read a long time ago in Russian. But they were beautiful with those hard covers and pictures. I was sad to leave without buying anything, but I couldn't. It costs a lot. However, we went to the library and bought four good books for only 50 cents each.

Dad saw a sign in the bathroom, "Kill all Jews, they are the first bankers," and, "Kill all blacks before 2004." I knew there was anti-Semitism and racism here too. But somehow it didn't scare me. It didn't worry me, like I was sure of something, like I didn't care. And then we were back out on the street again, looking at those huge buildings, those skyscrapers, and somehow I felt protected. I don't know why I felt that way.

Raimonda

AUGUST 12

Hi, dear Kitty,

Yesterday and today we celebrated Papa's birthday. Uncle Pavlik and Aunt Tanya came. Mama cooked and I came from work at 3:00 P.M. I was really tired. We worked handing out fliers for eight hours.

We watched movies that we had rented from the video store. All day Saturday and Sunday, we watched. Then I slept the whole day like the dead. We just watched Pink Floyd's concert, *The Wall*. I love it.

I miss my grandparents. Mom called them recently. When Mom asked them, "What are you doing?" they answered, "Getting ready to leave." And then there'll be nothing left there for me.

Raimonda

AUGUST 17

Hi, dear Kitty,

It was a hard and a hot day. I woke up at six and left for work. At four, I was tired, and rested at home. That's the last time that I will be working because all the original workers will come back from camp.

This is a true story: "Capitalists and Communists."

The day was Saturday, and we, like Jews who came from a Communist country, went to work. I woke up at six in the morning and got ready for this day, not drinking tea, which would only have reminded me of a warm dream. The street was still sleeping, but only two passersby talked to each other and they had a huge dog. "Hi," they said to me. "Hi," I answered, not smiling or breaking my stride. When I was a half block away, they cried out, "Cheer up." I mechanically smiled. I could hear from far away, "She's smart."

I came inside where Lisa and her mother were, and in several minutes we all waited on the street for the car. When everyone was ready, we drove to another area. There was a big building without windows or doors, where poor emigrants lived. The cars were filled with fliers from different stores. It got hot. It was one of those hot days. The boss had left and said that we had to do "doorknobs"—climb up the stairs and put a flier in the door—on such a hot day. The Russian manager screamed out: "What are you, crazy? They are all fucking gonna die! Don't you understand, it's gonna be ninety-six degrees today!"

The American boss didn't listen. He was scared of his boss who paid us all money, but made money on us. We sat in the car and listened. There was an old man standing next to us, waiting, hoping for work. Where did he go when he gave up? All of us waited. Some tried to laugh, but most of us kept silent. We seemed alien. We already knew that we were going to do the doorknobs. Capitalism won. But we were glad for that.

After work, being hot and tired, I still remembered the words: "What are you, crazy? They are all fuckin' gonna die!"

Raimonda

August 19

Hi, dear Kitty,

Today, the most important event happened in the Soviet Union. I heard my father calling me this morning. I was still in bed. It was very early. I opened my eyes, and the first thing I did was rush to my parents' room. The radio was on, and a loud voice was talking about a coup in Russia. I heard that Gorbachev was ousted, and that tanks were coming into Moscow, and, most important, that people were making barricades with their bodies. I was shocked. We all were shocked. Papa rushed out to buy a *New York Times,* where his pictures are published, and there he saw articles about the coup. We didn't turn off the radio. A few hours later the publisher called from *The New York Times,* and Papa went to the offices to make an illustration about the coup. Simon went to work. Mama and I stayed around the television. We stayed the whole day, and still I could not believe it. I couldn't believe that for so long people were staying at home, keeping silence, and now they were going out to fight. I was so surprised.

When Papa and Simon came home, we were still watching the

news. When we lived in Russia we always expected something to happen, though we couldn't expect this.

Love,
Raimonda

AUGUST 21

Dear Kitty,

We have heard that the people won! We have been crying and crying. We were crying not only with joy but because, in that moment, we all understood that we had lost something. My parents lost more than forty years there, living in a grand deception. They felt like their lives were for nothing. For nothing, they have lost their time and their lives, first to the deception of communism and then to the humiliation of emigration. When we were coming to America, they believed that they had lost their lives to an overwhelming power. And now they understand that they lost them for nothing, just a grand deception.

Love,
Raimonda

AUGUST 22

Hi, dear Kitty,

Grandmother Sofa called today from Chernovtsy. We thought she had news of the coup. We've been so anxious for her. And now we knew things must be bad if she was calling—it costs more than a month's income. But instead she was anxious for us because she had heard on the television that there were pogroms in Brooklyn, in a place called Crown Heights. We could only talk two minutes. We tried to explain. It's true that in Brooklyn, blacks are against Jews. It all started when a Hasidic Jew drove over a black boy who was seven years old. The boy was killed. His brother was injured. Some say the emergency car took the driver to the hospital but left the children by order of the police. That's what they said on the news. Blacks started a fight. They injured many people, even cops. Of course in Russia, the propaganda machine—with great enjoyment—showed it to scare Soviet Jews. We told Grandmother Sofa that it doesn't bother us. Grandmother Sofa talked to us for two minutes because it costs an enormous amount of money.

My parents have agreed to let me have a kitten after all. I have asked them for so long and finally convinced them. Thanks to mice! They scare me too, so I jump on my bed. At least I have a bed. But my parents have been sleeping only on a mattress on the floor. However, after a mouse got into their room, they bought a bed from the same store where we bought the mattresses a year or more ago. And the owner remembered me.

Love,
Raimonda

AUGUST 24

Dear Kitty,

I still remember what life was like before the people won: It is winter—dark and cold. But I have to wake up. My grandmother is softly trying to wake me. I want to stay in this bed for the rest of my life, but she says I must get up. I know that I must. While I am washing, my grandmother is preparing a hot breakfast, my favorite fried potato with eggs. But I am still very cold and dizzy. I am trying to talk with Grandmother, but my eyes are looking through the window, onto the gray street, where snow is falling. My grandmother looks at me with pity and tries to cheer me up before I close the door behind me. Outside, it is still snowing. I love snow. But now it is plaguing me, making me cold and wet.

I am so wet when I come into class. The snow is on my hat, and there is icy water in my boots. The teacher arrives. All the students are sleepy, and the teacher is angry because the chairs are still on the tables, where we left them when we swept up on Saturday after class. Everyone takes down only one, for themselves. The teacher gets mad and screams at the boys for not helping. But the boys ignore him. And suddenly the teacher falls to the floor on his knees and starts begging them to do it. They are absolutely still in their surprise. Then finally, they help with the chairs. And everyone sits.

Year after year, the teacher teaches Politinformation this way. Every Monday, we must all come to class one hour early, at 7:00 A.M., so we may learn about politics. Year after year, we listen to nearly the same thing, again and again. My parents listened to teachers who talked about the "great" Stalin. I listen to teachers who talk about the "great" Lenin, about the Party.

Now, everyone knows who Stalin was. The statues of Lenin are broken. The Party is gone. But I still remember that lesson in Polit-information. Everyone listens. But the "bad" student is asleep. How right he was!

Love,
Raimonda

AUGUST 25

Hi, dear Kitty,

Papa has drawn another picture for *The New York Times*. It shows people breaking the statues of Lenin. And they really did.

In the Soviet Union, the Party and Lenin were everyone's belief, everyone's life, everyone's way to live. And now it's all gone.

My father felt sad for all the insults he had suffered in that country. My parents' teachers and my teachers were so sure when they were telling us about Lenin, about the Communist Party. They were so sure.

We cried when we watched the funeral of the Jewish boy who was killed standing against the tanks. The American reports showed the rabbi at his graveside, and the mourners saying the *Kaddish*. But when Papa got the Moscow newspapers, they didn't mention that one of the three martyrs was Jewish. So some things never change. And maybe nothing changed at all.

Love,
Raimonda

SEPTEMBER 2, 1991

Hi, dear Kitty,

Chess became my hobby, in the morning, in the afternoon, and at night. I won from Papa.

In Russia, Latvia became a separate free republic. Raisa [Gor-bachev] couldn't speak for several hours after the coup.

SEPTEMBER 4

Yesterday, in the evening, Simon and Yoko came. Yoko is leaving to Pennsylvania today. She gave us a computer to use for a year. In the evening we ate Russian food and Japanese candies.

Raimonda

P.S. We have a big mouse again. Pretty soon I'm gonna have a kitten. Yoko has probably left already. Simon was at the university again. He starts on September 7. He took the program but again it's bull-shit. We don't know what to do. He can't get the classes he wants. Where's he gonna get the money? And what's he gonna do? Now he went to smoke, the only way to escape.

P.P.S. I couldn't sleep. I went to the bathroom and wrote a story called "The Eighth Wonder of the World."

SEPTEMBER 4

Hi, dear Kitty,

Honey is our new member, the fifth one. Andrew brought us a little kitten which has the color of honey. It took some time to guess whether it's a boy or a girl. We stopped on a girl, but we aren't sure. I didn't sleep the whole night, watching her. She's yellow, warm and alive.

Yoko left for Pennsylvania. This is where she goes to college. Simon has problems with entering college, but can't solve any of them. He went to smoke.

Raimonda

SEPTEMBER 12

Hi, dear Kitty,

Yesterday was my first day in school at Fort Hamilton High School. It's so big that I can't find anything without help. It's so big that I got into the wrong class and stayed there for the whole lesson before I realized my mistake. But I have an excuse, because it's just the first day.

It's night. I am almost asleep. Tomorrow is Friday, and then comes the weekend and my birthday. I'll be fourteen. I like this new school, even from the first day. You feel free and more like a grown-up. I have to study in school for four more years, whereas in Russia it would have been three or even less. I didn't like McKinley from the first day, but only at the end of the year did I realize that I got used to it. I like Fort Hamilton immediately. Maybe it's because I got used to Americans—teachers and people. Or maybe I've just soaked up America itself.

Russia? Not any more. Now it's an alien country. I have even

forgotten the address where I used to live. I think of it rarely; it seems
so far away. My parents are getting used to America, but they have
lost a lot, lost more than they are getting used to now. Simon? He
has more problems, fewer friends. He's not sure of his dreams. But
he's young and everything might still change.

The coup happened in the Soviet Union. But did it change anything? I am not sure anymore. Today in class the teacher asked about
religion and asked if any of us were Jews. There were four Soviet
Jews in class, but I was the only one who lifted my hand. I didn't
care anymore. I asked the Russian kids in surprise, Why? They called
themselves Russians. They were scared maybe.

In Russia, we knew we were Jews and wanted to know the religion. But we weren't real Jews, and most aren't becoming so now.
Maybe there's no need anymore. I myself think more of English, of
my American future, of study, than of that past life. Sometimes I pity
myself because I didn't learn Hebrew and everything, even now when
I can. Sometimes I am looking for a defense, like the Soviets used to
look for a scapegoat, and now I want to blame them, but I don't. I
am a stranger. But I am lucky, too.

SEPTEMBER 15

Hi, dear Kitty,

Today is my birthday. I am fourteen!

Yesterday, Pavlik, Tanya, and Ilona came. Mama cooked everything, and they left at night. I got $55 from everybody, a black leather
schoolbag, and other presents.

Today at one o'clock my friends will come, but there aren't many
of them! Them means three girls—Lisa, Natasha, and Luba. At six,
Kelli and Andrew will come.

Raimonda

SEPTEMBER 20

Hi, dear Kitty,

Simon has a lot of problems with the university. He has to pay
$2,000, which he doesn't have. He owes $16,000 but doesn't study.
He hasn't studied for three weeks. He always rushes, but then it's too
late.

Papa is doing homework for English classes he takes in Manhattan. He told me: "Don't interfere; I am doing my homework." It seemed funny to me because he finished school, got a medal, studied in the university, knows math and physics, worked on an electrical station, is a famous artist who publishes his works in many countries and finally has been published in *The New York Times*. A man of forty-five is doing homework. Mama says, "What have we come to?"

Raimonda

SEPTEMBER 28

Hi, dear Kitty,

I miss my grandparents, like a part of me is waiting and part of me lives. I called them today. Everything is fine.

Tomorrow it is two years that we have been away from the Soviet Union. And Russia? I am beginning to forget. Memories are in me, but they are asleep and I don't have time for them. I don't awaken them anymore. And emigration? I have forgotten all about it. Or, I remember all of it, but don't recall it anymore. It is like a big part of my childhood has passed. America stopped being my dream. Now I am here, and it seems I always have been, always went here to school, always slept on this bed, and only you have gotten bigger—pages are getting filled with black and blue ink, one after another. And I forget about the last page and start a new one. A new page of life. A new one for me. And what was behind is not mine, it's yours. It's kept by you, not by me.

Something has happened in my life that happens to many, but not to a girl who was born in Russia and will live there forever. And not to an American girl who was born here and her whole life is here. Only to immigrants.

Sometimes I feel that emigration has taught me to understand life better and people, too. At least I know I am not as empty as I was at nine. I don't hate anybody. I have no enemies. I believe in God, but then there's always a question in my head: "Why did millions die when they believed?" Papa says it's because the first god in a person is his mind. The higher your mind gets, the closer you get to God. The mind will show you the right way. So, did they have to fight, or run? But what about children who didn't have minds, who were not able enough to think of anything, not able to choose any way?

We went to synagogue. I wanted to go, to go for myself. But I don't believe in synagogue, not in this one where people talk, come in any clothing, and where even the rabbi talks fast like he has to hurry up. I don't see them believe, even if I am sure they do. This synagogue is alien to me. I only remember the tiny synagogue in Chernovtsy, which was always closed for me so that I could only look at it from outside—until once it was open and I came in. I saw a small room with hard chairs; old men sat in front and prayed. Somewhere were written Jewish letters. Sounds of Yiddish were heard there. And I didn't understand, but I could feel. I believed.

Today I saw a photo from a Russian newspaper, *Bukovina,* from Chernovtsy. They showed Chernovtsy, and I didn't recognize it at first. I didn't understand. And then I saw Lenin's Square. And there Lenin's monument has been taken away. There I became a Young Pioneer. There I put flowers. There, it's empty now. It feels strange, and I am in disbelief. How can it be? How?

I am here on this bed, in this room. It's warm, and Honey is beside me—my sun. America is outside my window. Not Chernovtsy. How? I ask again. Not Chernovtsy, so fast. Life, page after page, which is turned over and over, and will end sometime.

Raimonda

Afar . . . (Of Russia)
Deserted, she seems sullen.
Turned off are all her lights.
Houses stand in cool dust,
her dreams carried by wind:
The authority of immortality extinguished,
and all the hopes dead.
Her elevated glory
moans deceptively afar.
Misty are her roads.
Her hostile ringing has subsided
and in her boundless grief,
alone she'll die.

SEPTEMBER 29

Hi, dear Kitty,
At school, my history teacher just jokes. However, his jokes went

too far when he talked of Jews and Arabs. It was an ESL class, and there were Soviet Jews and Arabs, too. No one cared until he talked of it. One Arab boy said, "I hate Jews because they are stupid." But we didn't answer. We kept silent. Was it because it was smarter to or because we always keep silent? He usually always talked of something bad about Jews, but only today, our teacher called me and him outside. I don't know why he chose me. He said to the Arab boy, "She's a Jew and how can you say this to her?" The boy answered something, and then said to me, "I don't hate you, but only the Jews that are in Israel." He didn't understand that we are all the same whether we were from Israel, Russia, or America. Then two Hispanic boys passed by and stopped to listen. So the teacher talked to them: "You are from Puerto Rico, but now you are in America. This boy would say to you, 'I don't hate you, but I hate all Puerto Ricans who live in Puerto Rico.' What would you say?" The Hispanic boys answered: "This is the same shit." To the Arab boy, they said, "Stay on your knees and ask for forgiveness." They meant forgiveness from me. They smiled at me and left. Then a Jewish teacher came up and listened, then scolded the boy and left. That boy apologized and kept silent, and suddenly I understood that I won. For the first time someone defended me. For the first time, there was someone by my side, and I was proud. Oh, I forgave the boy. Of course I did. I didn't hate him. I knew it didn't teach him anything, and he'd leave with hate, but I didn't care. Not when I wasn't alone, not when I won. Not when I felt so good.

Raimonda

OCTOBER 1, 1991

Hi, dear Kitty,

The first time that I was jealous and wanted something, I wanted a writing table to do my homework on. We have it, but all the space is busy. I don't have bookshelves, but when I was in Russia as a child and was crazy only about fairy tales, I had so much space. It's a year and a half that I've lived in this tiny room with Simon. Our music systems stare at each other. I can imagine how annoying I am to him. He's angry in the morning and so am I. I scream, he curses. In the evening, he plays the guitar and I can't read. Angry Papa is screaming at him for not letting him study in silence. "Close the door!" screams out Papa. "What door?" I ask, laughing. "We don't have any door."

Somehow I am annoyed about it today, and Honey seems the only lucky one here.

But then I forget that I am lucky too. I am here and bookshelves can wait, just as everything else can. How could I forget? People can't stay at one place. They want more and more until they have everything or lose everything.

Raimonda

OCTOBER 5

Hi, dear Kitty,

I was handing out fliers today for someone who was sick. I woke up at six in the morning, and Mama made a breakfast. When I waited outside, the streets of Bay Ridge were asleep. And it seemed it would never wake up. I worked all day and came back home at 3:30 P.M. I bought some food too, so we ate dinner and nuts that I bought and watermelon. I wanted to do something else today, but I chose to work even when I don't know on what to spend my money. And it would be impossible anyway because everything I do want costs millions! If I were a rich man . . .

Raimonda

OCTOBER 6

Hi, dear Kitty,

It's already two years we have been away from Russia. What has changed? I don't remember Russia anymore, just know that we lived there. But it seems too long ago. Emigration—I don't remember it anymore, not even when I feel like it. What was it all? A dream or truth? Or a trusting dream? I saw Vienna, great Rome, Florence, San Marino, tiny Ladispoli, God-sent Venice. It seems so wonderful now. Was I that blind, and it just seemed to me the wrong way and everything was really that beautiful? And to check it now, I have to awaken my memories, my thoughts, but I don't want to. I want them to sleep and even to die in me.

America itself has changed something in me. Now I want to go forward, to get to my goal. I am in a good mood and feel lucky, too. Lucky for everything, for my new friends and for my old friend, Lisa. And for chess, which I only started to play here.

My parents, they change every day. When Papa is published and has a job and gets money, they are happy. When he doesn't, they seem to get older, sadder. But what for? I know money means everything here. These green papers, how much meaning they have inside us! Simon needs money, too. He doesn't get lucky much. He can't find a good start. He struggles.

Two years have passed, and the grandparents aren't with us yet. And I wait. Two years have changed so much in our lives—country, language, mind, dreams. They have changed everything. Two years in America can change as much as ten do somewhere else.

Raimonda

OCTOBER 10

Hi, dear Kitty,

It's unbelievable that it's Thursday already, but I wait for Friday. Just like Mama waits for me to get rich. Everyone waits for something. I already have $140, but I don't spend it. I don't listen to music as much as I used to and don't watch movies as much.

Poor Simon is leaving New York University because he doesn't have money and will work for about a year. He says I have more money than him. He will have to owe $10,000 if he doesn't leave. That's why he's leaving.

Papa studies English again and is black from worrying because no one called from *The New York Times.* And he waits. He's afraid to have false teeth, even though he can't eat with his own anymore. Every time he comes to the hospital, some medicine or tool is missing or the doctor is too busy for the operation. Even his doctor says surprisingly that this is the most unlucky patient of his. Dad says yes, it is unlucky. But he is more than just a little happy inside.

OCTOBER 11

Hi, dear Kitty,

Simon left the university and lost $1,000 on all of it. I pity him. He got used to another life, much easier, too. But here you have to struggle for everything in order to become someone. Here you have to fight to get higher. There's no ending to poverty, nor to wealth. We live and sadly laugh when one of us says, "When we are rich . . . " And knowing that money isn't happiness, we still think of money as happiness, as happiness to buy something, to walk easily into the restaurant and easily leave a tip and easily ask in English without Russian accents.

"Will we ever be able to become like this?" I remember how sure we were to find everything free here and rich, too. Clothing which was still good we left in Italy, and Mama left her new coat in the American airport. We waited for more. We all were naive children, believing in a kingdom. Now we know America, at least most of it. Maybe it's a kingdom where dreams come true, but only if you yourself fight for it. I loved this country when I first saw it from the airplane window—a big village. And now I don't want to go anywhere else.

Raimonda

P.S. Today I finished my second diary, the beginning of American life. I don't remember what has happened during this year and six months, but maybe much has changed. There are five of us now. Honey is our new member of the family. I don't want to remember what has happened because all of it is a part of our lives. My grandparents are still there, and I was sure I would have seen them by now. It has been already two years that I wait.

We haven't changed much. We are just the same crazy, talented family of unemployed people. However, Simon has started to work already. Today, Papa got a picture to do for *The New York Times,* the first one this month.

That's all. I finish my second diary and now I am thinking of the future. "Will we ever become Americans?"

Streets, avenues—places
black, white—gentlemen
poor, rich—people
sad, cheerful—fates
joy, grief—day
laugh, cry—life
rude, kind—I
joyous, tender—my dream

CHAPTER FOUR

BECOMING AMERICAN

OCTOBER 13, 1991, TO JUNE 7, 1992

"I DON'T KNOW WHAT SONG TO SING"

As Raimonda's homesickness lapsed, she felt more comfortable in loosening her grasp on old ways. Significantly, as she accepted her new life, she started writing her diary in English. And though she had a scholarly command of her new language, the English she used in her diary was not by the textbook: She was being folded into the typical urban diversity of her inner-city high school, Fort Hamilton, and her experience there was reflected in her slang-filled vocabulary and in her spontaneous references to pop culture. She even began referring in the diary to her parents as "Mom" and "Dad," though she still called them "Mama" and "Papa" when speaking to them. Raimonda still wasn't sure if she was a Russian girl or an American one. But she had an adventurous approach to her adopted culture.

Her newfound security coincided with a change in the family's fortunes. For a time, Igor maintained a job designing earrings for a Brooklyn factory owner; in addition, his freelance career was booming. Simon, having given up college again (until the fall of 1992), was working steadily at the music store and having a relationship with the young Japanese student, Yoko, who stayed with the family during vacations from her college in Pennsylvania. Klavdia, though still not earning an income, was going in every day to an Italian-American real estate office. There, she was learning to understand New York's quirky dealmaking, with the promise of a commission when she sold a property (which she finally did, much later, in November 1992). Raimonda lifted everybody's spirits when they received word that her diary would be published. Such good fortune buoyed them, but also made them restless. Prosperity seemed tantalizingly close, close enough to indulge some fantasizing, but too far away to make any lasting change. The Kopelnitskys said over and over again how slippery it all felt. And it *was* slippery, compared to their old life in the Soviet Union, where the one thing that had always seemed certain was the future. There, no one had much reason to worry about performing well to keep a job or making a lot of money that couldn't buy much anyway.

But even that Soviet stasis had by now proven to be an illusion. The Soviet Union was dissolving, and by 1992 would not exist at all. This was disconcerting for the family: What they had fled from no longer exerted any power, while the place they had come to did not always seem a pleasant escape. Instead of being secure in the rightness of their decision to emigrate, they now had to question it. Might they have been better off in a culture where at least they comprehended the choices and the consequences? Still, they persisted in believing that the anti-Semitism would erupt more virulently now in the Ukraine. Their parents complained of miserable conditions and sent letters full of longing for reunion in the United States.

For Raimonda, the sense of upheaval was compounded by events at school. School had always been a welcome escape from the emotionally overwrought confines of the tiny apartment. She relished her time with the other newly arrived students, but her academic excellence was propelling her beyond them and into the roiling mainstream of big-city education. There, she began to profoundly question her identity. She worried about her accent, which distinguished her from the American teenagers who baffled her with their cocksure attitude. She looked for deeper meaning. She looked to religion. If she had come here because of being Jewish, why did she not feel a religious fervor, some evolution of the spark ignited during her stay in Italy? She began to believe that her spiritually bereft upbringing in an atheistic society had stymied her soul: How could she ever be a Jew?

OCTOBER 13, 1991

Hi, dear Kitty,

Today I'm starting my new diary. It's a third one now. I can imagine how many mistakes I'm going or I already made, but I'll continue writing, as I promised, in this terrible and difficult language.

I got this notebook as a present from Audrey. It's about a year since we first wrote to each other, after she read about me in *The Village Voice*. And she is coming to New York on November 23, so I'll see her soon. She read about us in the newspaper. That's how we started our friendship, even though she lives in Florida.

Today was a great day. I played tennis with my new friend, Luba, a Russian from Odessa. She's sixteen. And she jokes a lot; even by her jokes you can tell she's from Odessa. She comes from an intelligent family. There are two groups of Russians at Fort Hamilton. One group doesn't talk to another. They are too different to be friends. I got to know Luba and her group because they shared their lunch with me before I had lunch tickets. Twice we went to the movies together. Once we rented a movie. Luba is really nice. She has a big cat, and she told me that Honey is a boy, not a girl. I am glad, because a cat-boy is usually cuter and bigger than a girl.

Simon is working now. And I'm sorry for him. He has no money, and because of that he doesn't go to NYU anymore. He has a lot of problems in America. He is probably too young and too old for this country.

My dad drew a picture for *The New York Times* today. It's about Russia again.

We are going to watch a movie now, *Oscar*. It must be funny.

Honey is jumping all over me. No surprise—it's a boy.

Talk to you soon.

> Love,
> Raimonda

OCTOBER 14

Hi, dear Kitty,

Today was Columbus Day. He discovered this country, where I live now.

I hoped my grandparents would come soon, but I guess it'll take one more year. I really miss them, but I can't write letters to them very often. I hate to write letters. Some people think that I have to love it because I am a "writer."

My father is my editor, who gives me a name for a story (any name he likes) and then I write a story about it. This way I get a lot of stories, and also he gives me a paper, like a real check. He promised to give me a real money, after publishing my stories. It's a wonderful game, and a wonderful dream.

I promised to write a letter to my grandparents.

Goodnight,
Love, Raimonda

OCTOBER 16

Hi, dear Kitty,

I spent a lot of time doing my homework. I got a 91 on my Spanish test, but I was sure just yesterday that I was going to get a zero. Well, I didn't.

I saw a horror movie and then the news. I like to see horror movies because they aren't as terrible and crazy as news from New York.

Goodnight, Kitty.

Raimonda

OCTOBER 17

Hi, dear Kitty,

I did my homework. I have four tests tomorrow. I have more than one test every single day. I'm getting crazy. I'm not used to it. My grades are from 85 to 95. It's fine.

Simon and I watched *Friday the 13th*. I like it. I really like an American horror movie. It makes me brave.

Dad and Mom are translating the article for *The New York Times*. Dad's picture is due tomorrow. Simon starts working full time again at the music store because he doesn't go to NYU anymore.

My music system isn't working well. Well, it cost just $100. I'm angry about it.

Uncle Paul and Tanya are coming tonight.

I got a letter from Anna today. I wish I could visit Israel as soon as possible. Thank God tomorrow is Friday. I'm tired already.

See you.

Yours,
Raimonda

P.S. My music system is working now, and it did before. I just forgot to turn the sound on! Sorry for my complaining.

OCTOBER 21

Hi, dear Kitty,

Today is Monday. I felt sleepy and cold the whole day. I don't really have time for adventures. Books are the only things that keep me in an adventurous world.

Goodnight, Kitty.

Love,
Raimonda

OCTOBER 27

Hi, dear Kitty,

This weekend, I simply stayed at home and watched my favorite movie, *Jane Eyre*. I can't believe I've found it in America. I saw the same movie in Russia. I love it. Yesterday, we saw a movie, *Green Card*. We loved it.

Love,
Raimonda

OCTOBER 29

Hi, dear Kitty,

We all live and all die. We often get sick and often feel healthy. We don't care or don't feel much pain reading sad books. But we always care and we are scared when we know that someone is in pain, someone who is close to us.

Yes, these two hard years passed already. They flew away, like wild birds do. But sometimes they leave some black feathers on the ground.

The day when we got an agreement to come here, we were scared and nervous. The day when we left our parents, our grandparents, we couldn't stop crying. Yes, we were screaming at each other, and even hated each other when the days were dark and nervous in Vienna or Italy. But still somewhere inside we were close. And we loved each other, as we do now. Emigration has its dark, black feathers. Myself, I became much older in my soul. I feel like I lost the peace of funny and gay days of childhood. I can see what is sad now. My parents, they became nervous, and older—at least they seem so to themselves.

Yesterday, my mother was crying because a doctor told her to take some tests, which means the doctor felt a sickness inside my mother. So my mother is making me angry and nervous by telling me every minute that she is dying.

Today, my father feels really bad too. He fears that it's a heart attack. I can't stand it. I am trying to eat, to read. I want to keep my mind off it. Oh! Yes, sometimes I wish to travel, to be somebody else, I wish. But my mind is here with my parents. I don't want to leave them. Never! I know that they'll be all right. Well, not as young, but young to me.

It was a quiet but nervous day. And I wish to forget it. Even Honey is quiet. I hope, I hope, I hope . . . I guess I have too many wishes. But maybe one of them'll come true. Who knows!

Love,
Raimonda

NOVEMBER 2, 1991

Hi, dear Kitty,

It's twelve o'clock at midnight, and I'm still awake. Pavlik and Tanya came. We ate Chinese food. And Pavlik went to see a movie with my parents. Tanya is asleep. I just wrote a letter to my grandparents. We called them this morning. Thank God, everything is all right. Oh! I miss them so much.

Poor Honey stays in this room the whole evening because Charlik the dog is here. Honey is so sweet and soft today, that's because he's scared of the dog.

I am so tired and so sleepy.

I'll go to sleep now.

I'm probably wrong because I started to write in English. I can imagine my mistakes! I could make them in this sentence also. But who knows. I can't check it!

Goodnight, Kitty.

I love you,
Raimonda

NOVEMBER 4

Hi, dear Kitty,

I'll continue writing in English. First, it's good because it improves my English. Second, it has to be my native language. Third,

I don't care much about mistakes because I made a lot of them in my old Russian diaries too. So I am going to continue writing this way.

Today is Monday. And I hate Mondays because it's the first day of the week. Mom is asleep, and she worries a lot about her medical analysis tomorrow. Dad is writing something again. My unknown genius. He knows as much about religion as only a rabbi can. He knows a lot about books and etc. He is unknown because there are a lot of genius people in New York. I saw a lot of great musicians eating from the garbage cans and so on. But Papa doesn't need to be known. He loves to know something, to study just for himself, sitting by his table.

This is probably strange, but I don't miss my Motherland and if my grandparents weren't there, I would lose all connections between me and that country. I don't know why, but I am already living here with all my mind. I know that I am not an American yet, but I'm not from Russia also. I don't remember anything good or bad, I don't really remember my childhood or my friends. I simply forgot and don't have time to remember again, to miss it again. Is it good or bad? I don't know. It's not my fault, it's life.

Maybe I'll be just like my dad is. My story, my hope and my dream will stay in me and live only for me.

Oh, I don't want to be selfish!

I love you.

Your unknown and unfamous young dreamer says goodnight!

Raimonda Kopelnitsky

NOVEMBER 9

Hi, dear Kitty!

I had a bad day and a bad mood.

My dad pointed a knife at me. He was playing. I wasn't scared, but I didn't like it.

Eating our supper we were talking about old days in Russia, about our adventures and so on. We all remembered some bad days. So after all we were laughing at each other. Simon and Dad told me that I am ugly. So what! I don't care! I know that. But they didn't have to tell me that.

I don't feel well.

Goodnight, Kitty.

Raimonda

Oh! Audrey called and she is coming on November 23 at 2:00 P.M. I am so glad to see her!!

NOVEMBER 12

Hi, dear Kitty!

Honey is so kind today. That's because he doesn't feel good.

I was arguing with Mommy today. And it was a silly thing to do. So I cried and then we kissed each other as a sign of forgiveness.

Simon had a day off. He went to the Brooklyn library because he wanted to take some books, but only in the library he remembered that he forgot a library card. Then, he wanted to go somewhere else, but he forgot something else again. So he returned at home and listened to the music for the whole day. He smokes again.

Daddy had some problems too. He went to the hospital for students where they make teeth for free or something like that. So they almost cut his mouth and burned it too. I don't go to school tomorrow. I'll go to Manhattan to get a green card because mine got lost. I have to reapply.

Yes, and I won't have a job on Saturdays. Oh, I am tired and sleepy. Well, do you like my day? I almost hate it.

'Bye.

NOVEMBER 13

Hi, dear Kitty!

First, about the job. I can't work anymore on Saturdays and neither can others because we don't have a job any more. I was only a replacement for some boys. They fought with each other and worked slowly. So the boss refused to give them a job because he probably thought that they weren't working hard. Well, it's not my problem. I don't need money this minute, and it was a difficult job. But I can at least try to find something else on summer vacation.

Yes, at 11:00 A.M. Dad and I went to Manhattan. So I woke up at eight in the morning. We waited at the City Hall from eleven till three o'clock for my green card.

Yoko is probably arriving soon. I think she'll come on Thanksgiving. She'll stay for several days. I'm glad: Simon was working, and I spent an hour and a half in his store doing nothing because I was waiting for him to take me home. I was doing nothing because I love music, but I don't know any groups or any names. At six-thirty, we went home. We had dinner and watched TV. Mom and

Dad are in Manhattan with Pavlik at a concert. They'll probably be back at twelve. We are listening to Frank Zappa. He is really funny.

Well, I guess that's it for today.

Goodnight, Kitty.

Raimonda

P.S. I forgot to tell you that my real name was supposed to be Raymonda, but Dad made a mistake in the airport in Italy. So I can't change it because on my green card and other documents it's written Raimonda.

Well, I don't care.

This language ruined my real name. I mean my dad did.

Still yours,
Raimonda

NOVEMBER 15

Hi, dear Kitty,

I couldn't write to you yesterday. I was busy and tired.

Yesterday at 2:45 I came home from school. I washed and then I dressed up. I wore white shirt, skirt, black tights, red shoes. At 3:00 P.M., Andrew came and we went to Manhattan. We met Kelli standing next to a huge and old building. It wasn't a skyscraper, but a huge building. I asked Kelli if she was nervous, but she said no. Then, she asked me and I said no. Was it true? I'm not sure. We went together upstairs, but Andrew left.

We met our agent, Daniel Strone, in the hall where we sat on the soft, deep armchairs. I was nervous inside and couldn't look around as I always do, but I did look at Strone and Kelli. Strone was really nervous. He was standing and jumping a little. He had nothing to talk about. He kept silence for five minutes, then suddenly said, "I am glad that it's not raining today." I was about to laugh, but of course I couldn't. But it was really funny the way he said it after thinking for so long what to say. But Kelli didn't lose control. She said something about rain and asked him some simple questions. Then they talked to me about school and so on.

Several minutes later a big and strong woman came. She is a publisher. She said Hello and asked us to follow her. We also put our coats in the closet. We came in the room and met another publisher.

It was a man this time. He smiled a lot and said that he was glad to meet me. We sat around talking to each other. Actually they asked me questions and smiled at me. I was answering and at the same time smiling at them. I was strong inside. I felt all my nerves staying together, like they were afraid to leave me. My smile was afraid to go away from my face and stayed there for the whole hour. So they asked me questions and every question meant something.

At last we said goodbye and we went back to the hall and took our coats. My coat looked childish, dirty and poor, when other coats looked clean, big and expensive. Now I had a chance to look around. The publisher gave to Kelli and me a Disney book. It's really a beautiful book. It's written about how they made a movie, *Beauty and the Beast*. Through the glass, I saw Mickey Mouse toys, watches and so on. Then we said goodbye to the woman and went downstairs. Strone wished us good luck and left. And suddenly my smile left me, and my nerves crushed and left each other alone. I was free, but nervous and very tired this time. And Kelli was too. I spoke with her about the meeting. We talked over several questions because I wasn't sure if I answered them right. But I did answer them right. I was glad. And Kelli was very excited about it. We told the whole story to my parents. We had a dinner with Kelli and Andrew. Then they left.

In the evening, Paul and Tanya came. We ate Russian food. Simon wasn't home. He slept at his friend's house. I don't know when Paul and Tanya left because I was asleep. It was a serious day for me. I met publishers and I talked to a businessman. They don't give an answer Yes or No, whether they are going or not to buy the book, which would be a book of my diaries. But they'll say it probably on Monday.

Good Luck!

p.s. On Saturday, I was home doing my homework. We saw a movie, *Godfather III*. I loved it. I was crying.

Today is Sunday. And I don't have any plans. 'Bye for now.

Love,
Raimonda

NOVEMBER 18

Hi, dear Kitty!!
And as I said, "Good Luck!" Good luck came.

Kelli called us about three hours ago. Her voice sounded very excited. She asked me as usual how is everything, and I hurriedly answered. "Do you have any good news?" I asked. Yes, she did. The publishers agreed to buy the book; they'll pay us. I am so happy, not just because of money. Of course money is a very important thing in this country; still, it won't be enough to buy an apartment. But it came from the air, right from the sky into our empty hands. My dad had to work for ten years to get that much. But the most important thing is that I'll have a book. A book about me. My name will be written on it. I remember when I first read *A Diary of Anne Frank*.

A Diary of Raimonda Kopelnitsky—it'll be published now. And my dad! He was the one who told me once, "You are going to publish this diary." And I was laughing at him. I still can't believe it. In 1993, I'll be able to touch my own book. In 1992, I'll be able to touch our money. You see something did happen. Something exciting and wonderful. My second dream came true.

I love you!

Raimonda

NOVEMBER 23

Hi, Kitty,

I didn't write to you for a long time.

Today, at two o'clock, Audrey came. I saw her for the first time, but she had sent me a picture before, when she had long hair. She has short hair now. She is really nice, and I was very glad to meet her. We had a dinner and talked. She presented us with a wonderful book called *America*. It shows the beautiful nature of America's cities. It's a huge book. About five o'clock, she left.

I wanted to wash my clothes, but I also wanted to go to the bathroom. And I couldn't, because the toilet didn't work very well. The water couldn't come through. But when I went to the bathroom, I thought that it was working again so I pushed the button, and suddenly water appeared from the toilet running on the floor. I got real scared so I called for Dad. But he was really crazy that moment because he had to draw a picture for *The New York Times*. He was very nervous. He appeared before me and screamed: "How many times did I have to tell you not to push the button?" He struck me in my face, especially in my nose so hard that I thought my face would explode from the pain. I started to cry, and only then he realized what he had done. So he asked me for forgiveness, but I was tired of it. I started to clean the floor, and Mom was just talking to me trying to make me feel better, but she didn't help me to wash the floor. I can't believe how lazy she is.

Well, anyway, then I forgave my dad. I remember when I was about four years old, I had a cold. And the doctor said that I had to keep my legs in warm water. So my dad prepared it for me. He simply poured hot, boiled water right on my legs. Of course, before that, I asked him to wait till it became cooler. Anyway he argued with me about one second, saying that hot water is better for my health. Well, of course he just burned my legs. I can remember me lying on the bed with my dad and mom and Simon all around me, fanning my legs. Dad was also asking me for forgiveness that time. And I forgave him. But somehow I still remember what had happened ten years ago. But I forgave him this time, and I hope I won't remember it when I am twenty-four.

At seven-thirty, I went to the dentist. We paid him $500, and we'll pay $1,000 after for the braces. Yes, it cost $1,500 for us. I am really glad that I am doing it. Beauty costs a lot, the dentist's wife said. And she sure was right.

Goodnight, Kitty.

Love,
Raimonda

NOVEMBER 28

Hi, dear Kitty,

I didn't write to you for several days, but there was nothing to write about. However, I had something to do. I was preparing for my huge tests. I had a test or two every single day. It's crazy. I didn't have enough time to sleep or rest. But at last the holidays came, and I am free for four days.

Today is Thanksgiving. We celebrated it yesterday with Pavlik and Tanya. They brought some Russian food and turkey. We were drinking and eating. Then Simon and Yoko came. Yoko arrived yesterday and she'll live with us till the holidays are over.

Today we are doing nothing. Everyone is resting. Simon is listening to the music, and Yoko is writing. We'll go to Manhattan tomorrow to buy Christmas presents. I feel like I am an American now. I celebrate American holidays. I'll buy presents on Friday, as all

Americans do. Oh, yes, I know it's a shopping day when you spend a lot of money for nothing, but still it is fun. "Fun!" I remember I hated this word. I couldn't understand people who were saying, "It's fun," but now I am saying it myself.

Yesterday Chung Won called. His name is Eddie now. He is my friend from McKinley who used to study with me. He's Korean, and I am sure he's a genius. He wrote me a letter, and I answered. He told me on the phone that he wrote to others too (from my class) but they didn't answer.

I have a bad news too. Our grandparents won't come in the summer as I thought. It'll probably take longer. I miss them, but I can't wait for so long. It's crazy. Who would think that I won't see them for more than two years? You won't believe, but I am still glad that they didn't come with us through the emigration. I guess I traveled a lot, but I want to travel again, not as an emigrant, but as an American . . .

Love,
Raimonda

P.S. I continue my writing to you today and it's something new. You know that when Pavlik and Tanya come, I say we are drinking and eating. It's true that we are eating, and the adults are drinking vodka and so on. Well, of course, I am just eating and drinking soda. My mom can't drink at all, she just touches a glass of vodka with her lips. My dad is drinking, but he never gets drunk because he doesn't drink a lot, but in the morning he has a terrible headache. Simon doesn't drink at all.

Raimonda

P.S. There is something else I have to tell you. You know that my book will be published. The publishers were talking to me, some other people were talking to me, and they are all telling me the same. They say that after reading my diary, they feel how much my religion means to me, how much I wanted it and needed it, and now I can be free to learn, to go to the synagogue. They say that they celebrated Jewish holidays, they had a bar mitzvah. That is how much their religion means to them. But that is not as much as for me, they say.

Oh, they are mistaken. They are very mistaken. I was brought up as a Russian girl, who knew and felt every time and everywhere that she was a Jew, but still she lived in Russian style, in Russian life. Yes, she knew that there was a synagogue in her town. It was a small, stone building that was just a mystery to her with no people in it, and no people close to it. And only once she came in, only once when it was a free thing to do, she saw Jewish people around her, and then she went inside the synagogue and she saw people, old people dressed in black praying there. She touched a Bible and quickly closed it, because she couldn't understand its language. She went outside loving everyone and everything around her, still looking at the synagogue—small, stone building that was open now, but still a mystery for her. Maybe inside it she felt heaven and God above everybody, but when she saw people dressed in black she felt their sadness, their pain. They were praying. They were saying something, but what? Maybe they were calling for death.

Now I am here. I don't feel anybody hating me. I don't feel anybody reminding me that I am a Jew. Do I remind myself? Do I go to the synagogue? Maybe once in a year, not to pray like the others do, not to sing like the others do. I don't know how to pray. I don't know what song to sing. I pray my way. I believe inside myself.

And I don't like this American synagogue that is always free and open to me. I don't believe in it. But I believe in the synagogue of my childhood, full of mystery, always closed for me. I believe in the old people who were praying there, dressed in black. I believe in that Bible that I quickly closed. I still feel their mystery, their voice, their trembling fingers praying and calling for death.

Raimonda

DECEMBER 2, 1991

Hi, dear Kitty,

I have two girlfriends. I guess I can call them mine now. I know a lot of Russians there at Fort Hamilton High School and a few Americans.

Today, actors from Broadway shows talked to us. They are playing in *Les Misérables* and *Cats*. They also sang three beautiful songs from the shows. They answered some questions. They get $1,200 a week. They have great voices, and I really want to see their shows. I can get a ticket for $16 if I have an I.D. card, and I have it.

P.S. I just stopped talking to my parents. Whenever they are arguing, I always know that I'm gonna be the one who will get in trouble. I'm the one who'll have to say "Sorry" and so on. I don't even have to cry, scream, laugh, or stop myself from doing it. It's already written on my hand or whatever that I'll get in trouble. This is crazy! I fear that we have to leave this crazy house in order to rest from each other before it's too late.

I don't know what to do now.

Should I ask for forgiveness as I always do? But I don't feel sorry, and what for? I don't even know what I've done. Dad is working today. He has to draw three pictures.

Well, let me make a pitiful face in order to get forgiveness. Only then, I'll go to sleep to dream. I hope they won't make me angry.

I am glad that no one is reading this, because they'll probably think that I am a crazy person.

Well, at least Honey is still normal.

> Goodnight,
> Raimonda

DECEMBER 7

Hi, dear Kitty!

I was trying to write with my gold pen today because Dad bought a black ink refill for it. But it doesn't write as well as it used to. Well, everything has its own time.

Honey is growing like an American vegetable. He gets bigger and bigger every day.

Yesterday, I watched *Mermaids* with my girlfriends Luba and Tanya. We had fun.

Today we are leaving at two o'clock for an exhibition where my father's and other Russian artists' paintings will probably be sold. Pavlik and Tanya are coming, too, but later. Tomorrow Kelli and Andrew are coming. We want to buy a green tree and we'll buy it. I can't believe it's finally the weekend. In ten days we have Christmas vacation. I'll be free for eleven days. Yoko is also coming on Christmas vacation.

> Love,
> Raimonda

DECEMBER II

Hi, dear Kitty,

I'm already in bed. I am tired and sleepy. I have tests every day, so I have to study. I like my school because I laugh there a lot. My girlfriends like to joke, so we joke as much as we can and we can't stop laughing.

My father just came back from *The New York Times*. He gave them a picture and he got another assignment to do. He also talked to other Russian people who told him that the Bay Ridge mafia is versus the Bensonhurst mafia. So it's dangerous. One boy was killed in the store by them accidentally.

What does Dad want me to do about it? Take my stuff and run away? It's New York City. What do you want? I don't have to watch any movies, everything happens on the streets anyway. I don't make a big deal of it. Still, I hope I won't have nightmares tonight. Even if it's gonna be about the mafia, I'll definitely win because it's my dream and my power to become anyone or anything I want. I can even stop dreaming.

Goodnight, Kitty.

Raimonda

DECEMBER I4

At last it's Saturday! But anyway I went to sleep at twelve last night and I woke up at eight-thirty today, because I couldn't sleep any longer. Yesterday I was so tired from school, but I had to clean the whole apartment. It was crazy. Everyone stays away from doing it, so the whole apartment was a mess. And I had to clean it. Me and me again. I was so angry. Then my mother came, and pretended to be tired from work at the real estate office. Well, I know that she just sits there and does nothing the whole day. When I finished cleaning I thought I'd die.

Then Andrew and Kelli came, and they brought a Christmas tree. It's much smaller than the tree last year. But I'm starting to like it. We talked and so on till twelve. When they left, I just went to sleep. I was tired as only I could be. In the morning I woke up feeling real bad and sick. I'm coughing now. Probably I caught a cold because the window was open. It's three-thirty now, and I can't do anything. Actually, I just finished doing a project for history, but I had been doing it since twelve. Honey's sleeping next to me. He likes the green tree more than anybody else in this family. He climbed on it and over it, he slept and jumped on it. Now, I am sure he's still a wild animal. He sleeps and eats and bites a lot. But when he sleeps he looks so cute and soft. My grandparents are going to be seventy-eight on December 31. God, time passes so quickly. Will it ever wait?

My mother is coming back from work. I am sleepy and weak. I probably waited for Saturday too long. Anyway, I am waiting for Christmas vacations now, so I'll be able to stay at home for eleven days. I love it.

Yes, I got a report card. My average is 90.73.

Yoko is arriving soon. And our relatives are coming, only two of them, Sasha and Stas. I have no idea where we are all gonna live. That's not my problem anyway.

Love,
Raimonda

December 17

Hi, dear Kitty,

And here I am, lying on this bed sick and tired when it's Tuesday, and I am not at school already two days. I got sick three days ago. Poor Daddy takes care of me. My mom went to work and swam in the pool when I had a very high temperature, 105. But when she came back, she got sick too. I take some pills and drink water or juice.

I am just home from the doctor's office. It's right in my building. They made an X-ray. Everything is all right. I don't have a pneumonia.

I'm not eating anything. It's already two days. I hope that someone will make something tasty and hot and soft. Daddy is getting sick too. It's a flu. I have a feeling we all are gonna die and no one will come to the funeral!

P.S. It's a day later. Simon is also sick. I guess we are all suffering from the flu. I still have a temperature, but not so high. Mom feels better. Dad is sleeping and he has a terrible headache. Simon is lying on the bed with 105 temperature.

The apartment is so dirty. Everything is on the floor. I don't care.

P.S. Day later, Thursday.

I'll be able to go to school tomorrow. I hope I didn't miss a lot. I'm not nervous, but happy this time to leave this house full of sick people!

P.S. I'm just home from school. It's Friday! And Christmas vacation began. I'm free for eleven days. In school we just talked and laughed and ate cookies. The teachers were so kind and lazy today.

Love,
Raimonda

DECEMBER 21

Hi, dear Kitty!

It's warm and clean. Everyone is up, the flu is over. Simon goes to work. I am doing nothing the whole day, but I'm pretty hungry and Mom doesn't care about it! I'll write to you later!

Raimonda

I'm still hungry, but Simon and Yoko are out for some food, so they'll bring me some. Yoko came just an hour ago. I hope I'll go ice skating with her tomorrow.

P.S. I wrote letters today, and we sent them. But I'll have to write to somebody else tomorrow. It's amazing that I know so many people. But only Christmas and New Year remind me about them!

Love,
Raimonda

P.S. Honey's sleeping, but I don't want to sleep. It's going to be 1992 so soon. God, time passes so quickly. So many things changed and some stayed. And I changed. I don't remember my emigration life and never remind myself of it. I also forgot about Venice and never talk about it as I used to. I don't dream about my hometown and I'm not homesick anymore. What am I? Russian, I answer. But I don't live in Russia, I don't feel like Russian. I just have a piece of sad and happy memories of my childhood somewhere inside of me. But I'm afraid to touch those memories, I'm afraid to awaken them, let them live in me. Why?

Maybe I don't want them anymore. Maybe it was just a dream, a history lesson, a favorite book. Oh, it couldn't be me. I don't feel myself in there. What am I? I can't answer that I am an American, because I am not. First, you can see my English, English as a second language. Second, there are so many differences: The way I speak, I live. At last, what am I? Who am I? Am I still an immigrant? I know I've changed, but I still don't know who I've become.

I'll wait till 1992. Maybe it will bring an answer.

Love,
Raimonda

DECEMBER 25

Hi, dear Kitty!

It's Christmas, but we don't celebrate Christmas. However, I want to. I want presents and Christmas dinner and everything. Of course, I'm gonna have all of these on New Year. But I still feel sad.

I miss my grandparents very much. Maybe it's because of the holidays—Grandma Sofa and Grandpa have their birthdays today. Maybe it's because nobody cares about me, because Dad has a picture to do for *The New York Times* and Mom is asleep and Simon is listening to the music with Yoko. And me? I can't do anything. I feel so lonely and sad. No one cares about me. I have a vacation, so I have to enjoy it. But how? I don't even have friends to play with. Yes, to play. I don't want to grow up, I don't want it. I want to play in the yard like me and my friends used to do. Oh, yes, we had fun. We had snow and we could skate right on the street. But not anymore.

I am angry, too. I broke up with Simon because I said something bad and he heard it. Well, so what.

Yesterday, Pavlik, Tanya, and Lesha came. We had fun at first. They brought food and vodka and other alcoholic stuff. Lesha gave me some chocolate candies and marmalade. Pavlik gave me $20. They talked and laughed. Then Pavlik and Dad went with Lesha to his home, I mean in the car because they were afraid he was too drunk. And he sure was!

Tanya talked about my poems. She said she loved them, but she also said that they remind her of Anna Akhmatova's poems. And she also read me some Akhmatova poems, which I think are very beautiful. (I don't think I know a good American word to describe the beauty and sadness of her poems.) But to come back, I write my own poems with my own style, and Simon can prove that I never copy from Akhmatova because it's impossible and because I didn't really read a lot of her poems. (It's a secret.)

Talking about poems, I think Pushkin is the best writer, unrepeatable and unforgettable. I wish I could write as he did. But he was a genius. And I am not!

Anyway, Pavlik and Tanya left the next morning at seven o'clock. Simon and Yoko went to Atlantic City with Sasha and Stas and their friends that day. They came back at seven o'clock, the same morning Pavlik and Tanya left.

Simon and Yoko spent $10 on gambling. They didn't stay in a hotel because it cost too much. So they drove back from Atlantic City the same evening. It took them about five hours in Sasha's friends' car.

I don't remember if I told you but I'll tell you now. Sasha and Stas came from Colorado. So we'll see them soon. I mean we saw them already but for only a little time. They just picked up Simon and Yoko and left.

God, now I want to grow up!

I feel left out again!

Why am I only fourteen? I remember dreaming to become fourteen when I was nine years old. I don't think I know what I really want!! I want something, that's for sure!

Goodnight!

Raimonda

DECEMBER 26

Hi, dear Kitty!

We had a good time. Me, Mom, Simon, and Yoko met Sasha and Stas today.

We went to the Metropolitan Museum, and because today is Thursday, we spent 25 cents for five tickets. Can you imagine? I guess only we could do that. I already saw this exhibition before, but it's still interesting. We took some pictures there.

Stas couldn't go with us because he couldn't park his car so he just waited for us in his car till seven. At seven, we picked up Simon.

We also watched a film—"Sasha and Stas's Wedding." They made this film in Russia. So we watched our relatives. I remember them from my early childhood in Odessa.

That's it for today!

Love,
Raimonda

DECEMBER 27

Hi, dear Kitty!

Sasha and Stas left to drive back to Colorado.

Simon brought home some stuff from Blake, who worked at the music store. Blake left to another city for good. He couldn't make it in New York!

Today was a special day in our family. We bought pizza pie and we ate it all. It was a special day because it was our *first pizza* in America. I mean the whole pie. I know that there's nothing special about it, but we felt good like when something good happens in the Bundy family in *Married with Children* on Channel 9 at 7:30.

'Bye,
Raimonda

DECEMBER 28

Hi, dear Kitty!

I had a great time today. Me and Yoko went ice skating today in the Central Park. We had so much fun! We would have had to stay about two hours in the line, but we cut in line and waited only thirty minutes. I know it's not nice. So what. We didn't waste any time on waiting. Some Americans were angry at us when we were buying tickets, but I saw them cutting the line to rent skates later. Nobody is perfect! They didn't have to argue, it's not a line for food in Moscow. Well, forget it.

We had so much fun. We skated, but Yoko skated only one time in her life, fourteen years ago. So it was difficult for her, but then she did a little better. But I couldn't skate with her because she was going too slowly. Anyway, I helped her some. I got so tired. I didn't fall on the ice once, but when we walked with our shoes on to pick up Simon, I fell down on the ground. It was funny. Now my legs hurt.

Goodnight, Kitty!

Love,
Raimonda

P.S. I guess I feel much better than I did before. And I decided to enjoy my fourteenth year. I guess I want to be sixteen now, but time passes so quickly. I don't want to neglect these years.

Love,
Raimonda

DECEMBER 29

Hi, dear Kitty,

I didn't write to you about the Soviet Union. But there is no more U.S.S.R. I am surprised to say it myself. But somehow it's true. Gorbachev is no longer a Soviet president. He finished his job smiling. I don't know why he was smiling, but he seemed happier being unemployed. After all, I think he did a lot for the Soviet Union. (I don't know about "for" the Soviet Union, but "in" the Soviet Union for sure.) First, he started Perestroika and Demokratia (I don't know how to spell that, sorry). Second, he let Jews go in 1989 (as you already know, we left too). Yeltsin is the Soviet president now. The Soviet Union is broken up into republics now. Some republics want their own army, and I think it's a beginning of the war in Russia. I mean, it's a first step to begin a war. And I'm afraid of that. Everything repeats, just like seventy years ago, it's the same record, over and over again.

I just wish my grandparents could come as soon as possible.

Dad is listening to the "News in Russia."

The New York Times Magazine published a photo where Gorbachev was closing the door after himself, and only his back and bald head were seen in the door.

'Bye,
Raimonda

P.S. I don't have time to tell you a long story now. But it's about my father's friend who went to Germany to meet his family. He says it's impossible to live and even rest in Germany because they hate Americans and Russians and Jews and they aren't afraid to show it and you can feel Fascism everywhere, in every German city.

It's awful, but I'm sure it's true.

We felt it in Vienna. I hope they won't start the war again.

P.S. Yoko and I will study tomorrow in the library the whole day. And my parents are leaving for Brighton Beach to buy food for New Year's. Simon is working tomorrow. I am so tired and sleepy.

Love,
Raimonda

DECEMBER 30

Hi, dear Kitty!

We had a great time this evening.

Yoko has a video camera. (Her grandfather gave it to her.) So we taped each other today. And then we watched a movie starring us, and it was really funny because Dad looked really crazy, Mom's teasingness is shining through. Simon said that he looks like an idiot (I do not think so). I think I looked ugly (but they don't agree). Yoko looked good, and Honey was wonderful. After all, it's just a crazy family. That's why it's funny. We laughed at ourselves.

P.S. Yoko and me studied from twelve till four-thirty in the library today, but we did very little because we felt tired and sleepy, so I'll have to study again tomorrow.

As you know, tomorrow is a very important and happy day, and it's a New Year. I can't believe it's gonna be 1992. I'm sorry that my grandparents won't be able to be with us this year. I remember writing the same phrase in my first diary in Italy, in Russian. I hope I won't have to write the same in 1993, and I'm sure I won't. Anyway, Dad and Mom went to Brighton Beach today and they bought a lot of delicious food (you know that I hate the word "delicious") for $110. That's a lot.

I have so many dreams and wishes for this new year.

My wishes are:

1. To pass all finals.
2. To get in regular English classes.
3. To see my grandparents.
4. To have my own room.
5. I hope Simon stops smoking.
6. I hope Dad won't be so nervous.
7. I hope Mom won't tease so much.
8. I hope we won't get sick.

9. I want to be able to write to you without making mistakes (you know what I mean).

I guess that's enough for one year. Oh . . .

10. I wish all my wishes to come true.
11. I wish to publish my Diary.

Well, that's enough.

> Love, still dreaming Raimonda
> Happy New Year 1992, Kitty!

DECEMBER 31

Dear Kitty!!!

Happy New Year!

We set up a table with (Russian) food. It sure looks beautiful. We are waiting for Simon and Yoko because they went into Manhattan to buy New Year presents. I already know what they'll get me, and I hope they'll find it. I want a book by Alexandre Dumas called *The Count of Monte Cristo.* And a watch.

I'll be back! (Hopefully tomorrow.) Yes, I also talked on the phone with Tova, Dov, and their family.

I feel great and happy.

I think I forgot how to write in English.

So, talk to you later.

> Happy New Year!
> Love, Raimonda

JANUARY 1, 1992

Hi, dear Kitty!

Just look at that date! I like it, and I don't like it at the same time—because my vacations are over. I can't believe that I'll have to wake up at seven and go to school tomorrow. All these days, I slept till twelve in the afternoon. And I ate so much that I hate food now.

Daddy is really crazy. He fights with everyone all the time. But he's better now. Simon works tomorrow. I'm gonna have tests and, in a week or two, "finals."

I got to bed yesterday at three-fifteen in the morning because Yoko and I were so full that we couldn't sleep. So we talked and laughed all night.

I'm going to bed now.
Happy New Year!

Love,
Raimonda

JANUARY 5

Hi, dear Kitty!

Tomorrow I go to school. My weekends are over. I was so busy that I didn't have time to rest. Yesterday Kelli came and we worked on the diary. She asked me questions about Russia, and I answered.

Once my teacher asked me a simple question, "Where are you from?" and I answered, "I am from the Soviet Union." But he told me that there is no more Soviet Union (and I for sure know that). Then he asked me the same question again, "Where are you from?" I couldn't answer. And at the same time I asked myself, where am I from?

There is another problem.

I'm often thinking about English and Russian languages. I talk English at school, and I talk Russian at home. In what language should I write a diary? I don't know which language is closer or better to me. Anyway, writing in English, I don't *feel* this language. I don't know if I write right or wrong. But pretty often I think I am wrong. I make mistakes and I hate to check them. However, English is a part of my life, the first way to become an American. It's a way to learn this language, to feel this life because it's an American life and nothing else. So should I write in my native language, which I can feel but not live in, or should I continue in the English language, which I don't feel and which I hardly know (compared with Americans) because this is a language of my new country, my new life which we chose and won't change? I know that I make mistakes (grammar and spelling and so on), but I make mistakes in Russian also. What should I do? I think I'll stay with English. And if I'm wrong, no one cares anyway because it's my diary and my decision.

P.S. I watched a Russian movie called *Mary Poppins*. As you know it's my favorite movie.

I have two tests tomorrow—Spanish and Science.

I have a problem at school. One stupid Russian girl who is fifteen years old copies every single history test from me and doesn't even read the assignment. Other Russians think I am so kind, so they just copy without asking or just ordering and I hate that. I become nervous and I make mistakes. Finals are coming. So I am gonna talk to that girl and there'll be no more copying. I mean, it's okay if you copy once, but then she became so rude she doesn't even study. She doesn't even open the questions. That's it. I am tired of being "kind and childish and small." I am in America, like my father says, and I am free from everybody. I am big and large and huge!

'Bye,
Raimonda

JANUARY 8

Hi, dear Kitty,
    I didn't go to school today because I had to go to the City Hall. They needed more pictures for my green card. I spent about an hour and a half waiting there with my mom. Why did they have to lose my green card? Why did they give my pictures back and ask me to make new ones so I couldn't go to school? God, people sure want to be in America, there was such a big crowd. Then, Mom and I walked in Manhattan. We had a great time. We came back at six and Simon waited for us on the street because he didn't have a key.
    Yoko left today to go to Pennsylvania.
    'Bye, goodnight, Kitty.

Raimonda

JANUARY 9

Hi, dear Kitty,
    I spoke to my great adviser today, and he changed my program card. In February I go to transition class, which means it's not ESL [English as a Second Language], but it's the last class before regular. So I skipped one class—ESL 8. Just listen to this, I'm going to have regular science and history! I'm so happy that I won't have to be in ESL anymore. They also changed my math to an Honor Class. I didn't want it because it's going to be difficult there, but what can I do? My teacher asked them to put me in Honor Class. I won't have English literature, but I will have Health Careers, and I wanted to have that class for a long time.
    My great adviser seemed nice to me. This is the first time I saw

him. He talked to me in a gentle way, but I was very surprised to hear it because all Russians say that he's bad and angry, that he doesn't like Russians. And I sure believed them, but not anymore.

Well, I think that's all about school, pretty good news. I can spoil it if I think about finals, but I won't.

Andrew came and he's talking with my parents now. Honey is so sweet. I love him. I just wrote a paragraph about you, Kitty. Our English teacher asked us to write a paragraph about one of these: 1) Something special from my childhood. 2) My special possession. 3) A special person.

And I chose Number Two and wrote a paragraph about you.

I'm very tired, but I have a good mood. And it's a rare thing.

Love you,
Raimonda

JANUARY 22

And finally, I am back!

Okay, first I know all my final grades. My grades are:

English—86
Spanish—94
English Lit—91
History—98
Science—87
Math—94

My finals are over! From January 24 until February 3, I have a vacation, and then I begin my new classes.

Okay, that's it about school.

Now, my family! Even my pen stopped writing when I started to write about my family. Whenever someone comes we look like a normal, happy family. But the "misery" is that this is definitely a crazy family. Nuts! They are all screaming and fighting because of money, because of food. And you know why? That's because everyone wants something. However, we don't have money for these "dreams." And we all have a lot of dreams because it's impossible not to have any in America! Dad says, "Oh, I read in the newspaper that it's so dangerous on the streets. I'm afraid for you. I don't want to let you walk alone to school. I'll walk with you, but as you know I can't wake up so early, so Mom will."

So I say, "Daddy, why don't you buy a car! I am tired of listening to those stories about NYC. Why don't we move?"

I memorized the answers: "I will buy a car someday, but we can't move because of my only job at *The New York Times*."

I know that! He repeats, telling me those "stories." But I don't need them. He thinks I am an "American." Why?

Yes, I want some things, but he wants too.

Then, Simon and "Them" (I mean my parents). Simon doesn't have enough money to live alone, and everyone knows that. I know we are tired of each other, and it's a big problem.

I am so nervous. I don't even write poems now. I am so tired of everything. God, where are my grandparents? I always could stay with them, but I need them *now*. I wonder what they are doing now. Where is my grandpa? My memories are dying, I don't remember all the things I used to, my room, my town.

> It's so far away.
> No people.
> No time
> No place to go
> No words to say goodbye
> Lonely wind will follow.
> Morning slowly passed by me
> Day and night are coming
> Can you feel the lonely wind
> Can you see me crying
> No sun and no sky
> No wings to fly
> No wind to save my dream
> Lonely will I cry
> —Raimonda

I just wrote it, but I can't check it. And I can't know if it is a poem! That's when I feel that it's not my native language. Anyway, it's my first English poem!

Love,
Raimonda

JANUARY 25

Hi, dear Kitty!

I feel so bad.

This house is a mess because we got furniture from the first floor where the Spanish people used to live. But they moved out. So I cleaned everything and Daddy did too. Except my lazy mom and Simon.

I don't talk to Simon anymore. I broke up with him. We curse each other and hate each other. I just wish I didn't have to stay in this room. I'm very tired, but I have a week to enjoy my vacation. I just have nothing to do with enjoying them. I'll probably stay at home cleaning or something like that while some lucky kids are skating on the snow somewhere far from N.Y.

I finished half a year of high school, and I think I did very well. I made good friends, but I'm not sure if I'll see them again next term because they are still in ESL.

I have a toothache, and I'm almost dying from it. I'm angry at Simon. I'm dying from toothache. I'm angry at my lazy mom. What else? Anyway, it's enough to stay in a bad mood.

'Bye,
Raimonda

JANUARY 30

Hi, dear Kitty!

Okay, my vacations are over.

I go to school tomorrow.

I spent these days cleaning, watching TV, sleeping, eating. I'm a fool! I didn't do anything to enjoy. No, I'm not a fool. It's my parents' fault. God, I didn't even read. Well, there's nothing I can do now. The phone is dead, and we don't know why. Dad called; they promised to come tomorrow.

Yes, I have braces on my top teeth, and I'll have them on the lower teeth the day after tomorrow. It hurts.

I'm sorry I didn't write for so long. It's because of these stupid holidays when you forget everything. I'm glad my English teacher can't see my writing 'cause I'm sure she'd be pretty sorry for putting 90 on my report card.

I can't believe I'll have to wake up with the alarm clock. I feel like tomorrow is another empty day when I'll sleep till noon.

'Bye,
Raimonda

JANUARY 31

Hi, dear Kitty!

And here I am, already in bed. Well, it's 11:30 P.M. anyway. I'm reading *The Three Musketeers*. Simon is listening to the "hard" music again, but finally with headphones. Dad is writing something in his notebook, probably thinking about ideas for the picture.

Poor Daddy got only one number right for the Lotto and nothing more. But he also lost one more dollar. He has spent about $30 on Lotto since he came to America. I played just once and lost. Every time he buys it, I tell him, "You'll lose. You have no luck." But he hopes, he buys, then he loses, then he understands and forgets and buys again. Well, "you never know."

Honey's sleeping on my bed as always. It's so hot in here, but terribly cold outside. You probably wonder why these days are so silly and empty. Well, we planned to go to skating in Central Park today, but Dad changed my mind when we were two steps from the subway. We didn't go because it was cold and Daddy is always nervous when it's cold and he makes me put on a hat (that makes me nuts). Then he cries because of the cold and it's not funny. So we just went back home. I watched a movie.

At 5:00 P.M., I went to my dentist. He finished my upper teeth and it didn't hurt when I came back. But it sure does now.

Daddy is so funny about the car. He wanted a big car, now he wants a small car. I certainly want a small car. I hate those tanks.

I am half asleep and my teeth are killing me.

'Bye

FEBRUARY 1, 1992

Hi, dear Kitty!

I am lying in bed and looking on the picture of my hometown on the wall. It's my favorite street. It's full of people and cars (sure it's not as full as in America). I feel sad looking at it. Before this day I probably understood my sadness, but today I don't. It's so far away from my daily life. It's so far away. I am starting to forget that life, those people. My memories are hidden inside so deep that I can't move them, I am afraid to move them, I don't have time to move them, and why?

I asked one girl to tell me about Russia. She came just three months ago, but she had nothing to say. She asked me to ask her questions first, but I had so many questions inside, but none on the outside. I asked her a few questions about the Russian weather, and then we started to talk about simple American things, like anything that happens every day. I saw her eating fast and a lot, everything on her paper plate. I remembered myself doing it when I just came to America. "I can't get used to it," she quietly said, and I smiled.

Then we talked with other Russian girls about school and our new teachers, and classes. We talked about movies and so on.

Today I was studying in regular English classes with Americans, with teachers who speak as native Americans because they are. And I was so proud to see that I can understand them without being afraid to talk to them. This was the time when I felt change, the biggest change probably in my life.

I'm listening to sad music by the French singer Mireille Mathieus; maybe that's why I feel sad now. And this picture on the wall, I just hope it'll never become just a picture for me. I don't have time to realize this change, my way of living. I don't even realize that I sleep in America and live in an American apartment, that I go to American "public" school, that I eat American food, that an American Honey is sleeping on the bed next to me now.

Well, I have nothing else to say. I am almost asleep still listening to the sad music I'll dream about . . .

Goodnight, Kitty
Love, Raimonda

FEBRUARY 2

Hi, dear Kitty!

I hate this life! I am probably the first person who starts to write to his diary like that. And you can see my handwriting says that I am not in a good mood today. First, I am sleepy and hot, but I have to study for a quiz tomorrow. Still, I can't even start. I don't know what's wrong with me. Second, I take Health Careers now. We are learning eye and ear, and now I think that I am becoming blind and deaf, but I still can see and hear. However, I pretend that I will be blind and deaf at thirty. Third, I am so tired of living with Simon. It's crazy! I can't stand it anymore, and neither can he. He curses and so do I. He laughs at me and so do I. But there is no escape. I have a lot of problems with this.

We read a story today in English lesson. I was really jealous, 'cause it was scary and fast and well written. I liked it. It was probably a mad story, but I really liked it. I laughed a lot today.

'Bye,
Raimonda

FEBRUARY 16

Hi, dear Kitty!

I know I should write more often, but sometimes the life is so miserable and so boring! For instance, Simon has a day off, which means that he spent all this day listening to the music, playing guitar for five minutes, eating, and finally cleaning the bathroom after we asked him a thousand times. Then he talked with someone on the phone for exactly two hours till Mom and Dad started to scream at him. Then he ate, and now he's in bed again listening to the music. Isn't it boring?

Now, Mom. She broke up with me in the morning. Then she took a driving lesson and went to work. In the evening she came back with three packs of sausages and without bread. She kissed me because she just forgot about the morning after her busy day and after she saw my cleaning.

Oh! Dad got a job for $75 a day. I'll tell you about it tomorrow 'cause tomorrow is his first day.

Now, me. I'm bored. I just watched movies and ate. I wrote a review paper for history and that's about it.

Anyway, what I tried to prove is that this life is boring. Nothing good is happening. I don't go anywhere. This diary is really boring, but what can I do? However it's not my fault, not life's fault. It's money!

When people say that money doesn't mean happiness and happiness doesn't mean money, maybe they are right, but not in America. If you want to buy something, if you have a dream, if you want to travel, if you want to see, if you want to live (I mean not on the street) you've got to have money. I mean, everything is money.

Money is an answer to your dream, to your wish (I don't mean completely in every situation, but in simple life).

I am not trying to say that money is happiness, but it's a great part of happiness. Well, I hope I can wait. Till what? I don't know, probably till my happiness.

'Bye,
Raimonda

FEBRUARY 18

Hi, dear Kitty!

I am crying, like all hell.

I just watched a movie called *The Shop on Main Street* about a kind old Jewish woman whose peaceful life ends with Nazi occupation. I can't even talk about it now. I don't know what to do. I guess I'd pray if I knew how. But I don't think I'd believe stronger in God. They believed, they prayed till the last minute. But did anyone hear them! Where was God when six million and even more people were destroyed? Where was he? Was he listening to his people? I don't think he was! My grandpa told me to believe! But what about him? Did he believe when his mom . . .

I don't want to talk about it. I will believe. I usually never pray. But when I do, I pray my way.

Just like a child.

'Bye

FEBRUARY 20

Hi, dear Kitty!

What about Dad?

He got a job for $75 a day as I already said before. He works in a factory that makes earrings. His boss is a fuckin' rich businessman. Dad has to give him ideas so he can make earrings with these ideas. That's about it.

Mom was really bad today. She was so jealous and so afraid of losing her powers. That really gets me. She couldn't forget the idea that she was feeding Dad for ten years in the Soviet Union. He was a freelancer, and she says if it weren't for her, he wouldn't survive. She was working every day at the museum. What a lie!

Anyway, I don't want to come back to it.

What a boring day I had! I don't want to talk about it. Yes, I am supposed to build a hot air balloon for a science project. Who the hell would do that?!

'Bye

P.S. What's becoming of my diary? My first diary was the most valuable one. I mean almost every day was new and full of something. My second and third diaries were pretty good—a new life in America. This is my fourth diary. I don't know how to call it. Nothing is really happening, but everything might. Let's hope. I mean a diary is a diary. Nothing should really happen; it's just life. And things don't happen so often, not as often as I wish them to. My fifth diary will be about "Americanism": me becoming an American. I think so, but maybe not. I have a clean book especially for that. Luba gave it to me last year. It has a lock, so it's supposed to be a love diary.

We'll see, we'll see!

'Bye,
Raimonda

FEBRUARY 22

I am lying in bed with a high temperature. I feel very weak. My dad is really upset, but he's always upset when I get sick. Anyway, I don't want to write about it now.

I've got much better news. My grandparents will have an interview with emigration officials in two months, on March 11th. We called to Grandma Galya yesterday. Her voice sounded young and happy. She told us that she's going to sell her apartment for $3,000. She's smart. Simon said that she'll have more dollars than he does! He doesn't have $3,000 yet. We are so happy, because the hope, my dream becomes a reality. And as you know this is my special dream.

Love,
Raimonda

FEBRUARY 23

Hi, dear Kitty!

Simon and I watched *The Gate,* a horror movie. It didn't scare me, but I liked it. And Simon had a good, funny mood after it. This happens very rarely. Thank you, *The Gate*!

You know, I'm glad I have you. I'm not scared to write about "it" (meaning all my secrets) to you because I know that you are mine and no one will have a nerve to open you, even though you don't have a key and you are written in English, an official language in America and some other countries.

Love,
Raimonda

P.S. I want to write to you about something good that had happened about five days ago. But I forgot to write about it (you know that I remember only bad things—just kidding).

Kelli and Andrew took me to a very famous American restaurant, Planet Hollywood. It's not just a restaurant, it's like a modern movie museum. I saw a mask of you know whom, but I don't remember the name, from the movie *Friday the 13th*. I saw a stick of Charlie Chaplin's. I saw a sweater and a scissor hand of Freddie (*The Nightmare on Elm Street*—my favorite horror movie). I saw Kevin Costner's clothes and arrows from *Robin Hood*. I love this movie, and I hate all other versions that were before it. I saw Edward's scissor hands. I saw a Schwarzenegger from *Terminator II: The Judgment Day*. He wasn't alive, but he resembled a real one. I saw Rocky's and Rambo's motorcycle and knife.

I really want to call Dov. I wonder if he still resembles a Schwarzenegger.

We ate real American food, which was much better than in McDonald's. That's why it was called a restaurant. We watched clips and my favorites were Michael Jackson's *Black and White* and *Do You Remember?* I just don't know why he made a plastic surgery and became white—and now he sings *Black and White*.

Kelli introduced me to her friend Meredith. She was a really funny and nice woman. I liked her a lot. She's a journalist and she interviews famous people and usually stars. She talked on the phone with Schwarzenegger and she interviewed the boy from *Home Alone*. He didn't want to answer her questions so they played ball! If I were as rich as he is, I would do the same thing.

I've got to go now.

Love,
Raimonda

FEBRUARY 29

Hi, dear Kitty!

Tomorrow is the first day of March. In Russia, it's called the first day of spring. However, I don't feel spring coming. It was freezing today and so windy that I had to wear a hat. And I hate it. Dad was reading me his morals about it. He used examples like Simon's hair, Simon's clothes and everything that Simon used to have or has now that is stupid. Because Simon thinks about others, how others will look at him, but he doesn't think about himself and so on. Dad also told me about his youth and his mistakes. That was interesting and I listened to his morals, but when he reminded me about the hat because it all started with the hat, I lost my great attention.

Simon just made fun of Mom, and I've never laughed so much at once.

Mom just left 'cause Simon was making fun of her and I laughed. Dad wasn't working today, but he moved all the furniture because he needed a space for the copy machine that he bought. It took him a whole day.

Love,
Raimonda

MARCH 8, 1992

Hi, dear Kitty,

I am so sorry I didn't write for such a long time, but I didn't write to my grandparents either. It's all I can say.

I've been in a bad mood all these days. First, I had tests every single day and I'm sure that my average will drop down because it's harder than in ESL, even if I don't feel it while studying. Second, we were supposed to have a dinner at Kelli's house and sign a contract, but the lawyers called and said that they didn't read the contract yet. So we can't sign it now. We cancelled dinner and celebration till the next two weeks. Third, if you still want to hear, Dad had an exhibition yesterday, but this time in Manhattan and in the temple. He didn't sell anything and no one even looked at it because there came only women with husbands to buy jewelry. And they gave my dad such a small dark place that no one could see anything. They just used this small space like an exit to get from one table with jewelry to another. I hated it! They looked like blind, small creatures. They didn't see my father's pictures. They didn't give him a good place. And I pitied him so much that I was angry enough to destroy everything. Yes, maybe I felt it because he's my dad. I didn't even want him to sell those pictures. I thought they were too good for those people. He sold four pictures at the last exhibition and I was happy for him. I was happy that those people understood. I know I can't explain my feelings. I have too many thoughts, so I mix them up. But I guess you got an idea why I am in a bad mood.

My school, this bullshit with the contract, my dad . . .

Maybe I should rest. I want to leave this house, this city, and rest somewhere in Florida, but it's all just a dream. You see, my bad mood isn't going away, instead it gets worse.

Simon says I should think of something happy and nice. My poor psychologist. Will he ever become one? I promise to write more often and have good news or no news at all.

Talk to you soon,

Raimonda

P.S. I forgot to tell you that Yoko came for a week. She has a vacation. It's fun, and I like her. Simon and Yoko went to Brighton to buy some Russian food. I could go too, but I have too much to do.

Kiss,
Raimonda

Yes, I got my green card, and it's written Raymonda on it, but I am kind of used to Raimonda now.

MARCH 15

Hi, dear Kitty!

I didn't write for so long, and I have so much to tell you.

I've been so busy at school that I didn't have time to read or write. I failed two Math tests, and I don't want to stay in honor class. I want to get 90s as I used to get in regular Math class. This week was so busy. My teachers gave us tests every day like they couldn't live without it. I got high grades on my tests except Math, and I'll know the results on Monday for some tests I had on Friday. Anyway, I don't feel like talking about school now 'cause tomorrow is Monday.

Yoko was living with us this week, but she's leaving today. Dad was really upset and I'm sure he is now because he gave Simon and Yoko his room and bed and they didn't thank him. He was tired from work, and when Simon and Yoko fought about some bullshit, he really got mad. Yoko likes to talk about racism in America, and Simon has nothing to do so he's just goading her. She starts crying and so on. It's so stupid to talk about racism in America. There are millions of different nations in America. Anyway, couldn't they find something else to talk about? Doesn't she get it? Simon has to go to college, but he's too lazy so he didn't even check to see if he was registered there for September—and only now they found out that he's not and it's too late for financial aid. He has so many problems, but he's not moving. I understood him when he was in a depression, when he said he hates this country. But not anymore. He wastes too much time. Nothing is gonna change if he just lies on that garbage bed and works at the same job where he just wastes time. He's not gonna make money at it. And Yoko is talking about racism?

Then they are fighting and she starts crying. What for, what is she crying for? She says American magazines lie about Japan. Who cares? Doesn't Japan lie about America? But what does it have to do with today?

I think everyone wants Simon to leave. He is twenty-one, he has to start his own life. I'm sure he's tired of all of us too. I don't think he wants to live with me in one tiny room and neither do I. Still, I don't see him doing anything about it, and I don't want to tell him anything either. I don't really want him to leave. Who knows what's "out there" waiting for him? It's scary, but the time is coming.

And here I am sitting in the kitchen. Why? Simon and Yoko are in that room, and I can't write when it's noisy. Mom is in "her" room and I can't be there either. Oh, God, I need my own room. I can't stand it anymore. I love them all, I do, but I need some privacy. I can't write and this is what I want. But I can't when people are around me. The same faces, voices! I just dream and most of my dreams have come true, but I want it *now* and my dreams never come true so fast. Instead, it takes them all years!

I'm never thinking about Russia now. I forget, only remember deep inside. Still, I don't want to awaken my deep memories. I'm afraid of them. How would I feel?

There is so much I want. Maybe it's because of America. I never had so many dreams in Russia, probably because there was nothing to dream about.

However, I have some good news for you. Some exciting news.

We signed the contract with the publishers and probably will get money in two weeks. I wrote you in two sentences all about this news, but for me it's unreal.

MARCH 22

Hi, dear Kitty!

There is nothing much happening in my crazy family. Everything stays the same. My school, Father's work, Mother's "work," Simon's work. It seems that "study and work" are two words that represent America. This is a major way to survive, to live.

I'm never bored at school, but sometimes I am tired from it. I get used to tests that are given by my teachers almost every day. I walk home with my new friend Natalie. She's black. She wasn't born here. She was born in Haiti, but she represents to me American teenagers: she doesn't like to talk about books, movies, and she's never ashamed to show it. That's why I mostly listen to her rather than talk. She talks about her ex-boyfriends and how she wants a new one and how she talks with guys on the phone. She saw a bus driver who is twenty-five years old and she always talks about him. I tried to change her mind sometimes, but she never listens. I just listen to her now, but we have fun talking or throwing snowballs at boys.

Yes, it was snowing two days ago and it will again. I love it; it reminds me of Russia. Most Americans think that Russia is cold and stays with snow the whole year. It's their way of seeing Russia. Cold, snowy, cold . . . They are wrong, but I was too when I thought of America: Kingdom, mirrors, skyscrapers, fairy tales, gums. There's a truth in those words, and maybe one day I'll be able to feel them. Maybe Russia was cold and snowy, maybe everything about it is cold and snowy. But what is it for me? I am so far away from it, from that life I lived there for twelve years. But these two years made them disappear, hid them so deep that my life became a history. I don't have time to come back to that history. I can't live in it, and a picture on my wall becomes just a picture.

I have some good news too. Daddy bought a car, and it will be ours on Tuesday. I haven't seen it yet. It cost $2,800, and I love it already.

Simon is still working. He's looking for an apartment. He'll probably leave soon. He told me that he wants to start his own life. It's a second time he will. He doesn't talk to anybody except me, and we like it because it's so quiet. We should have started it from the first day of immigration.

Honey is so lucky. He can sleep whenever he wants. He never has any problems. I wish I could be a cat sometimes!

Love,
Raimonda

MARCH 28

Hi, dear Kitty,

I've been reading books. Some are Russian, some English. They're different, but they are all exciting and interesting. I always imagine myself *in* there. I miss being there. It probably sounds strange because I always want something, I always miss something. When I was a child I wanted a doll. Then I wanted an apartment. Then I wanted to be in America. Now I have everything I've dreamed of, but not. I don't need those things anymore. I want more because I know that someone has it and that I can get it one day. I'm restless. I never stop dreaming. Isn't it enough . . . one immigration? No, is my answer.

Here I am running from one room to another, wishing to find a quiet place where I can be alone. I'm angry at everybody. I'm tired of my parents, who never stop fighting. I'm tired of Simon, who comes from work angry—or maybe it's my face that makes him angry. I want to hide in the bathroom, but it's too hot in there—Simon just took a bath. And these faces, these people walking front and back before me. There's no place to hide. I'd give all my money, I'd give my sneakers to my mom, I'd give everything for them to leave, I'd even have them go to Florida (this is where I want to go most).

What's my life? It's mostly school: Tests, homework, lunch, friends, stress from Monday till Friday. What's the reason to study for tests if there'll be tomorrow and what's the reason to live if you die? But you continue on studying, living, and wishing.

What's up? This is what I ask my friends, and this is what they ask me almost every time we meet. Nothing, I answer. Is there really nothing?

Dad bought a car, a Buick. And he drives me to school. It's great.

I don't even want to mention Mom and Simon because they haven't changed a bit. This is probably why I hate to write letters.

Letters are usually boring and empty. It gets harder for me to write letters to my grandparents because they are always the same. No one would be able to read them, except my grandparents. They can read my letters over and over again. My grandma Sofa is probably reading it over at night. She's blind, but she uses a microscope glass. My grandma Galya is probably reading it to her best friends and then crying at it. My grandpa is probably reading them loudly because he can see, but he can't hear. Maybe it's so. This is how I feel. This is how I imagine them. Grandma Galya's letters are always the same (filled with pity for Russia, a little anger at Mom, a few questions for Simon—which he never answers). Sofa is always writing about death and how old they are. She usually complains about something in every letter. This is when she reminds me most of Mom. Grandma Sofa always teaches me something that I already know or heard from her millions of times. She teaches me how to live here even though she has no idea about this life or about America itself. She talks about clothes or things that I've never done, over and over again. It makes me mad, but I never have a power to explain, to change their views. I never do that. I am powerless because I respect and pity them, because I love them and miss them.

I failed math. Yes, I did and I'm so embarrassed. I knew it. They put me in honor class. I hate math. I don't understand it. I'll try my best this time.

However, all of my teachers (except math) said real nice things about me in parent conferences. Daddy was proud of me, but I wasn't. I love Health Careers, English, History, Science, everything but Math.

Today is Friday, but it's eleven soon. So I'll go to sleep now. It's a pity today is over. I have to study tomorrow.

Love,
Raimonda

Even though I failed, I am not a failure.★

★Rationalization—explains what is done by making an excuse. Goodnight!

APRIL 9, 1992

Hi, dear Kitty!

Dad makes $100 a day and brings food sometimes. Mom is "unemployed" and as always is teasing me to death and Simon and Dad too. Then, Simon is a rude, lazy worker and a bad brother. And Honey, he's just my love.

Dad is driving me to school every day. I am off from school in a week for Easter vacation or for Passover (for us). Today I drank milk from a carton that said "Happy Passover" in English and He- brew. We smiled and one guy (a Jew) kissed the carton with such freedom and happiness. I guess everyone wanted to kiss him after that.

I feel like being somewhere else. Maybe in Florida . . . Please don't think I'm mentally ill, 'cause I do study "Health Careers." Don't forget, I am a future doctor. Maybe I'll find a cure for cancer . . . only if no one does it before me.

> I am a dreamer, that you know
> I am a day, when it's dark
> I am a cold, when it's hot
> Don't wake up, and see me so
> I am a wind, a rain, a snow
> I'll make you cry and wet and cold
> Don't wake up, I'll be a sun
> that'll make you smile.
> I'll be as fast as light,
> I'll be as strong as wind
> I'll be as big as earth
> But you woke up, to see . . .
> To see me small and weak, but so
> I'm surprised you aren't sorry
> I'm a dreamer, yes, you know.

> Raimonda
> Love you, Kitty
> Goodnight

APRIL 18

Hi, dear Kitty,

And finally, I write to you again. It took me a long time to get my memories together! Anyway, there are a couple of things that are very important to me, but I forgot to write about them.

First of all, I found out about a week ago that I passed a lab test.

I am in American classes now, and I'll be in regular "English" class next year. They would put me in now, but it's kind of too late. The school is over in two months, and I am having a lot of fun in transitional English. Talking to Russians and doing nothing for forty-five minutes or reading stories is better than doing something else in school.

Anyway, I was very happy about it, but I was very surprised when my parents didn't respond to it. I mean I didn't want them to cry from happiness and etc., but they were much happier when I didn't pass that test before. When I first came, I had 6 percent. Then, 23 percent. Now, I was the only person in my class who passed it. Well, I don't care! They continue on teasing me, especially I wanted to say Mom, but it's all of them. I'm sick and tired of them. That doesn't mean I don't love them, but I am sure that they are pretty tired of me too. I told them to take all the money they want from the book contract and leave! Just for one week or so. But, no.

And listen to this, they promised to go to Florida (Disney World) every single day before my vacations started, and now when I am free from school, they found out that it's too expensive. I know, I know . . . I understand, but I don't want to understand. We are poor, but I don't want to be. I want so much, now, every minute I want something. But, no. I wish I were twenty now. I would study and work till I became a doctor and then "Party Time!" But I'm just fourteen. I hope there's a girl out there who wants to become fourteen. I always wanted to become twelve, then I wanted to be fourteen, now I want to be sixteen. Never stop. But I don't want to be one hundred years old, that's for sure.

Simon, poor Simon, he's wasting his time and he knows it. He doesn't even struggle with this life. He's sitting in this tiny room and listening to the music. I'm already tired of it, but he's not. Maybe I don't understand, maybe there's something special in music. But I don't think it's special enough to fill your life with everything you need or want. Doesn't he want his own place, especially where he won't see me writing about him? Doesn't he want to travel and start his own life? I bet he does. He just can't start, and I don't see him trying. Will he ever try? I think he should. His long hair, millions of records and tapes, it's all that he owns. He gets angry when my parents or I talk about it. That's why I stopped talking to him about it anymore. Even though he's my only brother and I love him and he's the best brother I could ever have. So let him decide for himself.

I don't have to write about my parents much in this diary, 'cause you already know that they are crazy, crazy, crazy. Well, I am, too.

This family is nuts, so sorry to say. I wish my grandparents to come soon, and then I'll live with them. I told my mom that I'll visit her once in a month!

Well, I am not as angry as my letter might seem to be today. I am not angry at all; I just can't be 'cause today is Passover.

We celebrated Passover with our lawyer on the book contract. He invited us to come yesterday at 7:30 P.M. It was great! We only came home at two o'clock in the morning. I'm glad we took the car. However, it took a long time for my dad to drive from Brooklyn to Manhattan, but he did it. At first we talked and waited till everybody arrived. At about ten-thirty we sat at the table. People that I saw were real, American Jews with young, pale faces and red hair. Not all of them had red hair, of course. I liked three of them. All three of them were very smart, knew Hebrew, and I felt very ashamed and stupid not knowing it. One of them was my lawyer (of course I like him), then his friend who looks just like him. When I opened the door to him, I thought that he was our lawyer. They have the same first names too. We ate traditional food for Passover, like matzoh and green vegetable and everything that's eaten to remind us that we became free and God gave us freedom and freed us from slavery and took us out from Egypt.

The moment they sang in Hebrew, the moment they talked in Hebrew, I hated Russia and the Russian language. I kept saying that it's not my fault that I don't know Hebrew in my head. And my knowing the Russian language was nothing compared to knowing English and Hebrew. I'm wrong to say that. I am happy for what I am and for what I know and I'll always be, because it doesn't matter in what language you pray to God and celebrate Passover. The most important thing is for a Jew to be a Jew. After all, who knew that I ever would be able to celebrate Passover in America! I could still be a Pioneer, and know nothing except Russian and Ukrainian languages, believe in nothing and in no one. I could still be a Jew, but have no idea of what it means and why some people hate me for it. I could have known only that for the rest of my life.

I have to be happy for being here. And believe me, I am! I am happy. Yes, there's so much I want, but I guess a person never stops wanting. But I am happy for what I have now. I thank God for what I have and for what I know and I pray for my grandparents to come. I easily forget all my wishes and dreams, except being with my grandparents. Let it be the only wish I have for this Passover.

My letter is over for today, and I'm surprised to say that it's already midnight, but I don't feel like sleeping. Mom and Dad are sleeping, but Simon's still listening to the music. Nothing has changed, and maybe things should stay the way they are. So, I just say Goodnight, Kitty.

Always yours,
Raimonda

APRIL 28

Hi, dear Kitty!

There were so many things happening in my life that I didn't really think about them. I didn't think as much about the good things that had been happening as about the bad things. How many times I was talking about us and fights between us and being poor and not knowing the language and in some situations being Russians instead of Americans and all the problems we had or still have in this country. But I so rarely wrote about the good things that had happened in this country, like just being here, living here, becoming Americans, finding so many new things, just walking on these streets.

Why does a person, why me, why can't I talk about it, enjoy it, love it? Maybe it's because I'm a person, a human being who sees mostly the bad things. But, no. Not today. Today I'm going to write about the good things and only about them. Living in this tiny room, which is white and American, looking through the American hard window and seeing an American street, cars, and people, I can finally say that I am glad to see it. I am willing to struggle and fight all the problems that I have or might have just to see an American street.

I love this country. It seems so funny, me saying that. Me who once was a girl, oh yes a Russian girl with a red tie, me a Pioneer with Lenin's portrait hanging on every wall in my classrooms. Me? Me who was surrounded by Russian people and Russian culture and me who knew and memorized the Russian poems and Russian songs. I was a part of that life. That life just pushed me away and crossed off my name, but I had been a part of that life and once I was a name. That was before, not now. Now, I am a part of another life, and I hope to be a real part of it. There's no one and nothing who will ever take me in, make me a true part of this life. It's me who will fight to get in, just for the name of this country.

And I will say again and again that I love this country because there are so many things you can love here. You can make your dreams come true, you can do so much and make your own choices. Yes, as a little girl I always wished to come here. I pretended that I would find a kingdom from a fairy tale. I imagined and dreamed of so many things. I guess I did find a kingdom. Of course it's not from a fairy tale, but close in some ways.

Sometimes, I feel guilty, being a Jew and not knowing anything about it—religion, customs, or language. I look at real Jews and I see men with black hats, long dresses, long beards, pale and wise faces, or I see women in long skirts, wigs, always surrounded by children that look like angels because their eyes are full with a strong belief in God. They are so different from me because you can always see that they are Jews by looking at them. Their language and customs are so unknown to me, but somewhere inside I feel that I know it. I feel love for them when I see them. Well, maybe there is no difference.

I am not going to write about my dreams in this chapter because it'll sound sad. Dreams are always sad because they are just dreams. I have so many dreams in America, maybe because America is a dream.

My story, if it is a story, may have no point. But it has to me.

Talking about dreams, I forgot to mention that some dreams come true, and mine did. We got a check. It's my first check for the diary from the publishers! I got a check for writing, being just fourteen years old. It's silly now to compare myself with that Russian girl who had never been to Italy. I don't get it. I really don't get it.

I was at the movies when the check came. I was with Lisa. We paid $4 for one movie, but we sneaked in and saw three movies from one o'clock till eight, until our heads exploded and a big bag of popcorn was almost empty. So I came back home and found my excited parents who gave me a letter and check that said I don't remember exactly what except two phrases, "Diary of Raimonda Kopelnitsky," and thousands of dollars. I was happy, but I didn't quite know for what. I kept seeing mixed pictures from those three movies and at the same time I was drinking Coca-Cola with my parents and celebrating. I got $250 for spending on my own and the other goes to my mom, or, as we call it, to our cash register for the future house in which I don't believe! I mean they could spend some of it on Disney World, but Mom thinks it's too expensive. I am not angry at it. I have just stopped believing them. They kept promising and promising about going to Israel on this vacation, then going to Disney World, then to Washington. And I believe there'll be more places we'll visit just sitting in here, moving and visiting, but only in our dreams. I sound angry, but I am not. I understand them and don't at the same time. They are afraid and they just want to keep money. Mom's favorite job is to keep money. But if I were them, I would travel and enjoy that money at forty-six years old. Who knows, maybe I wouldn't.

Tomorrow is Thursday and my vacations are almost over. I have to do my homework tomorrow and so on. I hate just the thought of it.

We saw a movie yesterday. It's a Russian movie called *The House Under a Starry Sky* by [Andrey] Solovyev. At first we got scared, because it was very anti-Jewish, but then we understood that it was a fantastic movie and it was against a Russian demon who was against Jews. The demon was killed at the end. Even though I felt bad especially at the beginning, when I suddenly remembered what I had forgotten about the Soviet Union. I forgot the bad, the bad that was hiding and surrounding us in Russia, or it was Russia itself. There was a piece in the movie when a man who comes to America kisses American ground. It's a Russian custom to kiss the ground of your motherland. I cried because I remembered and understood that even if America has its dirty subways and some crazy people or scary places, it doesn't matter. What matters is its freedom. I understood that it is always better than Russia. I forgot the bad: I remembered only the trees and the sky, everything but the people. Some people could come one day and be our enemies, and Mom even named some names of our ex-neighbors. That brought some memories back. But my life is not the movie anymore. It's me being sure in my new land. And it's the only land I'll kiss if coming from the long journey.

Raimonda

MAY 1, 1992

Hi, dear Kitty!

Simon has a day off. Poor Simon, he's watching *Jaws* on Channel 11. Dad is drawing as always and I just finished my history homework. Everything seems as quiet and calm as it usually is! But L.A. and Manhattan weren't that calm for the last three days.

In L.A., cops beat up a black man because he didn't stop his car. Someone had a camera and saw how the cops beat this black man. At the trial, the cops were told not guilty and blacks started a "war" as they might call it, but I never would. They killed innocent people that had nothing to do with it. They burned L.A. They robbed stores. They say that it's like in the sixties, but it's not. They don't protest; they don't starve themselves. Instead they rob stores. They steal toilet paper, fried chicken, TV sets, sofas. Who the fuck would do that? They don't prove anything. They killed innocent people for nothing, and [N.Y. Mayor David] Dinkins asked them to stop the violence. Who was he talking to? They are never gonna listen to him. They robbed Korean and Chinese stores too. But what did they have to do with anything? Blake called yesterday. He said that he saw blacks beating up a black woman. They burned their own homes in L.A. When Simon rode home on the subway yesterday, a black man came in and said to kill white men because they are demons, etc. There were a lot of people on the train, but no one answered, of course.

Now it's almost stopped. L.A. is damaged in $200 million. Some innocent people will never come home to their families again. Stores are damaged and robbed. And what about the people who worked for twenty years to have a store? In N.Y., some places are damaged too. What did they prove, after all? Nothing or maybe everything they could to get attention.

Raimonda

MAY 5

Hi, dear Kitty!

My family is crazy, but I understand them. Living for two years in America and having just a little more money brings so many dreams. First, everyone is tired of each other. It's normal! Mom is too lazy to find a new apartment, or maybe it's because she teases too much. Simon wants to live and rent another apartment. Who doesn't? I just wish to close the door and be in my room. Oh, man, then there will be no one there except me! Take everything, just leave me alone. We are really a loving family. Still, we're too weak, too old, too tired to move, to start again. There are so many thoughts in me. I'm probably deciding whether I should or shouldn't write about my dreams. But there are so many of them!

Dad, Mom, and Simon are in the kitchen now talking about apartments, etc. Poor Dad and Mom, they want to buy a house. They don't understand. I don't want to be poor here, because I can have so many dreams and so many may come true. America is a country of dreams and riches . . . I want it all.

I am waiting for summer vacation 'cause I'm tired from school.

Some Russians just arrived in our school, so it's amazing to hear them saying that an airline ticket now costs 96,000 rubles, and bread instead of costing the equivalent of 20 cents, costs $6. I laugh, 'cause I can't believe. It's funny. Man, it's so far away . . . They flew straight to New York and don't believe me when I say that I stayed real close to the Father of Rome and the Vatican. They've never seen Venice, of course. Now, I've seen a lot! But now it seems so quick, that I can't really remember anything.

I don't want to sound sad again 'cause I am not. Just yesterday, I finished reading all five books from *The Three Musketeers*. Each book has 700–800 pages. Yesterday was the last book so I cried every time someone died.

In a week or so my grandparents will have an interview with emigration officials in Moscow. I hope, I pray everything will be all right.

Love,
Raimonda

MAY 8

Hi, dear Kitty!

I finally passed my Math test and got 94 on it, so I'm really proud of myself, but not for long 'cause I have another test on Tuesday. On my English tests, I get really high grades because my poor teacher is too old to teach. She forgets things. She can't really teach. She almost never answers my questions and mixes up everybody's name. But she's very sweet. My science teacher is about forty. He's a real type of American man from the seventies. He reminds me a lot of Russian men. He's a nice teacher, and he knows a lot in science. However, he mostly talks, which is a lot better than writing, but not for me!

I guess I stepped into another world being in regular classes. It's not that easy. Most of my teachers, especially my Health Career teacher, like me. Still, I guess I think more about students themselves than about teachers. Sometimes I'm "ashamed" to read aloud, even though everyone knows I have a Russian accent. Some kids laugh at my accent, but in a friendly way. I don't get mad, but they never stop to think that they would never say a word if they were to come to Russia. I haven't made any "real" friends. I am trying to understand American teenagers, but I just can't. I got used to my yard in Chernovtsy. I used to have so many friends, just to fool around with. Here, it's impossible. I know that I'm fourteen and I shouldn't probably "play games" anymore, but what about my weekends when I go out with Lisa and the only places I can walk on is from 74th Street to 86th Street and back on those hot streets where there is nothing to see or do.

Movies? Yes, I go to the movies once in a month and I pay $4 for one movie, but watch three without stopping till my head blows out. I don't want to pay $4 for one movie. Not when I used to sneak in without paying a penny because I'm so small and a ticket was really cheap in the Soviet Union. Like 5 cents.

You might get the wrong idea. I'm trying to say that there's nothing to do on weekends. I'm not trying to say that Russia is better. But there is a difference in our lives. I hope one day I will understand or get to know their way of being a teenager, being an American. Take Spanish. I've never studied it before. I never looked at it. But I get high grades on it. Well, how come American kids and Spanish kids that speak Spanish at home fail it? How come American kids laugh at my accent, but fail their History test which is written in English? And I get 97. Is there anyone here who can explain that to me? No . . . My mom is sitting on the bed, but she can't answer! Sorry, Mom. I won't even ask you.

After tomorrow, it's Mother's Day. I wanted to buy her flowers, but she doesn't want it. So I'll give her $5 and Dad will give her $8 because she wants to buy a "bra"! It's funny!

Poor Simon is working. He says he's looking for an apartment. Man, it's tough out there. It's too tough for him. He's not ready and he'll never be for America . . . You have to be strong, but he's not. He's not even trying to be. He got used to that empty, easy life where you smoke, talk in some Moscow slang, hang out with some lazy idiots who are geniuses at the same time. You smoke again, drink coffee, talk some shit, and that's it. You don't need money, or an apartment. You have everything and nothing at the same time. But here, no way! You need everything—money, apartment. You are too tired from work to talk fool shit and go out. There's always tomorrow. Well, what's it gonna be? Your choice, Simon's choice, no more easy, dirty life for him. Of course, he can have all of it, but what about tomorrow?

Mom and Dad, they aren't tough either, but who would tell

them. They are perfect. They're the best for being just Mom and Dad, for coming here. It's our time, and it's our turn to be tough, to be strong, to think about tomorrow and to be Americans.

MAY 15

Hi, dear Kitty,

My grandparents were about to have an emigration interview on May 11, but they got a telegram that said that their appointment was canceled till May 26, and that it might be canceled again. I hate when they do that, even though I have no idea who did it! So now we have to wait again. Is there a justice in this world? I hurriedly say no, but then I remember that a girl I know has a grandfather who is dying from cancer and she found out about it just one sunny morning when they called to Russia. Her family can't see him, and they won't see him. So maybe I should be happy to know that everything is all right with my grandparents and that they are ready to go, ready to leave everything behind—their life, culture, language, everything they own and have known since they were born sixty and seventy years ago. If it was hard for me being just twelve, how will it be for them?

I am glad to be here and have nothing to do with Russia. I have nothing to hate there, but soon there'll be nothing to love. As time goes, I forget, and when my grandparents come there'll be nothing to remember, nothing at all. All of my friends—which are friends of my childhood when I stole flowers from someone's garden, laughed at dirty jokes, climbed and stole apples from the trees—are all far from Russia now. We all found two countries where we could live in this world, America and Israel.

It doesn't look like my grandparents will come while I'm still writing in this diary notebook. There are not many pages left even though I haven't written every day. I guess many things happened this year. First it's a new year. I'm about to finish my first year in Fort Hamilton High School. Simon has a girlfriend, Yoko, and I have a "boyfriend," Honey, my cat, whom I truly love. We have a car. Dad is working, and Mom is still teasing everyone. So I guess this year in America, the year I described in this diary, was pretty good and maybe better than the previous one.

And if I ask myself again if there is a justice in this world—well, maybe there is because we live. We all wait for something better. This is where the justice still lives.

'Bye,

I'm not "Lenin,"
nor God to talk
about life, so if my
writing doesn't make
sense it can be ignored by everyone
except me and
Honey!

P.S. Dear Kitty,

Dad's and Mom's friend and his wife came from Israel to visit. They met at the same university, but haven't seen each other for twenty years. So he saw Simon as a little boy and didn't see me at all. They drank a little vodka for the sake of old days. Now he tells about Russia and about how he decided to leave.

MAY 20

Hi, dear Kitty!

I have so much to tell you.

First of all, Yoko came and now there are five members of our "Addams family," or six with Honey.

Today I had a lot of fun. Since Simon was working today, Yoko and I walked in Manhattan and watched the best movie I've ever seen, called *Europa, Europa*. After crying and laughing for a while during the movie I decided to marry a Jew. This movie truly showed how stupid this world is and how stupid people were and are. But it's understandable because I'm one of them. Just like the kids in the movie, I also wore a red tie, memorized poems, looked proudly at Lenin's monuments. Why? Because it was the only way to survive through that culture. Even though that movie showed time in the 1940s, I still don't see any change. When I say there are only two places for Jews in this world, America and Israel, my mom disagrees. She says there's no place in this world. But maybe in heaven there is one.

Both ways, we all live and will continue living till the end. When Yoko cried a little about racism—about anti-Japanese sentiment and magazine commercials with white-haired and blue-eyed women—I didn't. I looked around the subway and saw so many people, and it was so hard to believe that each of them has a different life, different beliefs, faith. Each of them can be an enemy or a friend. But who cares, I think. There's no real war today so you live. But if tomorrow there is war, in my childish thoughts, I see excitement, romance, adventures, and heroism. Even if I have changed, many Russian kids are still saluting, if not Stalin or Lenin, someone else. There'll always be someone else.

Dad is watching news. I never do 'cause they never show good stuff, just killings. Mom is asleep. So are Yoko and Simon.

Yoko and I "visited" a very expensive delicatessen store, where we weren't able to buy anything. But we did sample—or maybe more than sample—fruits like watermelon, strawberries, and cherries. At first, we walked around a lot and just tried bites, but finally we just stopped walking and ate. It was fun.

Yesterday, it was 100 degrees outside and Mom, Dad, and I went to the Robert Moses beach where I've been already with Kelli and Andrew. The water was cold, but I fooled around with the waves a little.

Love,
Raimonda

MAY 27

Hi, dear Kitty!

I decided to write to you even though I have nothing important to say and just because for no reason I feel extremely happy. I don't know, but maybe it's this music written by the known genius Mozart that makes me forget about school, finals, exams, people, and everything that is so boring. The music has turned it all into an exciting world.

First of all, I stopped watching news, and it's the best way to keep me from New York's horrors. I don't respond when someone argues, especially my parents. I get to know more Americans, and even my lazy accent doesn't always stay in my way, especially when it comes to tests or grades. I remember being so surprised when I found out that Lenin knew fifteen languages, but now it doesn't seem so difficult and genius. Of course, sometimes I'm happy to understand Russian without needing to read and concentrate on the words written on the movie screen. Still, I don't feel proud because it's just natural, my faith I guess. What's Russia to me now? I'm scared to ask that question. Soon it will remind me of nothing, of nothing at all. I catch myself forgetting all songs, poems, holidays, maybe everything that unites me with the Russian culture. I have no wish to betray or even to forget, but living here every day, fighting to survive, to get into society, to maybe even get into culture, takes all my time and maybe it takes all my unknown thoughts.

I'm not sorry, not at all. I left my childhood, kindergarten, friends, enemies, and so I have a right to forget all of it. I guess when my grandparents come, they'll remind me, but they'll be the last thing that preserves my memories, my way of thinking of Russia itself.

On May 29, my grandparents will have an interview in Moscow, and they are ready for that. On that day, I will decide if there is still something that can make me happy. I know that I'm not powerful enough to make my grandparents appear right here, right now, because if I was, they would have been here three years ago. I don't believe in government; I guess they are just playing with human lives. But there is a hope in God. And even though it takes me something special or a great need to pray to him, I'll pray now for my grandparents, for my happiness. God, help us—Just like my grandpa says.

Love,
Raimonda

JUNE 6, 1992

Hi, dear Kitty!

I haven't written for a long time.

First of all, I have finals, but compared to finals that I had in winter, I don't study at all. My finals begin tomorrow, but I'm not thinking much about it now. Maybe summer makes me think about going out and forgetting all about school. Maybe it's because I'm about to finish school in a week or so. Anyway, I just forgot all about it and looking through the window on green trees and breathing fresh air seems more important to me than studying.

My dad finished working at the factory for which he used to draw, and now Mom keeps teasing him too much and keeps complaining about us being poor and an American failed dream about the house . . .

The movie we watched yesterday, *Journey of Hope,* reminded me of immigration, and my eyes were red from tears. I guess I never cried so much before. Our dream about America didn't fail me. I hope to make this dream come true for me and my parents. Mom laughs at us "being poor," having no furniture, no apartment. I mean real stuff that we used to have, like expensive furniture; a cheap apartment, but our own. She laughs because now there are four people in these tiny rooms where most of the space is taken by Simon's records and Dad's books. The truth is that money is everything here and everything else doesn't matter as much. In Russia, friends were everything because of the way of life where you couldn't get much with money and because of the time you spent with your friends because there was nothing to do, just talk. In a way it's boring, but you never have to worry about tomorrow, and the future. Here, tomorrow is why you live, or what you worry about. That's why when Mom dreams about a house or what is easier to call the "rich life," she laughs at America, at her failed dream.

But if you forget about America, about Russia, about everyday life, and just remember the two facts that one day you live and one day you die, then what do we live for, what do we dream for if one day you die and your dreams die? I still want to live, to survive, to get a house if that's what my mom dreams so much about. Yes, I still want to do all of this, and I still have dreams that will keep me awake for the future day, for tomorrow. Well, maybe that's why we live the American way in America.

Yoko lived with us for two weeks. It was too crowded and dirty, but it wasn't bad. My parents didn't complain much this time. However, Simon can be pretty sure that it was the last time. I'm sure that would be all right if we weren't poor Russian immigrants. She's leaving tomorrow morning.

Simon had a birthday on June 4. I gave him $22 because he's twenty-two years old now, and that was what he wanted for his birthday. I cooked, and Pavlik came with Tanya. I bought the wrong vodka, but at least it was cheap!

Simon is getting old, and I didn't feel the excitement this time. We went to Brighton today, and I bought two Russian books. I love both of them, and now I'll have something to do during summer. I really want to get a job, and I'll try to find it as soon as the school is over.

Honey got lazy and he can't open the door like he used to, so he just starts screaming and I have to get up.

Well, I guess that's about it. I didn't write for a long time, but I didn't feel the time passing so soon.

If I could be a bird to fly away, then life would be so easy. But I guess I would have to hide at night and fly from big birds. No one gets an easy life in this world. I wonder if there's a heaven. But I'm not depressed, nor desperate tonight to ask for the answer.

Love,
Raimonda

JUNE 7

Dear Kitty!

I'm sitting in the bathroom now because there's no other place. Mom is asleep, Simon is listening to music, Dad is watching news, and Yoko is packing up her suitcase. So I guess it's the only place where I can stay alone, even though music and news are coming through the walls like they don't want to leave me in quiet. It's pretty hot here, too. The main reason why I'm here with you is because there's just one page left that I'm hoping to finish today. This is the end of my fourth diary, 1992, the end of some dreams which I probably forgot, but never stop dreaming.

Much changed. My school. My English has improved, I hope. My grandparents had an interview and I hope to see them all in six months. I have Honey. My parents haven't changed, but that's okay.

Most of my dreams came true from the last year.

I still love America even though it has nothing to do with the kingdom of my childish imagination. And immigration, it has become a piece of memory that I will never forget. It proved that all people are looking for the paradise but most of us don't get to find it or just don't find it—because there's no such place!

It's getting so hot. It reminds me of last summer when it was about 100 degrees and I couldn't sleep at night.

God, so much happened this year, but it wouldn't fit on this last page. I want to tell so much, but because I'm sleepy and I mixed up my thoughts, there's nothing to say.

Simon is going to study this September, and he stopped smoking.

Dad is reading some books about God and he has gotten so far that it's completely unknown to me.

Mom is asleep. We call her a bird because she is teasing everyone and she gets very upset when someone stops her.

My grandparents aren't here with me now, but after three long years, I still have hope.

If it seems to you that we are the "perfect family," you are very wrong because in reality we are the "Addams Family," the poor ones, the crazy ones, and still the Russian immigrants who are trying not to fail the American dream. Most of us are too lazy, too slow, too old. But my parents are hoping for me. And because they brought me here, I don't turn away. I go forward.

Love,
Raimonda

JB   copy 1
K $10

Kopelnitsky, Raimonda
No Words to say Goodbye

	DATE DUE		